# The
# Purest
# of
# Bastards

*American and European Philosophy*

GENERAL EDITORS: CHARLES E. SCOTT AND JOHN J. STUHR
ASSOCIATE EDITOR: SUSAN M. SCHOENBOHM

Devoted to the contemporary development of American and European philosophy in the pragmatic and continental traditions AMERICAN AND EUROPEAN PHILOSOPHY gives expression to uniquely American thought that deepens and advances these traditions and that arises from their mutual encounters. The series will focus on new interpretations of philosophers and philosophical movements within these traditions, original contributions to European or American thought, and issues that arise through the mutual influence of American and European philosophers.

EDITORIAL ADVISORY BOARD

David Farrell Krell, *The Purest of Bastards: Works of Mourning, Art, and Affirmation in the Thought of Jacques Derrida*

David Farrell Krell

# The Purest of Bastards

Works of Mourning, Art, and Affirmation
in the
Thought of Jacques Derrida

The Pennsylvania State University Press
University Park, Pennsylvania

Library of Congress Cataloging-in-Publication Data

Krell, David Farrell.
    The purest of bastards : works of mourning, art, and affirmation in the thought
of Jacques Derrida / David Farrell Krell.

        p.      cm. — (American and European philosophy)
    Includes bibliographical references and index.
    ISBN 0-271-01991-3 (cloth : alk. paper)
    ISBN 0-271-02999-4 (pbk. : alk. paper)
    1. Derrida, Jacques.    I. Title.    II. Series
B2430.D484K74    2000
194—dc21                                                        99-32685
                                                                CIP

It is the policy of The Pennsylvania State University Press to use acid-free paper for the first printing
of all clothbound books. Publications on uncoated stock satisfy the minimum requirements of
American National Standard for Information Sciences—Permanence of Paper for Printed Library
Materials, ANSI Z39.48–1992.

*for louis and reiner*
*in memoriam*
*and in gratitude to judith walz*


Gut ist es, an andern sich
Zu halten. Denn keiner trägt das Leben allein.
—Hölderlin, *Die Titanen*

# Contents

# List of Illustrations

# Preface

The song of the End and the Beginning—"My Lord, what a
mourning! when the stars begin to fall."
—W. E. B. Du Bois, *The Souls of Black Folk*,
"The Sorrow Songs"

Works of mourning and art, yes. But *affirmation?* In the United States and
England the name Jacques Derrida has for so many years been associated with
*deconstruction,* and *deconstruction* with *nihilism,* that it may seem strange to
insist on the affirmative character of his thought. Yet when Catherine Malabou
and Yvon Brès invited philosophers a decade ago to contribute to a special
"Derrida" issue of the *Revue philosophique de la France et de l'étranger,* they
requested that *affirmation* be the common theme.[1] They proclaimed Derrida's
thought one of the most affirmative examples of affirmation in our time. To
be sure, if Derrida's is a thought of affirmation, that only makes the connections
between *art, philosophy,* and *mourning* in his thought more mysterious than
ever.

The present book tries to show how the works and labors of mourning,
art, and affirmation are intertwined in Derrida's thought from the outset. It
refers to some of his earliest work, in *Voice and Phenomenon* and *Of Grammatology,* though only after having discussed some of his more recent work on
visual art, literature, religion, and philosophy. My chapters usually focus on a
particular Derridian text, not always among those texts most commonly
discussed, and they try to read closely what it is that the labors of art and
mourning in Derrida are affirming. I have not aimed at anything like
completeness in the present volume and have eschewed an exhaustive inventory
of references to mourning, art, and affirmation in Derrida's oeuvre. Rather, I

have tried to invoke instances where the interlacing of the three seems to me particularly intricate and intense.

   Among such instances are the following ten, constituting the Introduction, Conclusion, and the eight chapters of the book. First, Derrida affirms *memory* as the first and last refuge of all the labors of mourning, including the mourning that seems to occur in our experience of the beautiful in works of art and philosophy (Introduction). Second, Derrida affirms the beauty of Kant's *Critique of Judgment* itself and of Kant's Critical project as a whole—no matter how inadequate Kant's own discussion of the *frame* and *framework* of both the artwork and his own *Critique* may be (Chapter 1). Third, Derrida affirms the work of art precisely as a work of blindness and as a work—or the ruin of a work—that mourns all narcissism (Chapter 2). Fourth, Derrida, in his earlier work, affirms the phenomenon of the human voice as analyzed in the phenomenologies of Husserl and Merleau-Ponty; his affirmation, however, is called upon to mourn not only the "I" that once seemed to be the agent of the voice's utterances but also the phenomenological project as such (Chapter 3). Fifth, Derrida affirms the traditional Kantian distinction between the transcendental and empirical realms, albeit with the mournful acknowledgment of an "absolute past," that is, a past that never was empirical, a past that not even an ultratranscendental passage can bring to presence (Chapter 4). Sixth, Derrida affirms the necessity of an *imperfect* future in Heidegger's classic analysis (in *Being and Time*) of ecstatic temporality; his affirmation joins Heidegger in mourning the mortality of humankind (Chapter 5). Seventh, Derrida affirms, I believe, the omnipresence of cinder and ash in seven figures of mourning in contemporary thought—Husserl, Merleau-Ponty, Benjamin, Heidegger, Irigaray, Nietzsche, and Cixous—all of whom one may take to be descendants of an eighth figure, namely, Empedocles of Acragas, Empedocles on Etna (Chapter 6). Eighth, Derrida affirms the death knell, the *glas*, in and of Hegel's philosophy of the absolute (Chapter 7). Ninth, Derrida affirms a circuitous confessional thought, on the model of Augustine, and a mourning by and of mothers as others, a mourning of (m)others, on the model of Monica (Chapter 8). And finally, tenth, to close the present volume, *The Purest of Bastards*, without legitimate issue, Derrida affirms affirmation itself as the principal thrust of his thought at least since *The Post Card* and probably long before that: a bastard affirmation that is essentially the purest form of mourning without cease (Conclusion).

Earlier versions of two chapters appeared in the following publications, and by citing them I want to thank the editors for their generosity: David Wood and Robert Bernasconi, eds., *Derrida and Différance* (Evanston, Ill.: North-western University Press, 1988), along with Donn Welton and Hugh J. Silverman, eds., *Postmodernism and Continental Philosophy,* Selected Studies in Phenomenology and Existential Philosophy, no. 13 (Albany: State University of New York Press, 1988), for Chapter 3; and John Sallis, ed., *Philosophy and Deconstruction: The Texts of Jacques Derrida* (Chicago: University of Chicago Press, 1987), for Chapter 4. Thanks also to David Thomas and Crina Gschwandtner for their help in preparing the book for publication.

Strobelhütte, St. Ulrich

# Introduction

## *Memoria in Memoriam*

> . . . and I've been put back to work.
> Translate this, you've got the code: I am working (myself),
> and it is always a matter of my mourning [*mon deuil*] . . .
> —Derrida, *The Post Card from Socrates to Freud and Beyond*

The narrator of Friedrich de la Motte-Fouqué's *Undine* reflects on his hero's heartfelt yet fleeting mourning of the water nymph Undine, and asks:

> Should we say it is unfortunate or fortunate that our mourning has no real endurance? I am referring to our most profound mourning, which draws its sustenance from the very womb of life, the mourning that becomes so united with the lost loved one that he or she is no longer lost to it, a mourning that befits a priesthood devoted to the image that it wants to keep in its company throughout life, until the obstacle that stopped the one we love also stops us! To be sure, good human beings persist in being such priests, but even so, it is no longer the initial mourning, the real mourning. Other, foreign images intervene after a while, and in the end we discover in our very pain the transience of all earthly things. Thus one must say how unfortunate it is that our mourning has no real endurance.[1]

Mourning demands both a keeping in mind or memory and a releasing or letting go. How could we mourn our friend if we forgot him? And how could mourning do its work if we adamantly refused to let her go? Perhaps psychologists understand mourning well; philosophers certainly do not. Is mourning classified as one of the passions of the soul in either Aquinas's or Descartes's or Spinoza's reckonings concerning *tristitia, dolor,* and *desperatio?*[2] Is mourning an affect, passion, appetite, emotion, event, process, fatality, or achievement? I am no doubt asking the question τὶ ἔστι too naively, assuming that one mourning or mourner is like another. Perhaps philosophers have never asked much about mourning, have forgotten about it, because mourning damages their confidence in a *modus operandi* that prides itself on its contact with the undying and immutable?

Yet some thinkers would affirm that there is nothing more human than mourning, or the capacity to mourn, and that to ignore that capacity is to overlook what philosophers love to call the *essence* of human being. Nietzsche, at thirteen years of age, writes: "It is a noteworthy trait of the human heart that when we have undergone a great loss we do not endeavor to forget; on the contrary, we try to bring this loss before the eyes of our soul as often as possible, as though by this frequent recounting to draw considerable con-solation for our pain."[3] Others would say that to be human is to mourn our distance from the Ideas, especially from the ultratranscendent Good, True, and Beautiful. Still others would observe that *all* living creatures gaze with a mournful look—the Pauline ἀποκαραδοκία τῆς κτίσεως (Rom. 8:19)—as though mourning universal demise. Schelling writes of the veil of melancholy (*der Schleier der Schwermut*) that is draped as a shroud over the whole of nature, the realm of birth and death.[4]

Homer sings something about this long before there were men who prided themselves on the title *philosopher.*[5] He seems to gesture toward the essence of the human—quite paradoxically—by telling of a mourning that does not pertain to human beings alone. On the contrary, the capacity for mourning is what binds immortals to mortals, perhaps confounding the very opposition of mortal and immortal, an opposition one might have thought essential to the phenomenon of mourning. In book xvii of *The Iliad* Patroclus dons the armor of his sulking friend, Achilles; he borrows too the team of immortal horses that Achilles inherited from his father, Peleus, who had received them from Poseidon himself. Homer does not pause to explain what an immortal horse is, a horse that will not die, but paints the scene of Patroclus's bloody death and the reaction of those deathless horses:

> Yet the horses of Achilles, standing apart from the battle,
> Weep the moment they learn that their master
> Lies in the dust, laid low by the hand of murderous Hector.

These weeping steeds surprise us, perhaps because, like Andrew Marvell, we are convinced that only human eyes can weep ("Eyes and Tears"). However, if Achilles' horses are immortal, they must be more like gods, although whether gods or goddesses can weep is an even more delicate question. These weeping horses—somewhat divine, somewhat human, somewhat animal, but in any case altogether daimonic—suddenly seem as though carved out of marble or granite; they are stone monuments guarding the undug grave of Patroclus. The driver whips them, trying desperately to move them from the spot:

> Yet just as funeral stelae stand fixed above the tomb
> As monuments to the dead man or woman,
> They stand motionless and motionless hold the splendid car.
> Their heads are lowered to the ground, tears of mourning
> Run hot from their lids, so painfully do they
> Miss their master. Their luxuriant manes
> Spill over the ring of the yoke and are soiled in the dust.
>     It was a painful sight for Zeus, Son of Kronos, to see
> These weeping steeds. Sadly he shook his head and said to his heart:
>     "Ah, you wretches! Why did we ever give you to King Peleus,
> A mortal, you who are ageless and deathless [ἀγήρω τ᾿ ἀθανάτω]?
> Was it so that you could share in the sufferings of these unhappy
>     humans?
> For, truly, there is nothing more wretchedly lamentable than human
>     being,
> Amid all the beings that breathe and creep on the earth."
>
> (lines 434–47)

Zeus's regrets themselves mirror a kind of mourning—for he rues the day he and his brother exposed those immortal horses to mortality. The horses' suffering, which is perhaps even more painful than the *vicarious* suffering of which traditional Christology is so proud, is still more mysterious, however; for these creatures—somewhat betwixt stone and flesh and ever-living fire—share in the mortality of the mortals, the most lamentable of beings. Whether they are stone or animal or divine, these deathless horses are the figures with whom we human beings who hear the singer's song identify most readily. The horses' consternation mirrors our mortality and our mourning.

The story of human mourning is repeated a thousand times in myriad cultures. We are uncertain whether the great king Gilgamesh is human at all until he mourns his friend Enkidu in the most tender terms:

> O Enkidu, the wild ass and the gazelle
> That were father and mother,
> All four-footed creatures who nursed you
> Weep for you,
> All the wild things of the plain and the pasture;
> The paths that you loved in the forest of cedars
> Night and day murmur.[6]

Evidence of elaborate rituals of mourning, whether among the preclassical Maya or the modern Maori, assures ethnologists that they are dealing with human beings. Even if the clay tablets at Uruk invoke the wild ass and the gazelle as father and mother, it is the defunct hirsute man, the wild man who was civilized by a woman, who is loved and mourned. In the archives of all historical peoples we find tales of what befalls the son or daughter who *fails* to mourn a deceased parent, or a king who forbids a sister to inter her murdered and desecrated brother. If—closer to home—the icy serenity of Ralph Waldo Emerson often leaves us cold, the chill dissipates as soon as we read the journal entries Emerson inscribed after the death of his son Waldo, and as soon as we remember the unhewn rock that weeps stonily over their common grave in Sleepy Hollow Cemetery. And the most poignant moments in the story of Leopold Bloom on that famous 16th of June 1904 almost always involve the memory of his defunct infant son, Rudy, named after his own mourned father, Rudolph Virag. Even the rollicking parody of "Oxen of the Sun" takes on a somber tone when the dead son comes to mind: "No, Leopold! Name and memory solace thee not. That youthful illusion of thy strength was taken from thee and in vain. No son of thy loins is by thee. There is none now to be for Leopold, what Leopold was for Rudolph."[7]

Bloom's mourning puts us in mind of all the Old Testament stories that revolve about themes of mourning or the failure to mourn, as though to affirm Hegel's claim that the essential role of the family in the history of spirit—and especially of the women in the family—is to prepare the human corpse for burial. Hegel would castigate a society such as ours, in which professional undertakers usurp this role, while politicians lament the passing of family values. It is not for nothing that one of the most intense confrontations with Hegel's philosophy of the family—I mean Derrida's *Glas,* examined in Chapter 7—is a book whose very title sounds a death knell.

Is mourning an emotion or a process, we asked, an affect or an event, a fatality or an achievement? Is it an idiomatic occurrence or a regulated public ritual? If it is a process, transpiring across time, indeed, taking its wretched old time, mourning nonetheless involves an affect or a combination of affects that seem quite different from regret, sorrow, or sadness. True, Spinoza seems to have brushed up against it in his account of *desiderium,* nostalgia, longing, or languor, what the German Spinozists of the late eighteenth century called *Sehnsucht.* Spinoza writes: "*Desiderium* is a craving or drive for the possession of a thing, a craving that is nourished by the memory of the thing in question but also oppressed by the memory of other things that exclude the existence of the thing we strive for."[8] For his part, Descartes seems to come closest to it in his definition of "Regret" in article 209 of *The Passions of the Soul:* "Regret is also a kind of sadness [*tristesse*]. It has a particular bitterness in that it is always joined to some despair and to the memory of a pleasure [*la mémoire du plaisir*] that gave us joy [*la jouissance*]. For we regret only the good things which we once enjoyed and which are so completely lost [*tellement perdus*] that we have no hope of recovering them at the time and in the form in which we regret them."[9]

*Tellement perdus*—those good things we have lost in so excessive a way. It is their being "so completely lost" that defies telling and incites the labors of mourning. The German language here seems rich in its very poverty: the words for sadness and mourning are so close—*Traurigkeit, Trauer*—that it seems impossible to say whether all sadness is in memory of mourning or mourning an intensification or distillation of the collective sadness of our days. *Trauer* derives from words that mean to fall, drop, or droop, or to lower one's head—presumably after the manner of Achilles' horses. It seems to have a root different from those of the words *trauen, Treue,* and *Trost,* which mean trust, fidelity, and consolation, and that is regrettable, inasmuch as mourning may have to do most of all with *fidelity, promise,* and redoubled *affirmation.* That at least is one of Derrida's most often reiterated ideas, the one I want to make clearer to myself in these pages.

If fidelity, promise, and affirmation appear to belong to what one might call an *ethics* of mourning, I want to approach the *Treue* of *Trauer* somewhat circuitously by way of several other philosophical domains, namely, *aesthetics, logic,* and *ontology.* It may seem that mourning has but little to do with logic, which is so austere; yet I want to relate mourning to our notion of the proper noun, the name (especially the Christian name, first name, or appellation), and the signature—perhaps it is not so much logic, but grammar and syntax, that I am concerned with here. I then want to raise the question of mourning in terms of that subdiscipline of metaphysics called *ontology* or *theory of being,* and in particular what Heidegger calls *fundamental ontology,* only then turning to what others call *ethics.* However, the least hospitable domain for mourning seems to be *aesthetics,* the philosophy of art and beauty, which should be a matter of delight rather than of mourning, and so I want to begin with it.

## Mourning the Beautiful in Art and Life

A kind of battle rages, since Kant's *Kritik der Urteilskraft* (*Critique of Judgment*), over the nature of what Kant calls *aesthetic reflective judgment,* a judgment of taste that makes no conceptual, cognitive, or existential claims about a being, yet does claim universality. If I adjudge a painting or a statue beautiful, and presumably a human being as well, I make no claim about the *existence* of these things, nor do I make a claim of *knowledge* concerning them. Yet when I proclaim them beautiful it is not as though I am satisfied to be in exclusive possession of "the eye of the beholder," allowing others to agree or disagree with my judgment as they like, *de gustibus.* No, what is beautiful for me is, or may rightly be claimed to be, beautiful for all, even if I can make no ontological or epistemological determinations concerning it. What gives me that right, or presumption of right? The very fact, Kant says, that I make no claim concerning the thing or person *insofar as they exist.* In that famous (or notorious) phrase, my spectation of the beautiful is *disinterested,* "without interest," *ohne Interesse,* such interest ostensibly including my interest in whether the beautiful thing or person *is.*

As we shall see in greater detail in Chapter 1, Nietzsche follows Baudelaire and Stendhal in having a good laugh at such "disinterested" appreciation of beauty. In the third treatise of his *Genealogy of Morals* he argues that the beautiful is *une promesse de bonheur,* where "happiness"—which is too vague a word, as Baudelaire insisted—really means erotic transport. "Disinterested," "aesthetic," "reflective" judgment, at least according to these jaded late moderns, is judgment concerning desires that are repressed, censored, screened, condensed, displaced, transposed, and postponed, as the discourse of psychoanalysis has taught us to say. "Disinterestedness" is unconscious interest, interest of the gravest and most intense importance, however cleverly disguised.

Heidegger, in his first lecture course on Nietzsche, presented in 1936–37, would have none of this. He rushed to Kant's defense: what is beautiful can never be the object of an interest, especially an interest as undignified as the erotic. Heidegger stressed the purity (*Reinheit*) of the radiant appearance of the beautiful being, a purity that is never sullied by our enjoyment of it. Kant made it possible for our appreciation of the beautiful to be "purer" than ever before, and also "more intimate and intense," *reiner und inniger,* than any "interested" experience could be. Heidegger took such purity as a sign of the *ontological* relation as such: what the "unconstrained favoring" of "reflective judgment" enforces on the beholder is nothing less than the rapture of being: the "pleasure of reflection" inspired by beauty propels human beings to "the well-grounded fullness" of their "essence." The beautiful opens the path to human history, institutes our historical being, constitutes the very being-there of human beings.

Derrida's intervention in the debate concerning "disinterestedness" and eros is peculiar. Derrida seems to step outside the bounds of the discussion between Kant, Stendhal and Baudelaire, Nietzsche, and Heidegger, in order to introduce something altogether uncalled for, something excessive that adds to the confusion rather than dissolve it. He implies that all three philosophers are right about the beautiful, as long as one adjoins to their accounts something about *mourning.* When Kant argues that reflective judgment has nothing to do with the *existence* of the object, Derrida takes this, it seems, in an excessively literal sense—odd for someone who is always accused of being so excessively metaphorical that the literal quite escapes him. Derrida suggests that a stunningly beautiful object or person, in its purest and most radiant presence to us, shining within the aura of being itself, is actually *lost* to us and is at some terrible remove, always already in an awful *inexistence.* We find something beautiful precisely as we mourn its *loss.* And if the beautiful is a *promise* of happiness, as Nietzsche avers, that is only because it tells us of another promise that is already being extracted from us—a promise of *memory,* a promise of *mourning* that has always already begun. Finally, if the beautiful initiates us into the well-grounded fullness of our historical essence, as Heidegger (following Schiller) believes, that fullness circulates about an emptiness and a loss of ground at the heart of being.

Is Derrida simply being lugubrious here? Is it absurd to say that when we stand in front of Nôtre Dame on a brilliant Sunday afternoon in July the building is *lost* to us? Surely, it looms over us—lapidary, dependable, unmoving? Yet what does it mean when we turn away and continue on our path across Paris with the thought "Yes, I really am here," as though the "really" were an affirmation rescuing us from our drab quotidian existence, to which Nôtre Dame and Paris—with their rich patina of culture and history—seem so utterly foreign? If Nôtre Dame causes the everyday to slip away for an instant, can the very power of its presence nevertheless also be described as a kind of withdrawal? Is it beautiful precisely *as a ruin,* and is all beauty always running to its ruin, hence, in a sense, ruinous?

Or, to alter the example, is there something in our rapture before a Pollock painting or our laughter before a Warhol soup can or an Oldenburg "soft sculpture" that, while not lugubrious, both draws us in and keeps us out—somehow slipping away from us even as we gaze? That we are transported into a state of mourning by the final strains of Mahler's Ninth surely has to do with the music itself, rather than with its "beauty." Perhaps it has to do with the way Leonard Bernstein toward the end of his life was reading the score, which instructs the orchestra to play *Sehr langsam und noch zurückhaltend,* "Very slowly and even haltingly, reticently," and then later in the movement, bafflingly, *Etwas (aber unmerklich) drängend,* "Somewhat compellingly (but unnoticeably so)," with the first word on the final page of the score *Adagissimo* and the last word *ersterbend,* "dying." Yet what can mourning have to do with our simply whistling a happy tune, say, the final cheery movement of Mahler's Fourth?

Derrida would reply that the moment we find Saint Anthony's jocular *Fischpredigt* beautiful, our relation to it is one of mourning. Do then even the happiest song, the most rollicking painted scene, the most exalted edifice, and the most harmoniously constructed piazza induce mourning? Does the most powerful *presence* of a beautiful thing, the commanding stature and status of a statue, for example, wield its power in and as *withdrawal* and *absence?* Does the "promise of happiness" in the limpid eyes and silky arms of a lover also pledge a period of mourning, a period that commences even now, and not later, initiating an intense periodicity of proximity and distance, a rapid rhythm of intimacy and alienation that is set by the most distant drummer for us two who are so close? It may well be that we know too little of mourning, and too little of beauty, to know what that could mean.

And yet, to Heidegger and to Kant, Derrida would rejoin that the very being of a thing, its radiant coming to appearance, is invariably bound up with the withdrawal of the object into an irremediable absence, an absence so stark that it defeats any thought of presence, whether of the present, past, or future—an absence that is of the *absolute past* (see Chapter 4). And, truly, what could Heidegger counter, he being the thinker of the *slipping away* of beings as a whole in anxiety, and of the *default* and *withdrawal* of being, *der Entzug des Seins?* One does have the sense that the tonality of the mourning process is very different in Heidegger and Derrida, that there is something still victorious in Heidegger's commemorative thinking, even when it responds to pain, mourning, and the capacity to die. However, once again, our failure adequately to think *Trauer*—the process, event, labor, or work of mourning—forestalls us. For, of course, such *thinking* itself would be something unfamiliar, something perhaps unrecognizable.

# A Mournful Logic

Let me turn from the exalted presence of the artwork to the sober presence of a proper name or a signature and its logic. When I sign for a house, before witnesses, initialing all the final changes the lawyers have written into the contract, the mortgage company (*mortgage* is an interesting word!), the bank, and the sellers will all insist that I am fully present to the event. Yet the very solemnity of the occasion (I recall in particular the poker face of a rather striking and stylish blond woman who represented the mortgage company and who never smiled and never uttered a pleasant word during the entire ceremony) betrays something about me signing, about me being never more anywhere than I am there at the signing, about me being threatened with fine or imprisonment or both if I should renege, if I should come to doubt in the slightest that I was truly and fully *there* in flesh and in blood and of sound mind. Yet there is something about the signature, about the signature every bit as much as the work of art or the beautiful lover, that induces or expresses a situation or operation of mourning.

I recall a series of biographies of German thinkers and writers that I have on my bookshelves: the final page of each biography is graced by a facsimile signature of the subject of the biography, expressing the aim of the series to provide a *Selbstbildnis,* a self-portrait or autobiography, rather than a mere biography. Occasionally these biographies also include a photograph of the handwritten entry of the subject's name into the local death records—an entry written, of course, in someone else's hand.

My own signature on the mortgage and on the property title is there, of course, precisely in order to outlive me. I am signing, am always signing, my own mortgage, my own death warrant. To be sure, a signature or proper name has value only if it is iterable, only if I always sign the same. The trouble one has in late adolescence when opening a bank account (or trying to make a withdrawal from that account) but still trying out dozens of signatures, seeking the flourish that will be "really me," whereas the teller would be much happier with some simple consistency, testifies to the paradox of signature: I always sign once and for all, every signature is my last, it is the signature on the release demanded by my surgeon before my final surgery, else I would never have to sign in the first place; and yet each time I sign—and I will have to sign again and again until I drop—that signature will have to be selfsame and identical, as we say. For once, *pace* deconstruction, *A* will have to equal *A,* and we will be allowed to write it only once—although never for the first time, inasmuch as even the first signature will have to have been recognizably mine. It is as though the only important part of a signature is the date, which, *nota bene,* they also want us to write in by hand, and as though each date is the one that is already inscribed on my tombstone.

It is not merely that I sign my life away, that I kiss all my money good-bye when I sign: rather, my signature kisses me good-bye. My own signature is in a foreign hand, is always allographic. I recall the strange feeling that comes over me when I pick up an old phonograph record that my dead father once owned and catalogued, recording in his own hand on the jacket the code number and letter that would enable him to locate this record—I recall the idiosyncratic, obsessive signature of a Germanic father who disciplined even his records, the father now so endearing, so long deceased, so late understood. His signature, held in my hand now, reminds me of my own flourish, as foreign and as finalized in its own way as his.

Let me try to formalize the movement of Derrida's meditation on the logic of the signature, in four not-so-easy steps.[10]

1. The proper name survives its bearer. Even though we take it to represent the very identity of this particular person, existent here and now, the signature has value only in that it lives on independently of the signer, of whom the world at large is, as Hegel would say, sensuously certain. To think through this dizzying first step, we would have to move forward to matters that will be discussed in Chapter 3; we would have to advance to the personal pronoun "I," the shifter, and to what Derrida in *Voice and Phenomenon* calls the "testamentary ego."[11] For the signifying "I" is essentially neither universal nor particular, although it *universally* invokes and even induces *my particular* death each time *I* utter the "I." However, that would be a long first step, the step you have to watch out for, as we say to someone who is about to step off the roof of a building. Let the following brief extracts from *Voice and Phenomenon* serve as a reminder: "The absence of intuition—and therefore of the subject of the intuition—is not only *tolerated* by discourse; it is *required* by the general structure of signification, when considered *in itself.* It is radically requisite: the total absence of the subject and object of a statement—the death of the writer and/or the disappearance of the objects he or she was able to describe—does not prevent a text from 'meaning' something. On the contrary, this possibility gives birth to meaning as such, gives it out to be heard and read" (VP, 104/93). Thus what Husserl called the "essentially occasional" expressions, "I," "here," and "now," seem to take on meaning whenever a personality enunciates them. However, as Hegel long ago demonstrated, at the outset of his *Phenomenology of Spirit,* nothing is less sensuously certain than the truth such shifting words aim to hit. Derrida asks,

When I say *I*, even in solitary discourse, can I give my statement meaning without implying there, as always, the possible absence of the object of the discourse—in this case, myself? When I tell myself "I am," this expression, like any other according to Husserl, has the status of discourse only if it is intelligible in the absence of its object, in the absence of intuitive presence—here, in the absence of myself. Moreover, it is in this way that the *ergo sum* is introduced into the philosophical tradition and that a discourse about the transcendental ego is possible. (VP, 106/95)

Derrida insists that it is not an extraordinary tale by Edgar Allan Poe that he is recounting here, but an ordinary tale of language. Language itself asserts the *testamentary* value of all ideal meanings: "My death is structurally necessary to the pronouncing of the *I*" (VP, 107–8/96–97). Signature engages the work of mourning.

2. A person's signature is presumed to be the equivalent of an enunciation, an instance of living, performative speech: "I, *x*, being of sound mind, do hereunto affix my name, so that you who have this document in hand years hence will know that I-here-and-now, with my own hand and of my own free will, will have signed with the name that is proper to me alone, and with my own hand, at this place, and on this date." Thus too an author initials, dates, and "places" the "preface" to his or her book—or at least used to do so, for now publishers are reluctant to continue this old, revered imposture. For, as in the case of the uttered "I," the blink of an "eye," that is, an instant or *Augenblick*, divides the presumed instantaneity of the terminal signature, not simply because the signature (like the book) takes time to execute, but because every signature is in memory of an earlier signing and in anticipation of a future one. Every signature depends on its being recognized as identical to my earlier signings; it demands what Derrida calls "the possibility of anniversary." Every signature necessitates a countersigning, as on a traveler's check. The same signature, in order to be the same, must always be repeated—will always have been repeated, in some sort of future perfect—in another, different, altogether singular event of signature. Thus there is something mechanical about the process. And that mechanism means my death.

3. *Reading* a signature or a text of any kind is also a kind of counter-signature, albeit often inscribed by another. Nevertheless, such alterity has always already invaded the signature and the writing. Rigorous purity in a signature, no matter how well rehearsed, is impossible. Signature is inherently susceptible of repetition, hence of mimicry and counterfeit. No signatory can

appropriate a signature—or indeed any text—wholly, no matter how willful and aggrandizing a person he or she may be: if the signature is written, that is because *it remains to be read.* Thus not even Plato's (literary and doxographic) signature is finally accomplished and fully *underwritten,* as it were, although a long and august philological tradition feels confident that it can recognize the marks of his signature, the distinguishing marks of his work. Plato's signature is never fully achieved, even though, each time he executed it, Plato invited his own impending death. Signature is legacy, passing from logos senior to logos junior, yet a legacy threatened—for internal reasons—with illegitimacy, forgery, bastardy, and patricide. Signature is (one of) the purest of bastards.

4. Signature enacts an indebtedness, is invariably bound up with the enigma of the *gift,* of giving and taking. And here the debt accrued by both the giving and the receiving is total: human beings, beings who sign, live in the unthematized awareness that in every human encounter one of these human beings will survive the other, or the other outlive the one, so that even in a solitary signing one lives in memory of others whom one mourns or is called upon to mourn. The purest of bastards, our sheer signature, links us to the legitimate world at large and to all the others who inhabit it.

For scholars, who read and write texts, the anomalies of signature that we have only now outlined seem to contaminate an entire way of life, infecting it to a point of ultimate morbidity. (Scholars, as we shall note at the end of Chapter 6, often do not love Derrida.) Derrida writes about the mourning and memory of an author's signature in *Signéponge,* that is, *Signed Ponge,* or, as though one signature can soak up all the names of history, *Signsponge:*

> We always pretend to know what a corpus is all about. . . . The academic conventions of literary biography presuppose at least one certainty— the one concerning the signature, the link between the text and the proper name of the person who retains the copyright. . . . All the philological fuss about apocryphal works is never bothered by the slightest doubt, on the contrary, it is set in movement by an absence of doubt as to the status . . . of a paraph [i.e., an initialing]. They certainly ask whether or not it has taken place, this paraph, but as to the very strange structure of this place and this taking-place, the critic and the philologist (and various others) do not as such ask themselves a single question. They may wonder whether a certain piece of writing is indeed assignable to a certain author, but as regards the event of the signature, the abyssal machinery of this operation, the commerce between said author and her proper name, in other words, whether she signs when

she signs, whether her proper name is truly her name and truly proper, before or after the signature, and how all this is affected by the logic of the unconscious, the structure of the language, the paradoxes of name and reference, of nomination and description, the links between common and proper names, names of things and personal names, the proper and the non-proper, no question is ever posed by any of the regional disciplines which are, as such, concerned with texts known as literary.[12]

It is not that Derrida rests content with such confusion, not that he is delighted to point it out in order to leave it all in a muddle. Indeed, the quagmire that philosophers most often open up with their hairsplitting and their axioms, corollaries, and addenda is in Derrida's view anything but tasteful. Philosophers, says Derrida, and he regards himself as one of them for the moment, "are a little disgusting" because they never know when to stop, when to abbreviate, terminate, and sign on the dotted line. A philosopher's consent is always halfhearted, Merleau-Ponty once said, in *praise* of philosophy; a philosopher's signature is always half counterfeit, half forgery, replies Derrida, and her or his dithering and prevaricating are always a bit contemptible. The philosopher seeks protection in generalities, in notions and concepts that are so universal that he or she feels relieved of the obligation to sign: "In order to sign, one has to stop one's text, and no philosopher will have signed his or her text, resolutely and singularly, will have spoken in his or her own name, accepting all the risks involved in doing so. Every philosopher denies the idiom of his or her name, of his or her language, of his or her circumstance, speaking in concepts and generalities that are necessarily improper" (SP, 32). That of course does not prevent Hegel, for example, from spending an inordinate amount of time in his *Philosophy of Right* (§§ 64–69) condemning plagiarism and shoring up the "spiritual ownership" that is so dear to him and to all philosophers. And the flow of unlimited ink in our own time does not prevent all the participants from copyrighting and competing very much in their own names. Thus a certain tension persists in Derrida's labors, between the obligation to sign and the impossibility of signature: unhappy to dither, yet not wishing to prevaricate, Derrida nevertheless cannot blithely sign. His relation to signature (although he may be signing here on behalf of us all) is one of *mourning*.

Something in the signature and the proper name remains an epitaph, a cenotaph, a mark of mourning. When an initialing occurs or a signature falls, it falls to the tomb—the nominal and verbal *tombe* of *Glas*.[13] If my signature remains after I am gone, after the remainder of my mortal remains scatter, that is because the signature always was "remains," always was a residue, always was a kind of cinder. Written in stone it may be, but the stone is calcined to powdery ash, to the barest possible trace.

Yet everything we have discussed so far—the mourning of the proper in the logic of names and signatures, the ontology of radiant appearance and irremediable withdrawal, and the aesthetics of the beautiful, because lost, object—is parasitic on experiences of mourning, concerning which, we have said, we are largely in the dark. All we can hope is that something of our logics, ontologies, and aesthetics will become clearer to us if we dwell on experiences of mourning—or, if not dwell on them, at least try to release them from the effects of an overwhelming repression. The final thoughts of this Introduction, on the *ethos* of mourning, therefore take us to Freud's famous 1917 essay "Mourning and Melancholy" and to the realm of something like an *ethics,* which is most often said to be responsible for that overwhelming repression.


## A Mournful Freud

Freud discusses mourning only tangentially: his real interest is depression, or *melancholia.* Yet the mere "parallel" he claims to be descrying and describing in "Mourning and Melancholy" belies the importance of mourning in and for psychoanalysis as such. Recall, for example, the final words of the foreword to the second (1908) edition of *The Interpretation of Dreams.* There Freud reminds us that his entire endeavor in *Die Traumdeutung,* this cornerstone of psychoanalysis, is in effect a work of mourning for his dead father—a father's death being, as he says, in words one might have expected to read concerning the *mother's* death, "the most significant event, the most lacerating loss, in a man's life" (2:24).[14] Years later, when his memory plays tricks on him during a visit to the Acropolis of Athens, it is the same mourned father who haunts psychoanalysis. The "parallel" in and of "Mourning and Melancholy" seems indeed to collapse, in spite of Freud's best efforts to sustain it: mourning and melancholy are often conflated and become indistinguishable precisely when Freud most wants to keep them apart.

Depression is supposed to be *pathological,* whereas successful mourning is said to be *therapeutic.* Yet just as the manic side of depression is missing from mourning, so the *work* of mourning seems to be missing from depression. Further, it becomes more and more difficult to see what makes successful mourning—that is, an accomplished withdrawal of emotional investment from the deceased object of our love—successful. Freud's rather desperate suggestion, to wit, that the mourner revels in receipt of "the consolation prize of survival," seems more a capitulation than an explanation, inasmuch as *survival* is only another way of stating the *problem* of mourning. If only the dead *would* bury their dead, we mourners would have nothing about which to be depressed. As Freud recognized at the end of "Mourning and Melancholy," but also at the end of his late work *Inhibition, Symptom, and Anxiety* (1926), mourning is an experience of real pain (*Schmerz*), pain as intense as any suffering that we associate with physical trauma: because we *long for* the object we have lost, we *languish* in mourning. (Freud uses the Schellingian word *Sehnsucht*, Spinoza's *desiderium*, literally, what seems to befall one "from the stars," that is, from one's *disastrous, unlucky* stars.) We languish in every situation that reproduces for us our connection with that beloved person who—as our reality probe demonstrates to us—no longer exists (6:305–8). (The existence or inexistence of the one who is dead *interests* us, Freud would insist, against Kant, even and especially if we experienced him or her as *beautiful*.) Unable to do justice to Freud's essays, I shall nevertheless attempt a general account of the mourning process, taking into account the further developments of Freud's thesis by Nicolas Abraham and Marie Torok.[15]

If the work of mourning is successful, according to Freud, the *world* may be impoverished by the death of my friend, but my *ego* will not be. I will, over time, albeit in ways that are not easy to elaborate, withdraw the emotional investment I have made in him or her. Quite often that investment is excessive, inasmuch as I am inclined to overestimate the very persons whose deaths will cause me most to mourn. If my labors of mourning are unsuccessful, the bereaved object may come to invade my body and my behavior phantasmically; I may *incorporate* the deceased in such a totalizing way that one might almost say that the dead one has incorporated *me*. We all laugh about the older brother or sister who is becoming "just like Dad" a decade or so after our father's death; yet our laughter is disturbed by the uncanny presentiment that a *Doppelgänger* always evokes, and we realize against our will that mourning, if "unsuccessful," may well produce zombie effects or, at best, that the "who's who" of our families and our selves may be gravely disturbed by the dead one, whom we precisely *have not* laid to rest. The best we can hope for, says Freud, is *introjection*, in which a modest dwelling for the deceased is prepared within the self—a self that consists largely of hyperbolic identifications and narcissistic or anaclitic object choices in the first place.

How fraught the theme of mourning is, how intimately bound up with the constellation of the family and the very formation of our selves, is betrayed by

the following early reference to mourning—along with the very first reference
to the Oedipus complex—in Freud's work. In Manuscript N, from the year
1897, Freud writes:

> Inimical impulses toward one's parents (the wish that they would die)
> are likewise an integral component of neurosis. They come into the
> daylight of consciousness as compulsive representations. In paranoia
> they correspond to the most severe delusions of persecution (patho-
> logical distrust of rulers and monarchs). These impulses are repressed
> whenever compassion for the parents predominates, during the periods
> of their illness and death. Then it is an expression of mourning to blame
> oneself by means of hysteria, suffering the very same symptoms that
> they suffered, as though by way of retribution. The identification that
> takes place in this instance is, as we can see, nothing other than a mode
> of thought, and it makes the search for a motive superfluous.[16]

Note that the labors of mourning are here associated with the gravest of
neuroses and paraphrenias *as well as* with the most normal of developments:
mourning is bound up not only with compulsive neurosis, paranoia, and
hysteria but also with the very structure and formation of the ego, with the
gestation of our problematic Narcissus (whom, or which, we shall meet again
in Chapter 2). Even if Freud declares that the identification with the dead
parent is "only a mode of thought" and that it therefore needs no explanation,
such identification is continuous since birth and is inordinately complex for
the duration of our lives. If the most profoundly mourned persons happen to
be our mother and father, brothers and sisters, lovers and spouses, not to
mention our own children, then no one can imagine that the withdrawal of
libidinal investment from every "memory and expectation" associated with the
beloved can go without explanation. If our memories and expectations are
invariably bound up with the human beings who mean the most to us, how
shall we dismiss our preoccupation or withdraw our investment without (risk
of) autodestruction? Who will successfully withdraw investments from an
account that has always been a *joint* account, indeed, an account with multiple
signatories? Even if one manages to avoid the extreme case of incorporation,
in which some "original narcissism" devours and consumes the self through
the mouth of the other who is now dead—the sacrificial meal by which the
dead one now rules supreme in the crypt of the self—is it not also the case that
where flesh and blood are *shared* no self ever absolutely manages to escape
incorporation by and of the other?

Derrida wonders whether mourning, the "successful," introjective mourning prescribed by Freud, is *possible*. He then wonders whether, even if it were possible, such success would be *desirable*. Pushing the thought, he wonders whether successful mourning is in effect *impossible* and, as the poet Hölderlin says, always in default. Finally, he wonders whether the very default of successful mourning is what gives *fidelity* and *affirmation* a chance, the slim chance of a *promise*.

## Memory Mourning Affirmation

Memory has always been a sign of life. When Chaucer, in "The Knight's Tale" (line 2698), wants to tell us that Arcite is still conscious after a fall from his horse, he writes, "For he was yet in memorie and alyve." Memory is also a sign of love. The Minnesingers were mnemonics, not because they memorized their love songs, but because they dwelled on their beloved objects: *minne* (love) is a form of μνήμη (memory). Yet the mnemic and "minnic" sign is also a sign of death and mourning. The Indo-Germanic *mer-* is the root of death, *morior,* while the Indo-Germanic *smer-* is the root of remembrance. The Greek word μερίμνα contains both roots: it means "care, sorrow, and solicitude." Heidegger seems to be equally indebted to Augustine's *cura* and to the Stoic use of μερίμνα when he chooses first the words *Kummer* and *Bekümmerung* and later the word *Sorge,* "care," as the name that is most appropriate for human being as being in the world. Yet if his "care" focuses on the death of being-there as in-each-case-mine, that is, if Heidegger's existential analysis focuses on *my own* death, Derrida (no doubt under the influence of Levinas) soon shifts the focus toward the experience of the death of the *other,* and only then back again to "my own" death. Not because of some altruism, one must say; not because of sanctity or an ethics of ethics; but because "the other" (which in Chapter 8 will necessarily appear as "the [m]other") has always already invaded the propriety of one's ownmost, birth-bound, moribund self. Heidegger hopes that Dasein will come back to a memory of being by means of undistracted focus on its own death; Derrida suspects that if *being* is in default, as Heidegger says it is, then the absence or default that being *is* will be more powerfully experienced in the death of an other—and in the default of successful mourning.

The very fate of memory seems to be at stake in what Derrida calls *impossible mourning,* which is also a mourning that is eminently *unsuccessful.*

What does it mean to be in memory of an other or to do something in "his" or "her" memory, when it is only "our own" memory that avails? It is clearly a sign of fidelity, a promise to keep the absent one in and for our own future, a sign of faith made particularly poignant by the ineluctable happenstance that the other knows nothing of this, is none the wiser or richer for it. No narcissism—which is itself in ruins—rushes to the other's or to our own rescue in impossible mourning. "In this terrifying lucidity," writes Derrida, "in the light of this incinerating blaze where nothingness appears, we remain in *disbelief* itself."[17] The *fides* of this fidelity is utter disbelief in both the death and the immortality of the other—as though the mourned other were somewhat betwixt immortal horse and defunct Patroclus. "And we sustain the blaze of this terrible light," Derrida continues, "through devotion, for it would be unfaithful to delude oneself into believing that the other living *in us* is living *in himself*" (MEM, 43/21).

Nevertheless, this desperate memory *in memoriam,* in memory of the other, is not one memory among others: in Derrida's view, it marks the *birth* of memory as such in us, if one can say so; memory *in memoriam* is a process of original separation, in Levinas's sense, but also separation "from the float forever held in solution," as Whitman says. It is a nascent sensation or intimation, scarcely ripe enough for the following words: *One of us will have died before the other; we will not go down together; one or the other will have to survive if only an instant longer, whether it is she or I; do not forget this; never forget this.*

Of course we will forget it. Memory is finite. If we keep mourning in mind, we must also mourn memory, and thus mourn mourning itself. John Llewelyn writes of "the mourning whose death we mourn."[18] We cannot forever remain faithful to the departed one, to the facade of Nôtre Dame de Paris, to the tempi so imperiously ordered by Mahler on the edge of his death, to the unmarked graves of Patroclus and Enkidu, not merely because our attention span is too limited but because, in a sense that is difficult to articulate but hard to deny, these loved others *were never fully there* for us when they were alive, never fully present to us, never palpable in the way our dreams promised—if only because *we* were never fully there *for us* while they were alive. Even when *they* were there for us, there never was any *there* there for us. Perhaps the other *as* other comes to us for the first time, therefore, in the experience of mourning, absence, default. The friend lives on *in us,* even though we ourselves have never lived comfortably there, in that uncanny home which from the outset was always invaded by the others. "This is why there can be no *true mourning,*" writes Derrida, "even if truth and lucidity always presuppose it" (MEM, 50/29).

The other's death abandons me to a terrible solitude, but it is a solitude I vaguely recognize. Rather than bestow on me the narcissistic pleasures of survival, it inaugurates a relation of self to self that was not possible before the cataclysmic event but that nevertheless did not entirely surprise me. The other's death finalizes what Nietzsche calls the "eternally wretched 'Too late!'" that was always already part of the way we constantly missed one another in life.

Derrida argues that what I so confidently call "me," "us," the "between us," "subjectivity," "intersubjectivity," and even "memory" are constituted by the labors of mourning. Or, at least, they are constituted by the *possibility* of the other's death, which is therefore not preeminently the possibility of my own impending impossibility and which cannot be met with either resoluteness or readiness-for-anxiety. Such constitution transpires in some sense "prior" to my relationship to my self and beyond all narcissism. To be more precise, the possibility of the death of the other as *my* possibility or *our* possibility *together* gives shape to my relationships with others and to my own finite memory. It is not the repeatable-insurmountable imminence of my own death, my own being toward an end, as Heidegger avers, that makes my being my own; rather, the very otherness that is impacted in my living beyond the other, surviving her or him, is what molds the eminently vulnerable self that is *my* self.

Yet Derrida does not acquiesce in the default of *true* mourning. In his refusal of default and defeatism, in his redoubled desire to remain truly true to the memory of the other, one may descry the most powerful possibilities of *promise* and *affirmation*. If in his funeral address to Levinas (*to* rather than *for*), Derrida struggles to avoid all the language of the self, which seems to him "indecent"; if he shuns any reference to "consolation," especially the consolation prize of survival; if he spurns "this confused and terrible expression 'work of mourning,'" it is in the hope of a greater fidelity of mourning, a certain promise of memory, along with the singularly uncertain chances of affirmation.[19] To be sure, the affirmation is and remains *of the other,* "who will have spoken first" (MEM, 56/37). The priority of the other—the ultra-transcendental authority of the other, as it were—is possible as *pain,* if not as *success:*

> We weep *precisely* over what happens to us when everything is entrusted to the sole memory that is "in me" or "in us." But we must also recall in another turn of memory that the "within me" and the "within us" *do not* arise or appear *before* this terrible experience. Or at least not before its possibility, actually felt and inscribed in us,

signed. The "within me" and the "within us" acquire their sense and their bearing only by carrying within themselves the death and the memory of the other; of an other who is greater than they, greater than what they or we can bear, carry, or comprehend. . . . Which is another way of remaining inconsolable before the finitude of memory. We know, we knew, we *remember*—before the death of one we loved—that being-in-me or being-in-us is constituted by the possibility of mourning. We are ourselves only from the perspective of this knowledge that is older than ourselves; and this is why I say that we begin by *recalling* this to ourselves: we come to ourselves through this memory of *possible* mourning. (MEM, 53/33–34)

It would be easy to trip up Derrida here with questions about what comes first, the *experience* of mourning or the mysterious *possibility* of this experience; it would be easy to accuse him of a residual Platonism, as though we were certain of Plato's signature; it would be easy for us to say that even when the pain of mourning is actually felt and "signed" in us, there is no guarantee against a counterfeit signature. However, it is Derrida who has best helped us to trip him up, for it is he who warns us about the legerdemain of transcendental/empirical distinctions, he who insists that ultratranscendental passage confronts the absolute past, he who warns us that every affirmation is vulnerable to negation and mockery. For him, the phrases *in memory of mourning* and *in mourning of memory* do not represent a mere clever trope of reversal. The subtitle of this Introduction, *"Memoria in Memoriam,"* tries to keep memory in mourning, which now means both to keep memory and to lose it, embrace it and give up the dream of possessing it; the subtitle also tries to keep mourning in memory, not in order to intone a lugubrious threnody, but to *promise* memory to oneself and to one's others, living and dead.

In the end, to be sure, there remains some confusion about the possibility of an impossible mourning, about the default of something that is more pervasive *in* us and constitutive *of* us than anything (else) can be. In the end, there remains some confusion between ontology and ethics, an *undecidability* that afflicts the nature of faithful memory, confounding the chances run and the obligations met by mourning. In the end, the double or multiple *yes* of an affirmation alone resounds: *Yes . . . you are no longer here . . . and yes . . . you were the only hope of my being able to keep all this in memory and alyve . . . and yes . . . the absence started while you were still here, because I was always a bit lost, gone before you, but now it's been exacerbated beyond belief, beyond relief, now you've really done it . . . yes. . . .*

The pain of contradiction is exceeded by the pain of an undecidable mourning. Yet affirmation never withdraws its investment on that account, never withdraws itself once and for all, and the pain of undecidable mourning is the birth pang of all that will have come to be, of all that is beautiful in everything that was.

# PART ONE

## Mourning the Work of Art

# 1

# Broken Frames

This is the place, it seems to me, to take up again certain
questions concerning fashion and adornment [*parure*]
. . . and to avenge the art of the toilette.
—Baudelaire, *Le peintre de la vie moderne*

We are not even close to having at our disposal rigorous
criteria for deciding . . . the limits framing [*encadrant*]
a corpus or what is proper to a system. . . . The very concept
of belonging (to an ensemble) will allow itself to be worked,
that is, dislocated, by the structure of the *parergon*.
—Derrida, "Economimesis"

In the Introduction I speculated on beauty as withdrawal and on our relation
to the beautiful as a relation of mourning. Two of my examples, mentioned
only in passing, were the Warhol soup can and Pollock's action paintings. I did
not pause to ask whether and how these paintings are *framed*, probably because
we have been taught that frames are inessential to works of art. Yet we also
know that Nôtre Dame is in some sense framed by its square, the Seine, the
archbishop's park, and the rue du Cloître. Even Mahler's Ninth is framed, each
time it is performed, by players, conductor, listeners, hall, and season; beyond
that, it is framed by the anxious silence of expectation before it begins and the
awful silence after it has ended.

Do works need frames? If not, why do they have them? Would literary and
philosophical productions be among the works that need a frame? Is Kant's
*Critique of Judgment* framed in some sense by its place and time, framed also

by the tendency of its questions, framed perhaps most decisively by what it wants, what it desires, what is its pleasure?

And is ours the time in which frames—borders, edges, frontiers, limits—seldom hold? A time in which frames fail to protect their contents, so that our works of art, literature, philosophy, fashion, and culture generally leak to the outside at all four corners? Is not the frame broken today? Must we also mourn the shattered frame?

"Parergon" is the title of the first chapter of Derrida's *La vérité en peinture,* or *The Truth in Painting.*[1] The selfsame rubric, "Parergon," serves also as the title of the second division of this first chapter. From the outset, then, the question of frames and frameworks is unavoidable with regard to this text: "Parergon" is a text within a text, folded back into and upon itself, or reproduced within itself, after the manner of a Russian Baba or Chinese box, but into abyssal infinity—the phenomenon that Derrida himself designates as *mise-en-abyme,* a mirroring without end. The word πάρεργον means byproduct, marginal side effect, mere avocation, addendum, or supplement. The word refers to the subordinate or secondary aspects of a matter, to incidentals or accidentals. In a work of art such as a painting, the word refers to everything that lies outside of the main figure or thematic center of a picture—the supporting characters, the limned background, ghosted figures, ornament, decoration, and most obviously *the frame.* In ancient Greek philosophy, τὸ πάρεργον is anything that has nothing to do with philosophy proper, anything that does not rise to the occasion of rigorous philosophical inquiry. For example—as though examples were not themselves essentially mere *parerga*—each human being should exercise only one τέχνη in and for the city, Socrates insists in the second book of *Republic,* an art or a skill that he or she "pursues in an orderly manner . . . and not merely as an avocation [μὴ ἐν παρέργου μέρει]" (370c 1). In *Theaetetus* (184a 6–7) Socrates expresses the fear that Father Parmenides' doctrine will not be understood if one "examines it merely superficially [εἴτε τις ἐν παρέργου σκέψεται]." In *Laws* it is said that one never dare take the education of children "as a secondary and subordinate matter [οὐ δεύτερον οὐδὲ πάρεργον]" (766a 4). In ethics, as in all disciplines, declares Aristotle in *Nicomachean Ethics* (1098a 32), one must make certain that "subordinate matters do not exceed the scope of the main work itself [ὅπως μὴ τὰ πάρεργα τῶν ἔργων πλείω γίγνηται]."

Why, then, in the philosophical discipline of aesthetics, take up the question of frames and frameworks? Is it to imply that, in comparison to logic, ethics, and metaphysics or ontology, aesthetics itself is a mere hobby? Would such a degradation also apply to Kant's aesthetics, as developed in the *Critique of*

*Judgment?* Like Kant, Derrida would deny it. Why the question of frames and frameworks with regard to aesthetics? Because, since Kant, aesthetics has steadily gained ground in philosophy, assuming ever-enhanced power to define, determine, and synthesize philosophy's essential problems. One might even suppose that aesthetics is relevant to the problem of mourning and mortality in general.

In our own time, aesthetics has assumed truly epoch-making power. Some would say that it has become coextensive with what used to be regarded as the exclusive domains of metaphysics and morals. Others would observe that the very notion of epoch and ἐποχή is itself a kind of frame or historical framework, so that the issue of what is epochal and epoch-making can never be shoved aside as a mere appendix, appendage, or side effect. Still others would note that just as a frame serves as the *boundary* or *limit* of the work of art, so aesthetics has advanced to the very limit of an enlightened philosophy, to the limits of Enlightenment as such.[2]

Derrida tries to pursue the question of art—that is, the question of the circle that encloses the artwork, the artist (or genius), and art as such—in the framework established by Hegel's and Heidegger's meditations on art, in the aftermath of the Kantian Enlightenment. What becomes problematic for Derrida is precisely this historical framework; the "epochal" in general comes into question for him. Further, Derrida concerns himself with how aesthetics finds its way into the circle of artwork, artist, and art in general; how philosophy comes to penetrate or crack the artwork, define and confine the artist, and inveigle itself into the "essence" and "origin" of art "as such"; how the philosopher effectively asserts himself or herself in the face of the artist, no matter how ingenious the latter may be; how philosophy always manages to encircle art, besiege it, and master it—in a word, *interpret* it. Precisely this competence of philosophy with regard to beauty and the fine arts is what Derrida brings under suspicion. For, as we have seen, his own response to art and beauty has less to do with interpretive confidence than with a mourner's consternation.

However, if in Derrida's view the two most important framers of the framework of aesthetics in the history of that discipline are Hegel and Heidegger, it becomes compellingly clear that the great Kant cannot remain unexamined. Hegel endeavors to show that Kant's aesthetics is a theory of subjectivity and subjective judgment, and that it is therefore one-sided and incomplete. In contrast, and in defiant opposition to Nietzsche's remarks on Kant in the third treatise of the *Genealogy of Morals,* Heidegger argues that the Kantian concept of "disinterestedness" contains a genuine anticipation of the "unconstrained favoring" and the "bestowal of being" that his own thought wishes to encounter. Whether one agrees with Hegel, seeking to overcome Kant's shortcomings, or with Heidegger, desiring no more than to cultivate the Kantian anticipation of the alethiological or revelatory character of art, one inevitably comes back to the question of art as developed in the third *Critique.* The second section of Derrida's *Parergon,* itself entitled "Parergon," consequently proffers a long and technically difficult discussion of Kant's *Kritik der Urteilskraft.*[3]

The frame of Derrida's own discussion constantly threatens to explode. Not only the field of force that has Hegel and Heidegger as its most potent poles, but also the Kantian Critical project itself threatens to burst asunder. Derrida does not involve himself here explicitly with either the Hegelian objection to or the Heideggerian adoption of Kant: he asks about neither one-sided subjectivity nor the disinterestedness of aesthetic reflection. Rather, he inquires into the Critical project as a whole—a whole that is dominated by the forces of humanism, anthropocentrism, and "culturalism," or ethnocentrism. Kant's foreword to the first edition and his March 1790 introduction (the second, revised *Einleitung*) are, at least initially, the most important documents for Derrida's reading. In the context of the first part of the *Critique of Judgment,* "The Critique of Aesthetic Judgment," it is initially neither the "Analytic of the Beautiful" nor the "Analytic of the Sublime" that draws Derrida's attention. (It is nevertheless true that the third and fourth sections of *Parergon* occupy themselves with questions of the unconstrainedly beautiful and the sublimely colossal.) And yet from the outset Derrida poses detailed questions concerning not only the pleasing character of the beautiful or the delight (*Wohlgefallen*) we take in it, which we express in judgments of taste, but also emotion (*Rührung*) and charm (*Reiz*), all of which touch on the question of *plaisir*— which, in Kant's view, ought to be banished utterly from the realm of such judgments. As I indicated, however, these detailed questions arise within the most capacious of all Kantian frameworks, that involving the sense and direction of the Critical project as such and as a whole.

Oddly, this fascination with the whole, with the broadest possible implications of the Critical project, realizes itself in what appear to be mere minutiae. Derrida undertakes to examine with painstaking care Kant's examples (*Beispiele*) of aesthetic reflective judgment, the examples that are elaborated in the *Critique of Judgment* §14, "Elucidation Through Examples." Derrida reminds his readers of Hegel's commentary on the word *Bei-spiel.*[4] He reminds them also of Kant's warning that the examples are there only for those readers who are incapable of rigorous conceptual thought. As far as the Critical project is concerned, examples are mere by-products, side effects, if not sheer play and frivolity. Parerga are for the parergonal. That is not to say, however, that examples cause Kant no grief. In the first *Critique,* the inaugural *Critique of Pure Reason* (A xviii–xix), Kant admits that it is the examples that have given him trouble and made him uncertain, indecisive (*unschlüssig*). Whereas the inventory of all the principles, concepts, and categories of reason and intellect proceeded under the stable and steady light of reason, reason shining its light *within,* as it were, the effort to produce clarity through intuitive examples faltered and failed. Perhaps it should not surprise us that examples are still causing Kant trouble in 1790, with the third *Critique.* To be sure, we find there the usual disclaimer: the Critical philosophy concerns itself with principles, not examples. Kant therefore presents his examples throughout the *Critique of Judgment* without a great deal of soul-searching, as though they were the most transparent examples in the world. They are not. Kant's *Beispiele* are what lend Derrida's text its title, its outer frame, its charm, its bite, and its substance. What amazes Derrida is the fact that Kant's examples are exemplary *and* execrable examples of the example. What astonishes him is the fact that in Kant's reflection on art what is most essential and least essential in the Critical project converge—precisely on exemplarity. What bewilders him is the fact that the most grandiose and most picayune matters of the project appear within the selfsame exemplary frame, as it were.

Let me try to follow Derrida's steps in "Parergon," that is, the second, smaller, more interior "Parergon" of the larger *Parergon,* with the requisite caution and circumspection. There are, as I count them, twenty-four steps. Each step is indicated by a blank space in the text, a space that is framed on the lower left and upper right by broken or exploded jointures, jointures out of joint, more or less like these:

—

|

|

—

At about the halfway point, by approximately the eleventh step, the reader suddenly comes upon an empty space that has no frame, not even an exploded one (66/57). Precisely here, in the frame that is not so much sprung as obliterated, Kant's examples are most intensely examined and discussed. However, before venturing these twenty-four steps, let us now cast a glance at the appropriate point in Kant's own text, in order to remind ourselves about the Critical intention with regard to the example.

## Kant's Example

In the very same manner as theoretical or logical judgments—which, however, they are *not*—aesthetic judgments can be divided into either empirical or pure judgments. The latter alone, the purely formal and formally pure aesthetic judgments, qualify as genuine judgments of taste. No mere empirical liking or being pleased or delighted dare mingle with the pure formality and formal purity of such judgments. Hence, no charm, no emotion need apply. If delight may be introduced at all, it must be kept "dry." For example, in our enjoyment of a painting, the only aspects that play a role are the drawing and delineation, that is to say, the compositional form, not color. Color (the German *Farbe*, which is color, pigment, and paint in one) is not dry but wet. *Farbe* is slippery. *Farbe* smears. *Farbe* makes obscene noises when the paintbrush is dipped in the pigment.[5] In short, form over color, as not only Kant insists, but also Socrates, inasmuch as the chromatic distracts us from the pure idea of the beautiful and soils the beautiful idea of the pure, from which we mortals are so mournfully remote.

Form constitutes the sole genuine object of the pure judgment of taste. Yet precisely in the context of pure form Kant turns to the *parergon*, the matter in Kant's text that so charms or irritates Derrida. Kant writes:

> Selbst was man Zieraten (Parerga) nennt, d. i. dasjenige, was nicht in die ganze Vorstellung des Gegenstandes als Bestandstück innerlich, sondern nur äußerlich als Zutat gehört und das Wohlgefallen des Geschmacks vergrößert, tut dieses doch auch nur durch seine Form: wie Einfassungen der Gemälde, oder Gewänder an Statuen, oder Säulengänge um Prachtgebäude. Besteht aber der Zierat nicht selbst in der schönen Form, ist er, wie der goldene Rahmen, bloß um durch seinen Reiz das Gemälde dem Beifall zu empfehlen angebracht; so heißt er alsdann *Schmuck*, und tut der echten Schönheit Abbruch. (KU, B 43)

> Even what we call *adornments* (Parerga), i.e., whatever does not belong intrinsically as a component of the entire representation of the object,

but only extrinsically as an added ingredient, whatever augments the delight of taste does so at all events by means of its form: as in the case of frames of paintings, or clothing on statues, or columned porticoes about ceremonial buildings. However, if the adornment does not consist of beautiful form, if, as in the case of the golden frame, it is added only so that its charm will win the painting applause, then it is called *ornament,* and it severs all relations with genuine beauty.

We observe two possibilities with respect to *parerga,* where we might have anticipated only one. These two possibilities—or, rather, the very possibility that there could be two of them—create(s) several difficulties. For that which works its effects extrinsically, and which therefore can be designated as a super-added ingredient, an addendum, which merely augments or enhances the delight we take in judgments of taste, also does so merely (*tut dieses doch auch nur*) by means of form. Although it works its effects extrinsically, those formal effects are, formally speaking, identical with the effects that work intrinsically. Although purely extrinsic, adornment achieves effects that are purely formal and formally pure, that is, intrinsic. First example: that which frames or encompasses a painting (*Einfassungen der Gemälde*). And yet the adornment that comes to augment a work can also be pleasing for reasons that lie outside form, whereby, to be sure, it charms or stimulates (or offends, if one is a Kantian) more than it pleases. Adornment, when it is merely ornamental, can thus also work effects that are not purely formal and formally pure. Kant's text immediately adjoins the counterexample: the golden frame (*der goldene Rahmen*). Strangely, what Kant condemns is not *der vergoldete Rahmen,* whereby the extrinsic nature of the "gilding" would be apparent: the scandal would be evident—as in Samuel L. Clemens and Charles Dudley Warner's *The Gilded Age: A Tale of Today.* However, for Kant the scandal is not simply a matter of fool's gold; no, not even gold itself is formally pure enough to satisfy Kant's dry taste.

What then is adornment, as opposed to mere ornament? The entirely un-Critical dictionary defines *Zierat* as "ornament, decoration, adornment, finery; (*as an objection*): baubles," as though presupposing but being unable to explain the difference between *proper* adornment and *inappropriate* baubles, bangles, bright shiny beads. The simpler word *Zier* is defined as "ornament, embellishment." The slightly varied form *Zierde* means "ornament; (*figuratively*): ornament, honor, credit to someone." *Zier* and *Zierde* are feminine, *Zierat* (Kant's word, and the most ambivalent of the three) is neuter.

Allow me to interrupt the account of Kantian adornment with a very different account, to which I alluded in the Introduction, namely, that of Baudelaire in "The Painter of Modern Life."[6] As though in response to Rousseau and Kant, Baudelaire eulogizes adornment, makeup, and costume as elements that grace a nature which at its core is corrupt. Section 11 of the essay, "In Praise of Makeup," condemns the eighteenth-century confidence that nothing can embellish nature. "Nature can only counsel crime," writes Baudelaire, in phrases reminiscent of Sade. "Let it all pass in review, analyze all that is natural, all the actions and the desires of the purely natural human being, and you will find nothing other than the frightful." Thus Baudelaire is led to regard adornment, *la parure*, "as one of the signs of the primitive nobility of the human soul." Woman plays a special role in such nobility, indeed, a fundamentally *religious* role: "an idol, she should adorn herself in order to be adored." No doubt, for Kant, though not for Sade (here the case is far more difficult), *adornment* and *adoration* combine only as a wicked parergonal pun. Yet in Kant's aesthetics, *some part* of adornment remains permissible, and is even essential to the (enhancement of the) work. And that is where the frame rubs.

How must Kantian adornment be disposed so that it can avoid the merely extrinsic nature of mere ornament? How is it that the adornment that supervenes in a work also works its effects purely formally and formally purely, *even though it must do so from the outside?* What is beauty, such that the delight we take in it *allows itself* to be augmented from the outside? More specifically, how can a frame augment or enlarge the impact of a painting? What separates the intrinsic inner core or interior depths of a painting or drawing from the outside, for example, from the wall on which it hangs? Does the purely formal and formally pure framework, including the *passe-partout*, both of which are (in Kant's example) *good* parerga, pertain more to the painting or to the wall? Does the frame belong to the picture as long as it is colorless, and to the wall as soon as color—even golden color—besmirches it? If the gilding were removed from a *bad* parergon, if the merely ornamental frame were stripped of its gold and smoothed of its whittled flowers and leaves, would the frame then better adhere to the work of art? Surely the unadorned frame remains an adornment with regard to the painting *and* the wall? Yet if this is so, are not *parergon* and *ergon*, with respect to their formal purity and pure formality, well-nigh identical—or at least indistinguishable, undecidable? If outside and inside are formally no longer clearly delineated, especially not by a frame, would not the power of reflective aesthetic judgment, the judgment that judges works of art, lose its pure and genuine object, the object ostensibly protected within the frame? Would one not have to mourn the loss of the work of art as such?

Derrida's twenty-four steps in the "Parergon" of *Parergon* may be divided or gathered up into three larger leaps or stages: first, consideration of the curious position of Kant's *Kritik der Urteilskraft* within the Critical philosophy as a whole—curious inasmuch as the third *Critique* represents *both* a forked, bifurcated, or dual middle member between the theoretical and the practical parts of the Critical project *and* a unified terminal point of the entire Critical, or predoctrinal, part of philosophy as such; second, analysis of the curious role of pleasure (*Lust*) and liking, or delight (*Wohlgefallen*), a secret "pleasure principle" implicit in the analytic of the beautiful; and third, discussion of the curious appearance of extrinsic by-products and apparently contingent supplements at the very center of the work entitled *Kritik der Urteilskraft*. All three leaps or stages interact with one another and are imbricated in such a way that they cannot be neatly separated or circumscribed—in a word, framed. Nevertheless, let me try to work my way through them step by step.

## The Third *Critique* as Endpoint and Middle Member of the Critical Project

Critique of *pure* reason must exclude everything that does not pertain to theoretical knowledge—for example, feelings such as pleasure or unpleasure, along with the entire faculty of desire (*Begehrungsvermögen*). Critique of practical reason must exclude everything that does not satisfy the free, unconstrained, self-determining will—for example, the concepts of the understanding in theoretical knowing and all feelings, especially the lower, empirical-psychological cravings (KpV, 16n). If the understanding is taken to be the source of the a priori principles of the theoretical faculty, the questions arise "whether the power of judgment, which constitutes a middle member [*Mittelglied*] in the ordering of our faculties of knowledge, between the understanding and reason, also has a priori principles for itself; whether these are constitutive or merely regulative . . . ; and whether a priori they give the rule to the feeling of pleasure and unpleasure, as to the middle member between the faculty of knowledge and the appetitive faculty (just as the intellect prescribes a priori laws to the faculty of knowledge, while reason prescribes them to the appetitive faculty)" (KU, v–vi).

What is the significance of the hypothesis that the faculty of judgment is a middle member (*Mittelglied*)? The only possible reply is that the power of judgment cannot have its domain *merely between* understanding (or intellect) and reason, *merely between* theoretical knowing and practical doing. For in securing its proper domain it would lose its power to participate in and exert influence on knowledge and action. Rather, the faculty of judgment must *take part in both* knowing and doing, must *partake* intrinsically *of both*. Or at least, as we soon read, such a faculty must be *able* to partake of both "in case of need," *im Notfalle.* Critique of pure reason is critique of the faculty by which we "judge a priori according to principles." Critique of practical reason contains a "typology of pure practical judgment [ *Typik der reinen praktischen Urteilskraft*]" that belongs essentially to it (KpV, A 119). Such a power of judgment is thus not *in-between,* but can be attached to both theoretical and practical endeavors as the case requires ( *im Notfalle jedem von beiden gelegentlich angeschlossen werden*). *Can* be attached? As the case *requires?* Does not such an ad hoc attribution suggest that the faculty of judgment is a kind of by-product, a faculty on the side, as it were, as though judgment were a subordinate supplement and merely superadded contrivance? When and where does the emergency, or case of need, transpire, the case in which this middle member finds its rightful place(s)? What kind of need, or emergency, strikes transcendental philosophy here?

All such questions touch on the matter of frame and framework; all are in pursuit of the frame of the Critical philosophy as such. They are therefore questions that renew our contact with metaphysics, reminding us of the Critical task of securing the ground for the metaphysical edifice, a securing that always demands of us that we have conducted our geological survey ahead of time in order to make certain that the edifice will not sink or topple. In *Kritik der Urteilskraft* Kant concedes that the correct use of the faculty of judgment is so "universally necessary" that the search for the "principle that is peculiar to it must be accompanied by the gravest difficulties" (KU, vii). Accompanied? Accompanied on the side, incidentally, as though the faculty of judgment were one example of difficulty in the Critical undertaking? No. Such questions touching frames and frameworks have as their target a genuine "quandary"— *Verlegenheit* is Kant's word—that ceaselessly menaces the entire Critical project.

Kant hastens to keep the damage potential within limits: the Critical quandary, or embarrassment, "is to be found mainly" in *aesthetic* judgments. *How fortunate!* the philosopher cries. The damage does not extend to theoretical or moral-practical judgments, or to teleological, purposive judgments; immense difficulties are ostensibly limited to questions of art or of beauty in nature. The philosopher can apparently afford such difficulties. For in the sensuous domain of aesthetics it is a matter of mere images, not of the actualities of the universe and the soul. Happily, a firm frame appears to separate the fantastic world of paintings from the firm support wall of the theoretical-critical and moral-conative architectonic.

Unfortunately, such cries and sighs of relief come to soon. For nature herself, admits Kant, has created this problem, this "tangle," so that a certain amount of "not entirely avoidable obscurity" remains attached to every solution attempted by a transcendental critique of the power of judgment. By now, in 1790, the tone is far less triumphant than it was in 1781, when Critique could boast its putative completeness and thoroughness. Even if Kant is bringing his "entire Critical activity" to an end in *Kritik der Urteilskraft*, and is in a hurry to pass on "without hesitation" to pressing matters of doctrinal philosophy, neither the end nor the new beginning is undertaken in the full light of day. The frame of the Critical project cracks at each of its corners. What opens there is what Kant himself sometimes calls an *Abgrund*, but here a *Kluft*, an abyss, cleavage, or cleft.

Kant's question in the introduction, which is so significant for the execution of the entire Critical project, is whether an "unsurveyable cleft," a kind of gap, gully, or chasm, irreconcilably separates the two traditional domains (*territoriae*) of philosophy, or whether there is a "transition from the mode of thinking according to principles of the one to a mode of thinking according to principles of the other" (KU, 29). Such a gap or cleavage is spotted twice by Kant in the introduction, first in the second section, quite close to the opening, and then in the ninth and final section. The cleft between the sensuous, that is, the realm of the concept of nature, and the supersensuous, that is, the realm of the concept of freedom, extends throughout the introduction of Kant's third *Critique*. It seems as though the image of the cleft itself is to serve as the transition, or the bridge, that spans Kant's text as point of origin, a bifurcated middle member, and end. Yet what sort of frame can encompass such an image? How can a cleavage function as a middle member? How can the cleft that sunders them serve to attach the two domains of philosophy? How can a gap serve as the Critical terminus and a springboard to the "doctrinal" areas? In what sense can an abyss be said to unite the theoretical and practical regions of the Critical philosophy? Can any sort of frame or framework circumscribe such a cloven member or bifurcated terminal point? Indeed, the difficulty is great, the quandary sublime.

One imagines one can hear in Derrida's *Parergon*, and especially in its "Parergon," the echo of so many voices—those of the entire generation of thinkers and artists after Kant, including Goethe, Schiller, Hölderlin, Fichte, Novalis, Schelling, the Schlegel brothers, and the young Hegel. One imagines one can hear the collective voice of German Idealism and Romanticism. For every thinker after Kant searches for a way to connect the regions of a totally conditioned natural causality and an altogether unconditioned freedom of will, a way that would lead to the sole possible Absolute, a way that would promise the termination of all emergency measures, makeshifts, and merely tactical and dilatory—that is to say, in Schelling's vocabulary at least, *dialectical*—contrivances.

## Interest and Happiness, *Plaisir* and Delight

Derrida does not yield to the temptation to run through the entire history of Romanticism and Idealism. In any case, if the historical frameworks are exploded and the epochs in a state of suspension, no such run-through would be possible. He also avoids a minute analysis of themes that in other texts have fascinated him: spontaneity in the play of the faculties of cognition, such spontaneity (which sounds very much like freedom, indeed, sounds more like freedom than the "freedom" of the second *Critique*) constituting the ground of *Lust,* or pleasure (KU, lvii); spontaneity, in turn, leading us to the *simultaneity,* the ἅμα that plays so large a role in "Ousia and Grammè";[7] and play itself, *le jeu,* which plays, as we know, a central role in *Of Grammatology, Voice and Phenomenon, Dissemination,* and "Economimesis," to say nothing of more recent texts.[8]

In this second stage of the "Parergon" section it is rather a matter of pleasure and delight, concepts that Derrida translates as either *plaisir* or *se-plaire-à.* Obviously, any translation that conflates the two German terms *Lust* and *Wohlgefallen* into one indistinguishable term is extremely irritating, since for Kant everything depends on our distinguishing quite precisely among the various pleasures and among the three specific types of *Wohlgefallen* (KU, § 5). The talk of a "pleasure principle" in Kant is particularly irritating—as though psychoanalysis had any call to meddle with Kant. Yet what about this delight in the beautiful?

Let us recall in greater detail now the scene that Heidegger paints involving the figures of Schopenhauer, Nietzsche, and Kant. The scene itself establishes a kind of leaky framework for Derrida's discussion as a whole. The depicted scene could be entitled "Derrida on Heidegger on Nietzsche on Schopenhauer on Kant on the Beautiful." If one were to believe Nietzsche, the entire scene could also be called "Feminine Aesthetics," that is, an aesthetics of *reception* rather than a ("masculine") aesthetics of *creativity*. At the center of the scene we find Nietzsche's scornful rejection of Schopenhauer and Kant, in the third treatise of the *Genealogy*, vigorously refuted by Heidegger (at least as far as Kant is concerned, although Schopenhauer is left to the dogs) in the fifteenth section of his first lecture course on Nietzsche.[9] Let us first attend to Nietzsche's ridicule of Kant:

> "What is beautiful," said Kant, "is what pleases *without interest*." Without interest! Compare this definition with that other one, formulated by a real "observer" and artist, Stendhal, who once called the beautiful *une promesse de bonheur*.[10] In any case, here we find precisely what Kant emphasizes as found in the aesthetic state alone—*le désintéressement*—*rejected* and deleted. Who is right, Kant or Stendhal?— Even if our aestheticians never tire of tipping the scales in favor of Kant, with the observation that under the enchantment of beauty one can *even* gaze at statues of undraped women "without interest," one may nevertheless enjoy a bit of a laugh at their expense:—the experiences of *artists* with regard to this rather delicate point are "more interesting," and Pygmalion was at all events *not* necessarily an "unaesthetic human being."[11]

Undraped statues of undraped women, *gewandlose weibliche Statuen*: in other words, freestanding sculptures without the added charm or stimulus of the *good* parerga, those sumptuous, sinuous folds of cloth or drifts of gauzy veil in stone—such would be *Nietzsche's* examples. Perhaps these are the very statues in Dublin's National Library in proximity to which Leopold Bloom tarries, not necessarily an unaesthetic human being, although almost always "interested," observing the statues of the goddesses purely aesthetically, albeit with a certain theological bias. First, in Bloom's anticipation earlier in the day: "Nectar, imagine it drinking electricity: gods' food. Lovely forms of woman sculped Junonian. Immortal lovely. And we stuffing food in one hole and out behind: food, chyle, blood, dung, earth, food: have to feed it like stoking an engine. They have no. Never looked. I'll look today. Keeper won't see. Bend down let something fall see if she." Then in Malachi Mulligan's mocking words, later in the day, when he catches Bloom in the act of his theological speculation: "O, I fear me, he is Greeker than the Greeks. His pale Galilean eyes were upon her mesial groove. Venus Kallipyge. O, the thunder of those loins! *The god pursuing the maiden hid*." And later still, in Bloom's crestfallen recollection: "God they believe she is: or goddess. Those today. I could not see."[12]

Like Derrida and Malachi Mulligan, Nietzsche too is irritating. No one knows this better than Heidegger. He writes, as a part of the scene described above:

> Whatever exacts of us the judgment "This is beautiful" can never be an interest. That is to say, in order to find something beautiful, we must let what encounters us, purely as it is in itself, come before us in its own stature and worth. We may not take it into account in advance with a view to anything else, our goals and intentions, our possible enjoyment and advantage. Comportment toward the beautiful as such, says Kant, is *unconstrained favoring* [die freie Gunst]. We must release what encounters us as such to its way to be; we must allow and grant it what belongs to it and what it brings to us. (N, 1:129/1:109)

Then, several pages later, in somewhat greater detail:

> According to the quite "imprecise observation" on the basis of which Nietzsche conceives of the essence of interest, he would have to designate what Kant calls "unconstrained favoring" as an interest of the highest sort. Thus what Nietzsche demands of comportment toward the beautiful would be fulfilled from Kant's side. However, to the extent that Kant grasps more keenly the essence of interest and therefore excludes it from aesthetic behavior, he does not make such behavior indifferent; rather, he makes it possible for such comportment toward the beautiful object to be all the purer and more intimate [*um so reiner und inniger*]. Kant's interpretation of aesthetic behavior as "pleasure of reflection" propels us toward a basic state of human being in which man for the first time arrives at the well-grounded fullness of his essence. It is the state that Schiller conceives as the condition of the possibility of man's existence as historical, as grounding history [*des geschichtlichen, geschichtegründenden Daseins des Menschen*]. (N, 1:133/1: 113)

Thus it becomes a matter of measuring the supreme pleasure of reflection, or the pleasure taken in the foundation of a history, against other sorts of pleasures, other kinds of enjoyment. It becomes a matter of discovering what are presumably the purest and most intense and intimate pleasures. True, Derrida does not cite these passages from Heidegger's 1936–37 lecture course. Yet he appeals to the scene created by Nietzsche and Heidegger more than once in his "Parergon." He remains discreet, does not try to arbitrate between the two. Nevertheless, his desire is to know how "the supreme pleasure" is to be measured against the other pleasures, "how" here meaning by what order of implication, what standard, what principle of pleasure. Derrida's proclivity to *plaisir* and his readiness to relate even the august question of truth to the question of woman imply a tendency that would doubtless please Nietzsche much more than it would Heidegger.[13] For Derrida, as for Nietzsche, the question of art *is* a question of pleasures and delights, of interests in and promises of happiness. Moreover, Derrida would claim that it is the question of *plaisir* that sets Kant's own great book in motion. Finally, the same would have to be true of Derrida's own *Parergon:* his own text succumbs to a sort of seduction, and it treats the *Kritik der Urteilskraft* as though it too were a beautiful object, a thought-provoking and stimulating work of art. Thus the pleasure we take in Derrida's Kant opens onto a still more encompassing framework, a frame extrapolated to the third power, as it were.

To begin with, it is a matter of the possibility of pleasure in general, pleasure in one's taste, with relation to the *subject* of pleasure as the site of αἴσθησις. However, because the pure reflective judgment of taste does not take into account the *existence* of the object, existence being a matter of *interest,* which is here excluded or neutralized, to adjudge something beautiful is always to experience a certain sadness and even grief in the face of a loss. As I argued earlier, such reflective aesthetic judgments of taste, *whatever their pleasure,* touching at a vast distance the object of beauty, indeed, touching every object that in any way comes to appear, always perform the work of *mourning.* In pure reflective aesthetic judgment we attend to a kind of existential interment, "a *mise-en-crypte* of everything that exists, in so far as it exists" (54/46).

Judgments of taste dare not appeal to the external (or should one say *extrinsic?*) existence of a thing; only the interior, intimate (*intrinsic?*) sense or meaning of the thing is relevant. Precisely this inner or interior sense rules the tradition, from Plato through Kant and Hegel, and from Hegel through Husserl to Heidegger. Presupposed throughout that tradition is a discourse on the borderline, boundary, or limit that separates the inner from the outer in the object—for example, the work of art. There would have to be a discourse on the frame (*sur le cadre*), a discourse that would know how to counterpose disinterested delight to the pleasure taken in what is merely pleasant, a discourse that could distinguish a pure but bittersweet pleasure, as it were, from ribald enjoyment. Such mournful delight, Derrida concedes, resists precisely the translation he is making of it: *plaisir, satisfaction, jouissance,* and so on—none of these translations suffices. Rather, *Wohlgefallen*—liking, or delight in, the beautiful—seems to have more to do with a pure *self-affection,* one in which the imagination (and not perception, not αἴσθησις) plays the definitive role.

And yet, although reflective aesthetic (or imaginational) judgments of taste provide us with no knowledge *of* their objects, the subject takes delight *in* a beautiful object, or at least in the free play of our powers, that is, in the unconstrained and harmonious accord that the *object* incites in us: self-affection is therefore pure hetero-affection, provoked by the beautiful object that has its autochthony out there in the world—even if not *as* an independently existing object at hand. It is this hetero-auto-affection that summons whatever it is that one will want to assert in reflective aesthetic judgments—what one will want to assert *universally* or *generally.* Derrida writes, quite pointedly, in italics, "*The entirely-other cathects me [m'affecte] with pure pleasure by depriving me both of concept and of enjoyment [jouissance]*" (55/47). Precisely this is one of those "great difficulties" foreseen by Kant: an irreducible hetero-affection lies at the heart of every auto-affection; even the most interior, most hermetically sealed preoccupation, formally pure and purely formal, imaginational rather than aesthetic, involves some relation to an other. *Plaisir* is, to be sure, not some kind of μίμησις, ὁμοίωσις, or *adaequatio;* it does not assimilate or nourish itself on something that is foreign to it. I do not *take* pleasure—I *have* no pleasure—in the beautiful; rather, I *give myself* the pleasure; and yet, to repeat, I am not alone when I do this, even if I am solitary; nor is such self-giving achieved *through* me alone. By means of my pure reflective judgment of taste I make a claim on all who are capable of making such judgments, precisely because the beautiful has nothing to do with me as such, precisely because it has to do with something altogether other, something purely out there in the world, something I cannot experience empirically, something that is even lost to me, *something whose very withdrawal I mourn,* yet whose dominion over me I cannot dispute. I sense this dominion at a distance, suffer it, if only in the most discreet, silent, elevated, and even elated bereavement. Precisely for this reason, the *experience* of delight in the beautiful is not a *possible* experience for me. The object of my delight lies farther from me than every conceivable thing-in-itself of cognition. The beautiful object is not a thing conditioned by space and time: in terms of the "Transcendental Aesthetic" of the first *Critique,* nothing is less aesthetic than the beautiful.

Only now do we get an inkling of what happened to Bloom, not only at the interment of Paddy Dignam but also later in the day, at the National Library. "Immortal lovely. . . . Keeper won't see." Yet Bloom himself does not see. "I could not see." One *never* sees.

And yet, never am I more affected than in the confrontation with beauty or magnificence: an αἴσθησις eventuates, whether powerfully (as in the case of the sublime) or tranquilly (as in the case of the beautiful). Such a manifestation occurs, Derrida insists, even as we read the book entitled *Kritik der Urteilskraft,* this beautiful, confident, and yet forlorn book of Kant's, beautiful enough for tears, tears of mourning. To be sure, this beautiful book is made only for the reader of refined taste, the reader who likes to ascend to the highest spiritual or intellectual registers—if such heights can be measured at all. Yet precisely such a reader is likely to spurn all facile distinctions between elevated and base pleasures. Such a reader may ultimately be forced to despise customary good taste and to quit all finely decorated domiciles, as Kant says, in order to escape to "the beauties of nature, in order to find here, as it were, voluptuosity for his spirit [*Wollust für seinen Geist*] in a path of thought that he can never fully develop for himself" (KU, B 224). That reader will be sadder, but wiser.

What is beautiful in the *Critique* can be determined without our having to stick our noses into each copy or exemplar of the book. Yet where do we find the original, the original *third Critique,* the *Critique of Judgment* in the wild, as it were, which once seemed so attractively framed by the moral dignity of the *second Critique* and adorned with all the impressive theoretical structures of the *first?* On what twisting, unpaved, uncharted path will we find this dearly departed book, in which we have found, taken, or given ourselves such *triste* delight?

## E.g., Examples, for Example

Derrida justifies his predilection for examples by pointing out that Kant himself determines pure aesthetic judgment to be *reflective* (as opposed to *determinative*) judgment. "Reflective," a word I have been using all along without defining it, means that only the particular, not the universal or general, can be subsumed under a rule, law, or principle. As a result, in reflection we have many examples, but no universal or general principle or law, no purposiveness, and no concept. The example occurs prior to that of which it will have become an example. The future anterior example is therefore the original, the primal and primordial, object of pure reflective aesthetic judgments of taste. This very anomaly "authorizes" Derrida's interpretation of Kant's examples—on Kant's own example, Kant's examples.

We met them earlier on: encompassing frames, for example, unadorned ones or flowery golden ones, the drapery of a statue, or porticoes of columns about a ceremonial or monumental building: *Einfassungen der Gemälde, oder Gewänder an Statuen, oder Säulengänge um Prachtgebäude.* Curious examples, all three of them, one after the other: the first relationship is expressed by the simple subjective genitive, frames *of* paintings; the second by the preposition *an,* which is difficult to translate, the cognate "on" actually suggesting something like "clothing as it is portrayed in the case of statues"; and the third by the preposition *um,* suggesting "surrounded or girded by." The subjective genitive and the prepositions *an* and *um* shed light only on the variety and vagueness of the relations of *parergon* to *ergon.*

The examples have a curious task to perform. They are meant to show that delight is augmented or enhanced only by means of inner form, never by external charm. *Parerga* should never become pure decoration or ornament, the French *parure,* whatever Baudelaire may have been dreaming. (The miracle of miracles in Derrida's lengthy text—some 150 pages—is that the author successfully avoids the temptation of writing *parergon* as *paruregon,* a temptation that only now has had its way with me. *Mea culpa.*) The frame of a painting, the drapery of a statue, the columns girding a building—these should never serve a merely decorative function, but by their form should adhere or cleave to the inner form of the work itself—the work of pictorial representation, the work of the body cast in bronze or chipped from marble, the work of the building's sturdy walls and graceful doors and windows. Derrida discusses the important role that the parergon plays in the addendum to the first part of Kant's *Religion Within the Limits of Mere Reason,* a role developed most fully in the fourth section, in which Kant acerbically criticizes the pomp and circumstance of the churches.[14] Yet for the most part Derrida keeps to the examples of the third *Critique,* developing perhaps most fully that of the drapery on or of sculptures. He cites as an example of this example the *painting* by Lucas Cranach that shows the naked Lucretia Borgia clutching in her right hand a dagger pointed at her heart and holding in her left a strategically placed veil of gauze. To be sure, the veil is transparent and leaves everything—or nothing—to be desired. (A marginal question to Derrida: Is it legitimate to take a *painting* as exemplary of the *statue* Kant cites? Is the transparent painted gauze quite the same as a marble or brazen veil cast or sculpted across the pudenda of a statue? Bloom would doubtless assure us that the painterly veil is more brazen than the sculptor's. *Mea culpa.*) Cranach's parergon is colorless, dispensing with the charm of color, in conformity with Kant's strictures; yet it is also formless and without substance, merely allowing the *inner* form of a portion of Lucretia's body to shine through. Yet precisely this clinging conformity evokes the question of frames and frameworks: where does one draw the line between inside and outside, the intrinsic and extrinsic, the formally pure and the formless impure? What separates or at least distinguishes *parergon* from *ergon?* What protects the good parergon, as a supplement to the form of beauty, from the bad paruregon, which is mere ornament, tinsel, and source of titillation?

Turning to Kant's third example, that of the portico of columns (one might think of the example that Kant refers to later in his *Kritik der Urteilskraft,* that of the Bernini Colonnade about the square of Saint Peter's Basilica in Rome), what decides whether a colonnade or portico belongs to the general plan of a beautifully planned and executed building within a magnificently designed transteverean piazza? What constitutes the parergonal character of drapery or column? Derrida replies:

> It is not because they are detached but on the contrary because they are more difficult to detach and above all because without them, without their quasi-detachment, the lack on the inside of the work would appear; or (which amounts to the same thing for a lack) would not appear. What constitutes them as *parerga* is not simply their exteriority as a surplus, it is the internal structural link which rivets them to the lack in the interior of the *ergon.* And this lack would be constitutive of the very unity of the *ergon.* Without this lack, the *ergon* would have no need of a *parergon.* The *ergon's* lack is the lack of a *parergon,* of the garment or the column which nevertheless remains exterior to it. How to give *energeia* its due? (69/59–60)

With these two examples—the clothing on statues and the columns surrounding buildings—we find ourselves revolving about the selfsame question: what in general is a frame? Derrida goes on to ask, with somewhat irritating emphasis, "And what about a frame framing a painting representing a building surrounded by columns in clothed human form?" (71/60). A glance at the illustrations that grace *Parergon,* the illustrations themselves being so many parerga, indicates that this unhinged fantasy is precisely what Derrida is trying to fulfill, so that the choice of Cranach as an example of statuary is no accident but a part of Derrida's irritating strategy. It is as though examples, either because of their apparent particularity or their claim to some kind of generality through exemplarity, encroach on and invade one another, willy-nilly. There is a kind of *swarming effect* with examples: such is their particular energy, their setting-to-work in and outside the work, their excessive, eccentric ἐνέργεια. Such is the lack both within and without the work. What is particularly irritating here is the fact that Derrida shows *convincingly* why and how the entire analytic of aesthetic judgment depends on the possibility of a strict distinction between the extrinsic and the intimately, intensely intrinsic—which means, he shows why and how such an analytic inevitably shatters. Derrida tries to apologize for this:

> It may appear that I am taking unfair advantage by persisting with two or three possibly fortuitous examples from a secondary subchapter; and that it would be better to go to less marginal places in the work, nearer to the center and the heart of the matter. To be sure. The objection presupposes that one already knows what is the center or the heart of the third *Critique*, that one has already located its frame and the limit of its field. But nothing seems more difficult to determine. The *Critique* presents itself as a work (*ergon*) with several sides, and as such it ought to allow itself to be centered and framed, to have its ground delimited by being marked out, with a frame, against a general background. But this frame is problematical. I do not know what is essential and what is accessory in a work. And above all I do not know what this thing is, that is neither essential nor accessory, neither proper nor improper, that Kant calls *parergon*, for example, the frame. (73/63)

Yet Kant himself forestalls Derrida's apology. For in the *Critique of Judgment* (§ 32, "The First Peculiarity Concerning Judgments of Taste," B 139) he stresses the importance of examples in precisely this area of philosophical inquiry: "However, among all our faculties and talents, taste is precisely the one that—because its judgment is not determinable by concepts and prescriptions—is most in need of examples [*am meisten der Beispiele . . . bedürftig ist*], examples of what in the course of civilization has been applauded over eons of time; in order that it [i.e., our taste] does not immediately succumb once again to formlessness, collapsing back into the crudity of its first attempts." When the work in question is the *ergon* of art, the *parergonal* becomes what is essential in the education of taste. Here, at the middle member and end point of the entire Critical project, parerga are not merely for the parergonal.

Does it pertain to the frame or to the core of the *third Critique* that *its* forms (whether tripartite, as in the table of mental and cognitive faculties, or quadripartite, as in the table of categories and judgments of quantity, quality, relation, and modality) derive from the *first Critique,* which involves theoretical, logical, cognitive, and precisely not aesthetic matters? Derrida does not push this question harder, yet one is tempted to ask: If the deduction of the table of the categories in the *first Critique* stems from the traditional table of (Aristotelian) *judgments,* should not the *third Critique* confess the essential homelessness of reflective aesthetic judgment? Should it not put in question the deduction of all the (judgmental) categories of the understanding as elaborated in the *first* and all the (judgmental) imperatives of pure practical reason as elaborated in the *second Critique?* Should not the *third Critique* itself be put in question precisely with regard to its own frame and framework, which is also to say, with regard to its ostensible center and ground? The fact that all three *Critiques* fit into one another like Babas or boxes, and that the question of the frame is no sooner raised than dispensed with or reduced to secondary importance, may of course be merely tangential, marginal, and off-the-mark. Or it may be the only essential *Critical* question. If it is the essential question, and if we can identify it as such, then the first, second, and third *Critiques* may in the end make for something more than merely charming reading. The *Kritik der Urteilskraft* may be simply the most stimulating part of the Critical project— this and nothing more—or it may occupy the very center of all Critical work. Or, if indeed the third *Critique* is somehow lost to us, having slipped through the cracks of its impossible frame, perhaps it is as beautiful as any work ever was. If the diaphanous veil of its examples—reminiscent of both Lucretia's self-revelation and Schelling's veil of melancholy—is not stripped from its place but allowed to cling to the vulnerable form of the whole, perhaps our reading of Kant might be enhanced and augmented.

The logic of the *parergon* "is mightier than that of the analytic," avers Derrida (85/73). What does he mean by "analytic"? Is this the "Analytic" of the first, second, or third *Critique?* For reasons we have already elaborated, an answer cannot readily be given. However, wherever the *parergonal* logic pops up, we can be certain that it involves "a certain repeated dislocation, a regulated, irrepressible dislocation, which makes the frame in general crack, undoes it at the corners in its quoins and joints, turns its internal limit into an external limit, takes its thickness into account, makes us see the picture from the side of the canvas or the wood, etc." (85–86/74). As is always the case, it is impossible to gauge how much such dislocation results from the operations of an ultra-Critical deconstructive reading and how much it results from a kind of fission already at work in the Kantian text—and in the Kantian Critical project—itself.

Beyond the frame of "Parergon," in the third part of the greater *Parergon* of *The Truth in Painting,* the explosion of the frame strikes the reader with full force. Within the framework of the present chapter, such impact cannot be demonstrated. Yet readers may permit me to offer a minor example by way of conclusion. This example, another example of Kant's taken up by Derrida, stands in § 16 of *Kritik der Urteilskraft*. It is an example of the purity of reflective aesthetic judgments of taste. It involves the freedom of the object of such judgments from intrinsic purposiveness and from every concept of the understanding and reason. It is an example of free or unconstrained beauty, *pulchritudo vaga*, literally, "wandering beauty," in contrast to dependent, nonautonomous beauty, *pulchritudo adhaerens*.[15] As an example of the free, unconstrained beauty that betrays no purpose and that no concept subtends, Kant refers to Greek decorative motifs, "designs *à la grecque*, [or] the leafwork on frames or on wallpaper, etc." (KU, B 49). Unconstrained beauty, that is, beauty that is most intrinsically and intimately in conformity with pure reflective aesthetic judgments of taste, is and remains parergonal—indeed, parergonal to the second degree, at the level of mere ornament and decoration! Now, the judgment of taste is pure only in relation to unconstrained beauty— hence, pure precisely when it is denigrated by what does not measure up to purely formal and formally pure beauty. Freedom and purity alike are therefore essentially parergonal and are to be found on the charming (or irritating: *reizend*) frame that is gilded and whittled but also cracked and broken. For the Kantian Critical project, that is parirritating. *Mea maxima culpa*.

Derrida does irritate. In *The Post Card* (as we shall see in the Conclusion), he calls himself the purest of bastards, and he knows himself well. Derrida irritates, like the leafwork on a gilded frame: poison ivy. He does not proceed modestly and obediently to Kant's major contentions in *Kritik der Urteilskraft*, but tickles us with examples. However, such tickling, taken in itself, could hardly cause excessive irritation. Derrida irritates because his exemplary play with examples, in combination with his respect for the impossible placement of prefaces and introductions, has an extraordinary impact on our reception of the Kantian philosophy. Two thousand pages of the most obstreperously difficult philosophy, the most astonishing philosophical architectonic of the Western tradition—can it really be made to tremble by such tickling? *That* possibility is what unsettles us, nettles us. Worse, Derrida's question concerning frames and frameworks has implications for Hegel's aesthetics and Heidegger's counteraesthetics; it even unsettles what Nietzschean genealogy would like to distinguish quite sharply—a "masculine" as opposed to a "feminine" aesthetics. Exploded frames frustrate every maneuver by which we would delimit and demarcate; they menace all our appropriations and challenge all our inclusions and exclusions; they undermine the entire politics of philosophy. We can only stand by and watch our confidence diminish as everything that overflows its frame rushes toward us as a veritable tidal wave.

Can it really be true that our advancement through a history guarantees us no privilege, no progress? Can it really be true that the greatest labors of philosophy can be undone by mere side effects and by-products? Are abyssal gaps and lacks to be found in every corner of philosophy and at the heart of all its objects? Will we never be finished with critique, precisely because crisis accompanies every endeavor to encapsulate, circumscribe, and frame? Is every critical and Critical endeavor tied to withdrawal, loss, and mourning?

No doubt Derrida irritates, as does the glandular secretion of a tiny insect that squats upon the leafwork, the Spanish fly—in German, *Kantharidin*. Derrida does not so much tickle, however, as strike with a whip, a lash that is woven from thick strips of leather—in German, *Kantschu*. Indeed, Derrida is angular, multifaceted, a man of many edges—in German, *kantig*, or, as the residents of the Palatinate are likely to pronounce it, altogether *kantisch*.

# 2

# Echo, Narcissus, Echo

What is *Echo* to do—she who is only voice?
—Novalis, *Fichte-Studien*

The blind seer Tiresias assured the mother of Narcissus—she was the first person ever to consult the seer—that her son would live a long and lucky life, provided he never came to know himself. Narcissus therefore became the prototypical antiphilosopher: if Socrates devoted himself to the Delphic prescription, "Know thyself," proclaiming self-knowledge to be the very goal of philosophy and life, then Narcissus, as self-absorbed as he proved to be, was the foe of all philosophy. At least until the instant—and one would like to know precisely when and how that instant advened—he came to know himself and thus to die.

Narcissus was irresistibly beautiful, and arrogant in his beauty, they say. By the time his boyhood had passed, a string of rejected lovers trailed wretchedly behind him. Echo was one of these.

Echo had distracted Hera with entertaining stories while Zeus dallied with the other nymphs. Hera punished her by depriving her of her own voice—now she could only repeat the final syllables of the shouts and cries of others.

Echo followed Narcissus into the forest one day. He, having lost his way, cried out to his comrades, "Is anyone here?"

"Here!" echoed Echo.

"Come!" shouted Narcissus.

"Come!" came the reply, and Echo rushed from her hiding place.

However, Narcissus repulsed her. "I will die before you ever lie with me!" he snarled.

"Lie with me!" Echo echoed. Narcissus fled, and Echo pined away, until only her voice was left, the voice that long since had not been truly hers.

Some time later another rejected suitor killed himself on the doorstep of Narcissus, calling on Artemis to avenge his death. The goddess heard his curse and caused Narcissus to fall in love with his own image in a quiet pool. No embrace or kiss of the image proved to be possible for Narcissus. In one way, the enraptured Narcissus possessed himself utterly; in another way, he never could possess that beautiful boy. Narcissus gazed and loved and grieved and could not quit the grassy verge by the pool. Concealed at a distance, Echo mourned with him. When at length he plunged a dagger into himself, soaking the earth with his blood and thus seeding the future with the white-blossomed narcissus and its red corolla, she too cried, "Alas, alas!"—she too echoed his final words: "Farewell, O youth beloved in vain." We have no news of what became of her after Narcissus's death.[1]


## The Louvre Exhibition *Memoirs of the Blind*

In the preceding chapter we mourned the loss of frames—of every enclosure that might contain and circumscribe the work of art—and even of the historical and transcendental frameworks that until recently organized the philosophers' world for them. In the Introduction we saw Narcissus invoked in the questions of ego formation and the primary love object, these questions themselves being evoked by experiences of loss and mourning. In the current chapter we will try to gaze into the heart of a work of art, at the very core of its *ergon* and *energeia,* supposing that there could be such a core. Our hypothesis will be that the story of Narcissus and Echo has something to do with that heart's core in the work of art and in us. One particular work in the possession of the Louvre will draw us into its seductive precincts: Félicien Rops's *Femme au lorgnette.* It is one of the works of art contained in the 1991 Louvre exhibit inspired by Jacques Derrida, *Memoirs of the Blind.*[2] Blindness and narcissistic beauty will be our theme—as further approaches to the mysteries of works of art, mourning, and affirmation.

The generosity of the organizers of the Louvre exhibition is impressive. For these curators insist that "art has a hard time accommodating itself to monopolies, even if erudite; that even historians [of art] would agree that their

exegesis stands to be enriched by other approaches, by another *gaze*" (7/vii).
How can I describe the uncanny effect the exhibition itself had on me? I spent
two full days there, from opening to closing time, reading the vast amount of
text by Derrida printed across enormous gray panels, and gazing at the strange
array of paintings and drawings. I recall the powerful effect of the very large
canvas that stood at the entrance to the Hall Napoléon, outside the exhibition
room itself, *Butades, or the Origin of Drawing,* by Joseph-Benoît Suvée. For it
is the nameless daughter of Butades who instituted the entire *iconography* of
drawing, an iconography that has to do with love on the verge of separation,
loss, and mourning—the love of Echo for Narcissus. When the daughter of
Butades learned that her lover would have to leave on the following day she
took up a stylus in order to trace the outline of his silhouette on the wall, as
though this shadowy outline of him would *draw* him, *draw him back* to her
one day. We do not know the daughter's name, for she did not sign her work,
not even with a paraph or monogram, but merely allowed it to echo in other
voices, other texts.

One of those texts is Rousseau's *Essay on the Origin of Languages,* and
another is Derrida's *Of Grammatology.* Even though Rousseau generally decries
the lethal impact of writing on speech, and even though he attributes the origin
of *speech* to the love shared by boys and girls who linger at the watering well,
the silent daughter of Butades wins over even Rousseau's loquacious heart:
"Love, it is said, was the inventor of drawing. Love might also have invented
speech, though less happily [*mais moins heureusement*]. Dissatisfied with speech,
love disdains it: it has livelier ways [*des maniéres plus vives*] of expressing. How
many things the girl who took such pleasure in tracing her Lover's shadow was
telling him! What sounds could she have used to convey this movement of the
stick [*ce mouvement de baguéte*]?"[3]

However, the nameless daughter of Butades herself, as the originator of
drawing, is a bit lost in the published catalogue of the Louvre exhibition:
number 1 in the exhibition, serving as an exergue or epigram on the very
threshold of the exhibition, she is number 19 in the catalogue, in a tiny black-
and-white reproduction. The place she occupied at the exhibition is represented
in the catalogue by the epigram from a love letter written by Diderot to Sophie
Volland: "This is the first time I have ever written in the dark . . . not knowing
whether I am indeed forming letters. Wherever there will be nothing, read that
I love you" (9/1).

Allow me to recount only one other detail concerning the exhibition, a
detail involving a conversation with the originator of *Memoirs of the Blind*—
if one can name a singular "originator" in the case of an exhibition at the Louvre

and the simultaneous publication of a catalogue. I would love to have written here of the series of *dual* structures in *Memoirs of the Blind,* the "two hypotheses" concerning the blindness of drawing, all drawing, but especially drawings of the blind (10/2); of the "two great logics" of drawing, the *transcendental* and the *sacrificial* (46, 96/41, 92); and—to truncate the list, which would go on into the duals and duels of a dreamworld before it ended—the two or more voices that make of the catalogue a dialogue or polylogue. I would also love to have related Derrida's project to other projects to which it alludes, sometimes overtly, sometimes covertly—for example, to Merleau-Ponty's *Eye and Mind* and *The Visible and the Invisible,* inasmuch as Derrida's confrontation with Merleau-Ponty here is the first fertile "public" meeting of the two; to Heidegger's *Origin of the Work of Art,* evoked secretly each time Derrida refers to a human gaze, to bedazzlement, to veiling and revealing, in other words, to ἀλήθεια, the setting-to-work of the work of art (60/56, 69/68, 117/112, 123/122, 128/126); and to Hegel's *Aesthetics,* which confronts the essential blindness of all philosophy of fine art, which incorrigibly seeks spirit in the realm of the sensual and sensuous.

In the end I have decided to tell a story (that of Narcissus and Echo) and to use that story as an excuse to gaze at an image; to allow myself to be called, arrested, and enthralled by that image, ultimately to be *drawn into it,* perhaps in multiple senses.[4] An instant ago I described the vast gray panels lined with text—difficult text, Derridian text—at the exhibition *Memoirs of the Blind* in the Hall Napoléon of the Louvre. Among the forty-four works of art installed there, embroiled in a text that went far beyond the usual sorts of data-plus-fluff we read at art exhibits, several drawings held a particular fascination for me, a fascination that my subsequent reading of the catalogue did not always help to explain. At the far end of the hall, a series of self-portraits by Henri Fantin-Latour seemed to represent the very core of the exhibition, perhaps its innermost crypt. Here the text and the works required hours of perusal, study, astonishment, and further study. Something about the "ruins" of these self-portraits, asserting themselves before me yet retreating from me, held me entranced for a long time. Eventually, Fantin-Latour's gelid eye released me, and I ambled on. After pausing over about a dozen works, I met Cigoli's "Narcissus." I remember being struck by the odd combination of materials used for this drawing, which was an elaborate sketch in the mannerist or baroque style. The description in the catalogue confirmed my sense of the technical complications of this sketch. It is described as "Brush, brown wash, pen and brown ink, heightened in white over black chalk lines, on prepared green paper," the sketch's "very colorful technique" suggesting "a late date"

Fig. 1.   Henri Fantin-Latour, "Self-Portrait." Département des Arts Graphiques, Louvre, Paris

Fig. 2.   Cigoli [Ludovico Cardi], "Narcissus." Département des Arts Graphiques, Louvre, Paris

(131/135).⁵ I noted that the artist had made several visible "corrections" of the central figure's two arms. The left arm of the figure in its final form is lower than Cigoli had originally drawn it, and the artist's chalk has only partly effaced the original arm, so that Narcissus's arm—the obedient organ of his absorption—seems to be in motion toward the arm reflected on the surface of the pool. Whether at that time I saw the ghosted figures of Echo rushing from her ambush on the right, or Cupid drawing aim with his bow on the left, about to shoot the arrow of a devastating obsession, I no longer remember. I certainly could not have seen the reverse side of the sketch, which the catalogue reproduces. It is an odd verso, with the torso of a standing man now prostrate and partly obscured by some five ghosted figures of Narcissus and Echo. It is difficult to make out the sex of these figures, just as it is impossible to see the sex of Narcissus's reflection. Indeed, some observers of the sketch may find in the lines of the abdomen and thighs, as muscular as they are, something distinctly feminine; they might also find something feminine in the languid

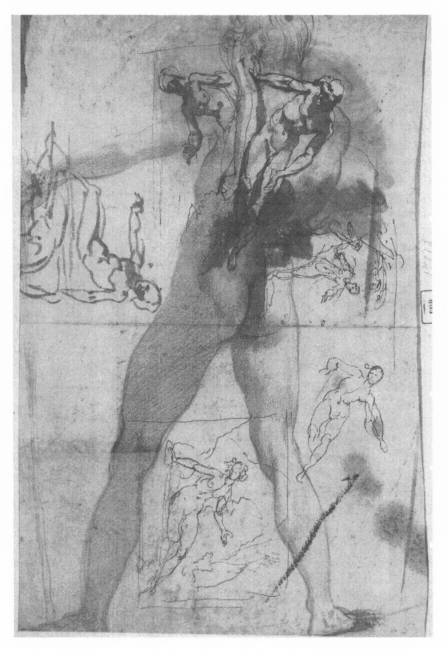

Fig. 3.    Cigoli [Ludovico Cardi], sketches. Département des Arts Graphiques, Louvre, Paris

pose, the rapture, languor, and languorous pining of Narcissus. Schelling, writing in the early nineteenth century, found God in that languorous position, the position of *Sehnsucht;* he never felt confident enough to publish the results of his reflections on such languorous, languishing divinity.

I passed by several exhibited items, then stopped in my tracks. Installed on a display rack below eye level and on the oblique was a charcoal drawing. I was to spend at least as much time with it as I did with the Fantin-Latour self-portraits, and much more time—in solitude, though not alone—than with Cigoli's "Narcissus." I cannot be sure when I first noticed the circumstance that astonished me more than any other thing at or about the exhibition: of all the forty-four works, this work alone had no text by Derrida anywhere near it; this work alone was absolutely devoid of commentary. Once I noticed the absence of text, the question began to haunt me: why, of all the drawings and paintings, did this one resist or defy comment? In the catalogue, the only object of commentary in the drawing—and a very indirect commentary on an apparently very marginal or parergonal object at that—is the pince-nez that jounces so jauntily on a black cord. It serves Derrida as one example among many others of the ophthalmic prosthesis or technical device, detachable from the eye and from "the body proper," devices such as "mirrors, telescopes, glasses, binoculars, monocles" (74/70). Not a word about the extraordinary wearer, her remarkable posture, her astonishing gorge, her face all shadow. I was certain that the innermost crypt of the exhibition had now retreated back beyond Fantin-Latour to Félicien Rops's "Woman with Pince-nez," who or which received or abided no text, the woman who echoed no words of others.

On the evening of the second day on which I visited the exhibition—and on that second day I spent even more time in reverie before the wordless charcoal of Félicien Rops—I met with Derrida. Late that evening, as I was about to leave the house, I asked him in some agitation why he had left this one sketch without text of any kind. Three years later, almost to the day, I asked my colleague and friend Michael Naas, who cotranslated the catalogue, the same question. Naas astonished me by answering, without an instant's hesitation, "Because it reminded Derrida of his mother, and so was the condition of the possibility of the entire exhibition." I was astonished for several reasons: first, because Michael Naas never answers any question instantaneously, inasmuch as he is one of the most careful thinkers and certainly not one to bandy about transcendental conditions of possibility; second, I was unaware of the fact that something in this portrait (perhaps it was only the perspective that places the observer well beneath the figure; but no, it was more than that) reminded me of my own mother, unaware of it until Naas invoked Derrida's

Fig. 4.    Félicien Rops, "Woman with Pince-nez." Département des Arts Graphiques, fonds Orsay, Paris

mother; third, Derrida and I often spoke of our mothers when we crossed paths (he had met my mother during the summer of 1986, and after that always asked about her, and even though I had never met his, he often told me about her, especially during the final months of her illness). And I suppose there was a fourth reason, a foolish reason that I ought to suppress, because it is one of those accidents or contingencies that only gossips or psychoanalysts but certainly not philosophers would find important. Two years after the exhibition Derrida and I met again. It was a Tuesday evening. As usual, we spoke of our mothers: he had just written a very strange text in which she played an important role, a circuitously "autobiographical" text entitled *Circumfession*, a text I examine in Chapter 8.[6] Again he told me of her illness, her apathy, her inability to recognize her own children. Two days after our meeting and conversation she died in Nice. Naas's words reminded me that I have always felt vaguely responsible for her death, somehow guilty on account of it, with that foolish logic to which only children and the mad are susceptible, or psychoanalysts perhaps, but certainly not philosophers. Naas had his own reasons for mentioning the mother, and I will return to them in a moment. But I have gotten too far ahead of myself. Let me return to that question I posed to Derrida at the time of the exhibition—why was this drawing alone without text?

Derrida had some trouble understanding what I meant. (Often when I speak French the French have trouble understanding what I mean.) So I described the drawing, which of course he knew perfectly well. He had no explanation for the absence of commentary. In fact, he told me that the curators themselves had seen to almost all the details of the actual installation of the exhibition. "Is there really no text there?" he asked me, incredulous, as though forgetful of the fact that there is precious little written about Rops's charcoal in his own text, precious little the curators *could* have exhibited, writ large for the exhibition. I encouraged him to visit the exhibition, in order to see for himself the emptiness surrounding the "Woman with Pince-nez." He explained that he had not been able to return to the Louvre since the opening night of the exhibition, when of course it was a matter of champagne and photographs, so that he had not yet really *seen* the exhibition, *his own* exhibition, the exhibition *of himself,* as one of the polylogue voices teases. "You should go, it's really worth seeing," I echoed. Whether or not he did, I do not know. We never spoke again of the woman with pince-nez.

I should have gotten over her long ago. Yet when the English-language catalogue fell into my hands, as a gift in a double sense from Pascale-Anne Brault and Michael Naas, there it was again, the same pointless obsession.[7]

When I showed the drawing to my doctor, who at the time was worried about my throat, he looked from the drawing to me and then back again to the drawing: "You really feel yourself *drawn* to this?" he asked. It was only then, with the English-language catapolylogue in my hands, that I examined the description that the curator, Yseult Séverac, had bestowed on Rops's sketch. She wrote of the woman with pince-nez that her "gaunt and gangrenous face echoes Baudelairean creations" (136/136). I was aghast. Of course I had seen the echoes of Toulouse-Lautrec and Dégas and had heard indirect echoes of Baudelaire's essay on the painter of modern life.[8] The obvious fact that the figure was gaunt and emaciated had not really struck me—but of course the taut musculature, the brilliant white of the clavicles, and the extreme length of the gorge yielded that concession from me: yes, yes, all right, *gaunt.* But *gangrene?!* I had spent hours in front of her, at the exhibition and later in the catalogue, and not once had gangrene crossed my mind. The Baudelairean echo of the *demi-monde,* yes, I could hear it; but the word *gangrenous* was a screech that grated against my heart's eye—a triple catachresis—whatever Baudelaire might be insinuating. Séverac noted further that Rops, "a famous illustrator from Brussels," was fond of "portraying women of little virtue," figures that he "rendered with his ferocious and provocative pencil." What naughty little boy would confuse this with his mother?

Michael Naas, who suggested that this charcoal drawing might have reminded Derrida of his mother, recalled Derrida's eulogy for Roland Barthes, "The Deaths of Roland Barthes," another text he and Pascale-Anne Brault translated some years ago. There Derrida writes about a book of photographs with extensive commentary by Barthes, *Camera Lucida.* However, one photograph to which Barthes often refers, "The Winter Garden Photograph," which is apparently a photograph of Barthes's deceased mother when she was a child of five, is nowhere present in Barthes's book. Naas reasoned that if Barthes could write of an absent photograph of an absent mother, Derrida could present an image that would defy all words, and that such an image would have to be of the mother—or at least of the mother as *other,* in a word, an image of the (m)other. After that conversation with Michael Naas, I read in Derrida's "The Deaths of Roland Barthes" the following passage: "Since I've read *Camera Lucida,* Roland Barthes's mother, whom I never knew, smiles to me at this thought [the thought of Barthes's *jouissance*], as at everything she breathes life into and revives with pleasure. She smiles at him and thus in me, since, let's say, the Winter Garden Photograph, since the radiant invisibility of a look which he describes to us only as clear, so clear."[9] Several pages later, Derrida describes the photograph of Barthes's mother as the *punctum*—beyond all *studium*—of Barthes's entire book on photography: "The Winter Garden Photograph: the invisible *punctum* of the book. It doesn't belong to the corpus of photographs he exhibits, to the series of examples he displays and analyzes. Yet it irradiates the entire book. A sort of radiant serenity comes from his mother's eyes, the clarity of which he describes but we never see. The radiance composes with the wound that signs the book, with an invisible *punctum*." It would not be possible to say that the "Woman with Pince-nez" is the *punctum* or *punctum caecum* of Derrida's *Memoirs of the Blind,* inasmuch as Derrida's book is perspicuous concerning the blind spot within vision. Yet it might be possible to think of Rops's drawing as a reverberation, as an echo of music, an echo of lunar voices, perhaps.[10]

At the Louvre exhibit I did move on from Rops's "Woman." The two drawings that followed were Bernard de Ryckere's "Head of a Dying Man" and the "Portrait of Margarete Prellwitz" by the German School, two sixteenth-century drawings. The old man whispered many things to me, some of them quite mordant and all of them sardonic, yet neither of the two could prevent me from turning back again and again to Rops's "Woman." The curators and guards might have doubted my motives, and rightly so. The Rops charcoal is not even a self-portrait—at least, not in any usual sense. However, it is precisely this usual sense that Derrida is about to undermine. He shows that a self-portrait depends precisely on the *nomination* "self-portrait," inasmuch as in any *soi-disant* "self-portrait" there is no internal evidence that guarantees the identity or even verisimilitude of drawer and drawn. Indeed, he goes so far as to say that "an act of naming should allow or *entitle* me to call just about anything a self-portrait" (68/65).

Just about anything? Surely not a figure of the opposite sex? Surely not an Echo of Narcissus?

## The Purest Type of Woman

Allow me at this juncture to introduce two texts by Freud: first, his "On Introducing Narcissism" (1914; 3:37–68); second, the three "Contributions to the Psychology of Love Life" (1910–18; 5:185–228). For these two texts will allow me to echo something concerning Derrida's use of the Narcissus theme in *Memoirs of the Blind.* If I have rushed in where art critics and art historians fear to tread, I may now compound the crime by broaching one of the most recalcitrant themes of psychoanalysis. Yet narcissism seems more like a terrible accident that happens to psychoanalytic theory than a graceful ornament—a mere parergon—borrowed from literature and art. Whereas narcissism originally refers to a male's homoerotic relation to himself, a relation encountered in the study of "perversion," Freud eventually takes it to designate an essential aspect of psychic development, indeed, an essential part of the life of everything that lives (*jedem Lebewesen*). There is, he insists, a "primary" narcissism beyond all the "secondary" narcissism that has to do with one's subsequent choice of love objects. Yet the way in which Freud first defines primary narcissism hints at its theoretically recalcitrant character. He calls it "the libidinal supplement [*die libidinöse Ergänzung*] to the egoism of the drive to self-preservation" (3:41). Why does the instinct for self-preservation—even supposing that it can be called an *egoism*—need a libidinal supplement? And if that supplement is essential to everything that lives, why is it *called* a supplement? In other words, what is libido, and what are drives?

These questions will unsettle Freud for the remainder of his career, and will induce one of the most far-reaching reformulations of the life (and death) drive(s) in Freudian theory—in *Beyond the Pleasure Principle* (1920). Nor will such a reformulation leave intact the theory of the ego, of perceptual consciousness, and the unconscious; it will in fact induce a second revolutionary reformulation—in *The Ego and the Id* (1923). There is no way I can do justice here to the intricacies of these reformulations. Allow me merely to mention the difficulty that Freud acknowledges in "On Introducing Narcissism," the difficulty that "the ego must be developed" over time in a human being's personal history and that a human being's "narcissism," no matter how "primary," must be "configured" (3:44). No matter how "primary" narcissism may be, this libidinal "supplement" leads a life of its own, a life that takes shape before or behind our own life, we egos must say. Such a life resists our inspection: according to Freud the most direct route to narcissism is study of paraphrenias— for example, schizophrenia—a route that is of course barred to psychoanalysis. Three indirect routes remain open: (1) observation of painful organic illness, and especially our response to open wounds, (2) inquiry into hypochondria, and (3) study of the love life of the two sexes. Allow me to take the third, clearly the most circuitous route, the route that psychoanalysis itself and as such pursues—not that I have anything against laceration or hypochondria.

Just as our earliest autoerotic satisfactions mimic self-preservation (as sucking one's fingers imitates nursing), so too the first object of the sex drives derives from the person on whom the drive to self-preservation depends. The "anaclitic" type of object, the type on which we depend (*Anlehnungstypus*), is

the mother and/or nurturer of the infant. However, Freud moves quickly to
the observation that there are fundamentally two types of love objects eventually chosen by a male: either the image of the mother or that of "one's own
person" prevails. The latter image he now calls "narcissistic," as though
forgetting that a *primary* narcissism would have to precede this secondary
type—forgetting, indeed, that the first narcissism would inevitably be bound
up with the infant's relation to the mother or nurturer. Why and how a
*secondary* narcissism gets its name from the *primary* narcissism that is
precisely bound up with the *mother* is unexplained. Yet the forgotten women
of narcissism—the other of all mothers, the (m)other and nurse of all
becoming, the Echo of an archaic past that was never present but that never
ceases to exercise its effects—will soon return to haunt Freud's text, and she
comes in a most remarkable guise. Whereas the male "overestimates" the
object of his affections, seeing her through rose-colored glasses or magnifying
lenses, such overestimation arising—once again inexplicably—from the
male's "original narcissism," the female develops in a different way. Freud
now continues in a famous (or infamous) passage on what he calls "the most
commonly occurring, and probably purest and most genuine type of woman
[*des Weibes*]":

> With the development of puberty and the formation of the female sex
> organs, which up to that point have been latent, there occurs an
> enhancement of the original narcissism. Such enhancement is unfavor-
> able to the formation of a proper object-love, characterized by over-
> estimation of the opposite sex. What is produced instead, especially
> when a woman develops in the direction of beauty [*im Falle der
> Entwicklung zur Schönheit*], is the self-absorption of the woman, which
> compensates her for the reduced freedom that society grants her in the
> choice of her object. Strictly speaking, such women love only
> themselves, and they do so with an intensity that approximates that of
> the man who loves them. Their need is not to love but to be loved, and
> they settle for the man who fulfills this condition. The significance of
> this type of woman [*Frauentypus*] for the love life of human beings must
> be estimated as quite great. Such women stimulate men intensely, not
> only for aesthetic reasons, not only because they are usually the most
> beautiful women, but also as a consequence of interesting psychological
> constellations. For it seems to be quite evident that a person's narcissism
> serves as an enormous source of attraction to those others whose
> narcissism is no longer granted free rein and who find themselves in

pursuit of object-love. The attraction exerted by children rests in good part on their narcissism, their self-absorption and inaccessibility, as does the attraction of certain animals that seem to pay us no mind, animals such as cats and the large carnivores; indeed, even the terrible criminal, and the humorist in his literary inventions, captivate us by means of the narcissistic consistency with which they are able to keep at bay anything that threatens to diminish their ego. It is as though we envied the way they have been able to preserve a psychological condition—securing their libido within an unconquered fortress—which we long ago had to surrender. However, the enormous attraction of the narcissistic woman has its other side: a good part of the dissatisfaction of the man who loves her, his doubts concerning her love of him, his laments concerning the enigma that is concealed in her very being—all these have their roots in the incongruity between the types of object choice. (3:55–56)

As though he could hear the howls of execration and indignation rising from future generations of liberated women and men alike, Freud hastens to assure us that his analysis—however reminiscent of Baudelaire it may be—is not at all "tendentious." Whether or not his assurances soothe us, we ought to find some delicious satisfaction in the way Narcissus has now switched sexes: whereas he was introduced to add mythic grace to the psychoanalytic account of male homosexuality and was then universalized and made primary in order to supplement every living creature's drive to survive, Narcissus winds up wearing the mask of the beautiful Baudelairean woman, the shadowy and shady sister to Echo. However, her (or his or its) very overdetermination and ubiquity disarm the master's discourse, perhaps in the way that works of art disarm masters and mistresses alike. For not even the most perspicuous analytical system can master the intricacies of narcissism. In the third section of "On Introducing Narcissism" Freud reminds us that the two most accomplished groups of system builders are those who thrive on the intense "inner search" for meaning by performing all the operations of speculative thought. The two groups are of course philosophers and—paranoiacs. Let me therefore turn in haste to the second aspect of my poor system.[11]

In the second of his "Contributions to the Psychology of Love Life," Freud cites a widespread difficulty in the development of libido in Western culture, the difficulty of experiencing a love that is both *tender,* as tender as mother care, and *sensual,* as disturbing and powerful as predatory Eros. He cites the ancients' division of love into heavenly and earthly aspects, the division that philosophers associate with the speech of Pausanias in Plato's *Symposium*. "Where they love, they do not desire, and where they desire, they do not love" (3:202). Freud doubts whether the schizoid love life of our culture can be repaired. The thought of "organic repression" already looms large for him, casting a shadow over all hopes for reform and for the transformation of erotic practices and attitudes. Yet through this very shadow shines the dream of Freudian discourse, as it were, the dream that even if anatomy is destiny, the destiny of women and men on this earth is a *shared* destiny—and that the streams of tenderness and sensuality will some day converge.[12]

The force of their confluence would certainly muddy the waters of all theories of narcissism: no clear reflection of self would be possible—at least in contours that we today would recognize. A consternation, some would say, devoutly to be wished. However, let me quit my paranoetic system altogether and return yet again, obsessively, to Rops's "Woman."

## The Spinning Librarian

While preparing the present chapter as a paper for the conference "Drawing from Philosophy," I showed the Rops drawing in the catalogue to my three children, aged at the time seventeen, thirteen, and twelve, the two older children girls, the youngest a boy. The oldest and the youngest saw the drawing together, and both asked, without hesitation, "Why is she crying?"

"*Is* she crying?" I asked.

"Yes," they insisted, adding after a moment's examination, "Or maybe she's singing."

The middle child, a thirteen-year-old girl, had much more to say:

> It's weird—her position is weird. She looks bored. No, not bored: she's worried about something, she's waiting for something. What is she? A librarian? She's got glasses. . . . She doesn't look rich. She's getting ready to spin. Her glasses are bouncing. They are a man's glasses, they are too big for her. Where are her breasts? [Pointing to the veil above the face:] Is that part of her hat? Oh! It's a veil, and it's sticking out—she's definitely moving. How old is she? She's got a long neck! Her nostrils are wide open, she is sucking in air. Maybe she's a singer, and a dancer, too.

Two medical doctors gave me their reactions to the sketch of the spinning librarian. "Look at that sternocleidomastoid," said the one mentioned earlier, a male, indicating the taut musculature of the throat. "She's got a severe case of torticollis," he continued, defining the latter infirmity for me as "wryneck," spasms in the musculature of the throat. Another doctor, female, noted that the neck (with its pronounced larynx, or Adam's apple), jaw, and chin were those of a man (just as the abdomen and thighs of the languorous Narcissus might have been those of a woman). She continued, and once again I took care to record the words: "Her body posture is somewhere between torture and ecstasy. She is turning away from something: the monocle hangs in midair because it has just fallen from her face as she averted her gaze. However, her hands are still on the object, and she does not want to disconnect completely, because her eyes are still open. The 'R' at the top of her head is strange: she is a woman with a monocle *and* a monogram."

Allow me to add my own fantasies to those of my colleagues and children. The "binocle" (not a monocle) is not merely detachable, as Derrida notes; it does not even seem to belong to the woman. She may have lifted it from some bourgeois gentleman in the audience—if indeed she is a singer, perhaps of cabaret—and flung it ostentatiously about her neck. Whatever the case, we ought to pay some heed to the *lorgnon* of the *Femme au lorgnon*, as Derrida does. *Lorgnon* is related to *louche*, cross-eyed, and the verb *lorgner* means to observe in a peculiar way, from the side, aslant, or askance, as it were, but always intently and insistently. The *Robert* offers us but one example: *lorgner une femme*, to look cross-eyed at a woman, to eyeball her, to ogle or gawk. Rops's *Femme au lorgnon* thus doubles back on itself in a strange way: it is at once the object of a gaping gaze and the subject who commands the spectacle(s), both monocle and monogram. As for the prosthesis itself, a *lorgnon* may be either a monocle or a binocle. In the present instance it is clearly a prosthesis consisting of two lenses. It is not a *face-à-main*, which is a binocle equipped with a handle or grip, but a *pince-nez*, a "pinch-the-nose." Yet it is not clear whose nose is being tweaked by this spectacle, nor precisely how the *femme au lorgnon*, herself gazing aside and aloft, with her entire figure and her veil swaying to the very edge of the drawing at stage right, will draw the beholder to herself. Perhaps she is waiting for the abashed monsieur in the front row to reclaim his pinched prosthesis. Perhaps she will take wing and abscond with monsieur's pince-nez, taking the spectacle(s) with her into the shadows that accent the garish light of this theater. At all events, the binocle is refusing to obey the laws of physics; it dangles halfway up the cord, straddling the dark cloth of the dress and the shadow that follows the line of the dress but is apparently unaware of any décolleté; it accentuates the luminous inverted triangle that has its base upon the clavicles and its apex at the sternum, or breastbone. The base of that triangle supports the narrower inverted triangle that has the sternocleidomastoids as its sides, with its apex in a deep, shadowy hollow or gorge—the suprasternal notch—below the site of the thyroid gland and above the trachea. Light from the footlamps strikes the clavicles, the tendonlike muscles of the throat, the underside of the mouth from jaw to chin, the so-called submandibular and submental areas. The entire face is cast in shadow. Yet once the observer's eyes have adjusted to the darkness of that space, as though having entered a dark cabaret, the gradations of shading reveal everything: the full lips, the upper teeth, the slender nose and flaring nostrils, the fine lines of eyebrow, the eyes at first difficult to descry but then the right clearly seen to be gazing up and to the figure's own left, while the left eye itself is altogether obumbrated. The veil casts its own shadow over the face: what at first seem to be flaws on the skin of the cheek (Séverac's gangrene?) are reflections of the veil's netting—provided *some* light projects from the top right-hand corner of the scene.

There may be some relation between the artist's monogram, paraph, or signature and the sketch as a whole: while at first the monogram seems to bar the beholder's entry into the drawing, as though it were a brand or a mark of ownership, the imbricated "FR" itself appears to be gazing to its left; it seems to mimic by some strange hieroglyphic animism a head, long neck, and wide shoulders, with the signatory flourish below actually following the lower neckline of the dress and the lower arm of the figure. And, to cap it off, at the upper left of the monogram too, a kind of plume. Perhaps the apparent narcissism of the *n.n. fecit* is here too totally absorbed in its object choice, itself determined by a narcissism so "primary" that the nascent self is indistinguishable from the (m)other, its Echo. Perhaps that problematic narcissism, drawn by the beautiful woman in the drawing, is what enables viewers of any and every sex to enter into the space of the drawing, and thus to withdraw from themselves and from us. Perhaps the ostensible alteration of sex, from the artist, "with his ferocious and provocative pencil," to the chosen object of his spectations, is not reducible to the usual discourses about either drawing or desire—even desire of the (m)other's desire. Perhaps the observer, the artist, the psychoanalyst, and the philosopher are stuck precisely at the blind point where the variously embodied human psyches are stuck—the radiant point where primary narcissism and its echo, to wit, its anaclitic object choice, are indistinguishable, indeed, radically undecidable. However, as the thirteen-year-old girl also said, "You'd have to see all the artist's drawings to know whether he always signs that way." So, I had better reign in my wanton steed, in order to say as clearly as I can what I take the drawing—and its with-drawing—to be about.

I suspect that the work of art, like the work of mourning, draws us to itself and into itself at a depth that defeats the proliferated discourses of sex, gender, beauty, need, and desire, whether those discourses are transcendental or empirical, political or psychological, litigious or aesthetic, emancipated or reactionary. I do not mean that it is a matter of indifference whether the onlooker or artist or mourner is male or female. Nothing about the human body is indifferent. Schelling reserved *Indifferenz* for God, and even God soon put it behind her. No one can doubt that the mode of our being drawn to and into the drawing is molded and shaped by our respective bodies, codes, histories, and phantasms. Yet I suspect that these phantasms of our embodied and codified desires are transparent only to those who either trade on them according to what the current ideological market will bear or curse and flee them, whereas the remainder of mortals find themselves ever and again bemused in the echoing spaces of an always overdetermined yet invariably undernourished Narcissus. ("Is anyone here?" he cries, not only when he misses his companions but also when he misses himself.) In the case of Rops's drawing, one observer may look up to the mother who still looms tall even as (s)he proclaims her sensuality; another may experience her torture and ecstasy as their own when wrapped in the arms of another woman or man; yet neither the tenderness nor the sensuality, neither the ecstasy nor the torture, will return the observer's gaze with assurances of knowledge, especially not self-knowledge, not if one's look has been arrested at eye or larynx or suprasternal notch or pince-nez.

Perhaps this lack of assurance is what must be affirmed. Perhaps the *work* of art is its drawing us into its drawing and withdrawing surfaces—with no assurances or confirmations concerning what we may think we know about ourselves. And, while I am at the outermost frame of my squalid system, let me add this question to the world and earth of drawing: is it only drawings, and figural drawings at that, drawings of human figures, that do this kind of drawing and withdrawing work? Or is there a way in which one could expand these musings to a Kandinsky, a Rothko, a Comtois, inasmuch as we are drawn into their shapes and swirls, layerings and texturings, juxtapositions and imbrications of hue, precisely in the measure that they slip away from us? For these things—however much they may be reduced to mere formalist surface—are after all the very flesh of our Narcissus and our Echo, engaging a body of desires to a body of laughter and tears.

## Narcissus in Ruins

If primary narcissism is the libidinal supplement of the drive to survival, then a meditation on works of mourning, art, and affirmation can scarcely ignore it. For if the mourner walks off with the consolation prize of survival, thanks to the libidinal supplement of the drive to survive, he or she will be plagued by the flagrant narcissism of such survival—which, as I said in the Introduction, is only another way of stating the *problem* of mourning. Yet how would matters stand if primary narcissism remained elliptical even at its most hyperbolic— that is to say, if in both life and art (as the expression goes) object choice and self-constitution or ego-formation remained indistinguishable and altogether undecidable? If Narcissus were always in ruins? If Echo, or Echoes, alone prevail?

There are eleven specific references to Narcissus and narcissism in Derrida's text, and what one might call three indirect, tendentious references. The tendentious references occur whenever a voice interrupts the predominant voice of the catalogue in order to object that the argument—and indeed the project as a whole—is suspiciously self-referential, the exhibition excessively exhibitionist. "—This really is looking like an exhibition of yourself," remarks the wry interrupting voice (38/32). When the dominant voice speaks of the ruin of the self-portrait, the interrupting voice says, "—You mean yours?" And when the dominant voice says that one can still see with one eye, the other voice reminds the dominant voice of an infirmity suffered by the author himself: "—Isn't that in fact what happened to you, as you explained earlier?" (128/127).

No doubt Derrida's recent work on blindness, mourning, the (m)other, and ruin will strike many critics as "narcissistic," and we will surely hear a hue and cry raised by hasty readers of *Memoirs of the Blind* and "Circumfession," readers who long ago were convinced that they know the difference between what is "objective" and what is "merely subjective" in philosophy and criticism. However, narcissism may be less an objection than an impossible project. Narcissism? Derrida, and the rest of us, should be so lucky. Let me now trace the thread of Narcissus and narcissism through Derrida's text, in order to work my way toward a conclusion. There are, as I mentioned, eleven direct references.

1. At the outset, Derrida develops his two hypotheses. The first is that all drawing involves an operation of blindness, inasmuch as no model, however unreservedly it may give itself over to inspection, can assist the artist's pencil the moment it touches paper. Whether looking up or down, the artist draws blind. The second hypothesis is that when an artist draws the figure of a blind

person, he or she is in fact fascinated by his or her own blindness, the blindness of his or her self-portraiture. Further, such blindness also involves in some uncanny and inexplicable way an alteration of gender: "Every time a draftsman lets himself be fascinated by the blind, every time he makes the blind a *theme* of his drawing, he projects, dreams, or hallucinates a figure of a draftsman, or sometimes, more precisely, some draftswoman [*quelque dessinatrice*]" (10/2). Why the Echo of a drafts*woman?* Why the Echo of Butades? It is still too early to tell.[13] Yet this Echo will immediately introduce Narcissus and the theme of an impossible or at best paradoxical narcissism, a narcissism in ruin and retreat:

> There is in this gift [i.e., the gift of blindness as a potency or potential of poetry and prophecy] a sort of *re-drawing*, a *with-drawing*, or *retreat* [*re-trait*], at once the interposition of a mirror, an impossible reappropriation or mourning, the intervention of a paradoxical Narcissus, sometimes lost *en abyme*, in short a specular *folding* or *falling back* [*repli*]—and a supplementary *trait*. It is best to use the Italian name for the hypothesis of this withdrawal [*retrait*] in memory of itself as far as the eye can see: the *autoritratto* of drawing. (10/3)

2. In a drawing after Lucas van Leyde, "Christ Healing a Blind Man," Derrida interprets the blind man, who is pointing to his closed, blind eyes, as a curious kind of Narcissus. The blind man returns to himself, gestures to his sense of infirmity, his kinesthesia tracing a gesture to his eyes that his own eyes will never see: "It is as if the blind man were referring to himself with his arm folded back, there where a blind Narcissus, inventing a mirror without image, lets it be seen that he does not see" (18/12). Several lines later Derrida emphasizes the mirror effect of the right hand of Christ and the left hand of the woman in the background: "Jesus' right hand is held out, but still at a distance; it sketches out or initiates a gesture to accompany—*like the woman facing him*—the right hand of the blind man: a mirror effect, around what we have called the mirror without image" (18/12). Derrida himself emphasizes the mirroring of this *woman*, this Echo, by italic type.

3. In the process of abandoning the oft-discussed Theban Oedipus and Tiresias for Old Testament stories of blindness, Derrida cites the first object of the blind seer's prophecy, namely, Narcissus. "Tiresias goes blind for having seen what must not be seen, the coupling of two snakes, or perhaps the nakedness of Athena, or perhaps even the Gorgon in the eyes of the goddess with the penetrating gaze (ὀξυδερκής [sharp-sighted]). He then predicts to Narcissus that he [Narcissus] will go on living as long as he does not see

Fig. 5. Lucas van Leyde, "Christ Healing a Blind Man." Département des Arts Graphiques, Louvre, Paris

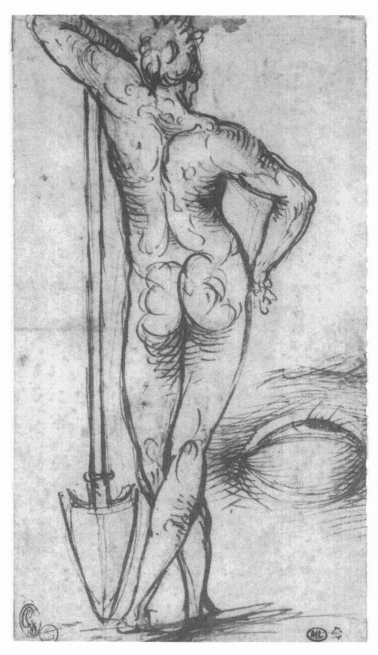

Fig. 6. Bartolomeo Passarotti, "Cain and the Eye of Abel." Département des Arts Graphiques, Louvre, Paris

himself, and to Pentheus that he will lose his life for having *seen* the sacred rites of Dionysos, or for having *let* himself *be seen* as a boar by the Bacchants" (24/17). Here Narcissus is brought into proximity with Pentheus, whose name means "grief" or "mourning" and whose peripety is occasioned by one line in Euripides' *Bacchae,* namely, the question put to him by Dionysos, "Would you like to *see* [ὄρεσι . . . ἰδεῖν] their revels on the mountain?"[14] Pentheus not only accedes to his desire to see but also dons the costume and adopts the gestures of a woman in hopes of spying on the Bacchae undetected. "Mourning" thus becomes what he hopes to see. Pentheus in turn is seen by his own mother as a large narcissistic carnivore. She bears home as a trophy his severed head.

4. Derrida reminds readers of his own lack of talent as a draftsman—his older brother had the gift, but all that brother Jacques can do is "draw nets of language about drawing" (44/37). This puts him in the position of Cain jealously contemplating the eye of Abel. (Note Bartolomeo Passarotti's horrific drawing, "Cain and the Eye of Abel.") The last time he tried to draw, Derrida tells us, was when he sketched his mother's profile as he "watched over her in her hospital bed" (44/39; see also Chapter 8). In the course of the ensuing discussion of Rilke's poem on a blind woman, "Die Blinde," and of Milton's *Samson Agonistes,* Derrida cites the theme of blindness as imprisonment and insularity, that is, separation by water. "The confinement of the blind man can thus isolate him behind some pretty hard walls, against which he must use his hands and nails. But the abyss of isolation can also remain liquid, like the substance of the eye, like the waters of a Narcissus who would no longer see anything but himself, nothing around him" (46/40). The pool of Narcissus reflects or echoes his image back into the pool of the eye itself, closing the watery circuit that is more like death than life, more like mourning and tears than anything else.

5. Merleau-Ponty elaborates a number of "Working Notes" on invisibility as a necessary quality of everything visible, everything seen. Consciousness itself has its *punctum caecum,* as though the ego and the self possess the structure of the retina of the eye. Derrida cites a number of passages from the "Working Notes" of May 1960:

> *What* it [consciousness] does not see it does not see for reasons of principle; it is because it is consciousness that it does not see. *What* it does not see is whatever in it prepares the vision of the rest (as the retina is blind at the point where the fibers that will permit vision spread out into it).

To touch *oneself*, to see *oneself*. . . is not to apprehend oneself as an ob-ject; it is to be open to oneself, destined to oneself (narcissism).[15]

Thus the blind spot becomes more than an anatomico-physiological detail about vision; it becomes a figure of human vision in general, "which, seeing itself see, is nevertheless not reflected, cannot be 'thought' in the specular or speculative mode—and thus is blinded because of this, blinded at this point of 'narcissism,' at that very point where it sees itself looking" (Derrida's words, at 57/53). To be open to oneself, destined to oneself, whether in philosophy or in life, is precisely *not* narcissism, *not* Narcissus locked into a gaze that closes him off to alterity. On the contrary, vision thrives only if Narcissus is blind, and consciousness advenes only if Echo interrupts the visualist revery of self and soul.

      6. This blind spot of vision is figured for Derrida in the self-portraits of Henri Fantin-Latour, which generally seem to "favor" one eye over the other, letting one eye disappear in the penumbra, as though in acknowledgment of the fact that when we gaze at ourselves in a mirror, or when we look into another human gaze, we look into one eye alone. Indeed, at the origin of drawing, the gazes of Butades and her lover never meet. In the case of Fantin, it is a matter of the monocular stare at the mirror of ourselves (for he looks at his beholder as if the beholder were his mirror); like Polyphemus, Fantin is in contact with Nobody; like Narcissus, he has lost his hunting companions and is answered only by Echo:

> the monocular stare of a narcissistic cyclops: a single eye open, the right one, fixed firmly on its own image. It will not let it go, but that's because the prey necessarily eludes it, making off with the lure. The *traits* of a self-portrait are also those of a fascinated hunter. The staring eye always resembles an eye of the blind, sometimes the eye of the dead, at that precise moment when mourning begins: it is still open, a pious hand should soon come to close it; it would recall a portrait of the dying. Looking at itself seeing, it also sees itself disappear right at the moment when the drawing tries desperately to recapture it. For this cyclops eye sees nothing, nothing but an eye that it thus prevents from seeing anything at all. Seeing the seeing and not the visible, it sees nothing. This seeing eye sees itself blind. (61/57)

      7. In a footnote dedicated to E. T. A. Hoffmann's tale "The Sandman" and to Freud's treatment of the tale in his 1919 essay "The Uncanny," Derrida deconstructs Freud's "most eye-striking formulation of the equivalence between

anxiety over one's eyes and the castration complex; it is there that we find his discourse on the genesis of doubles, the effects of primary narcissism, etc." (65/63 n. 59). One might fault both Freud and Derrida for ignoring a detail of Hoffmann's tale that especially in the present context is of considerable importance. I mean the fact that the eyes of the automaton, Olimpia, with whom Nathanael has fallen in love, are *Nathanael's own eyes*. Whenever Nathanael looks through the spyglass (*Perspektiv*) that the *Doppelgänger* Coppola has sold him, espying his beloved in the distance, the gaze of love that she returns to him is the gaze of his own eyes. In other words, Hoffmann's tale can be read as a tale of impossible narcissism *and* impossible object choice, in which the hero's very self-relation is obliterated by the echoes of the puppet-woman he loves. Indeed, there are indications from the outset of the tale—from the moment Coppelius unscrews the boy's hands and feet and then reattaches them—that the child Nathanael is as much an echoing automaton as Olimpia is. Nathanael himself is a child without flesh, a child of the gaze, but without eyes. Much could be made of this, had we time and world enough, and all of it would be uncanny.

8. Uncanny, for *we* are the mirroring eyes of the self-portraitist, "or the double of his eyes," and yet, far from reassuring us, the lessons of the *Doppelgänger* are "just as petrifying [*médusante*] for us as for him" (66/63). Indeed, one sees in Derrida's treatment of Freud's "Uncanny," or in what that treatment ignores in Freud's essay, *something like* a blind spot in Derrida's own text. Derrida does refer to the most extraordinary achievement of Freud's analysis—namely, his ability to integrate into one very powerful reading the two parts of "Der Sandmann," first, the boy's loss of his beloved father, and second, the hero's madness and death through the loss of his eyes and his love to Olimpia. Yet Derrida does not speculate whether Freud's achievement has implications for his own desire to abandon Oedipus and Tiresias in order to turn to the heroes of his own father's (and mother's) tradition, the tales of all the blind fathers of the Old Testament. I suspect, though I cannot demonstrate, that the deceptions visited by Yahweh upon Abraham and Isaac, by Jacob and Rebecca upon Isaac, by Ephraim upon Jacob—all the ruses that disenfranchise the elder son in favor of the younger, in other words, the entire *sacrificial* logic of *Memoirs of the Blind*—have Freud's "Uncanny" as their prophetic text and Hoffmann's "Sandman" as their sacred poem. And the logic of sacrifice—the son's being forced to adopt a "feminine position," a position of tenderness, before the father—would somehow be bound up with the way in which the *spectator* who at once occupies and obfuscates the *mirror* that is demanded by the self-portrait vanishes in the black hole of infinity.

Such infinite withdrawal—in which even the purest type of woman recedes in the face of the fathers, as an apparent homosexuality reclaims its rights in the theory of primary narcissism—is particularly visible, writes Derrida, in those artistic productions that are in effect "self-portraits" *manqués*, inasmuch as they are portraits of something or someone else:

> For a mirror is also necessarily inscribed in the structure of self-portraits of draftsmen drawing *something else*. But in this case, one must suppose, in addition to the mirror, *another object*, one that does not look, an eyeless, abocular object, or at least (since it may be a third being supplied with eyes or an optical apparatus) an object that, from its standpoint, its place, takes nothing into consideration, has no views. Only the topic of an abocular object, only this topical remedy, rescues Narcissus from blindness. And this to infinity, since there is no object, as such, without a supposed spectator: the hypothesis of sight. (66/63)

Abocular rescue is itself a ruse. Neither the self-portrait nor any genre of drawing can escape the *ruin* that drawing will have been since its inception. There is, as we saw in the preceding chapter, a kind of leakage into and out of the frame of any work, the signature, monogram, date, title, and dedication interrupting the blessed solitude of the work that would blind us to all else. The origin, emergence, and setting-to-work of the work of art is this process of ruination or, as Heidegger would call it, *ruinance:* "the performative fiction that engages the spectator in the signature of the work is given to be seen only *through* the blindness that it produces as its truth" (69/65). If the work of art blinds its beholder as it draws and withdraws, it enacts a scene of mourning: the work of art affirms the work of mourning.

As for the "apparent" homosexuality, stemming from relations to the father, we will have to wait for a final word from Zipporah—the Echo of Moses— whom we will meet in Chapter 8. For Zipporah, the Gentile wife of Moses, is the *punctum caecum* that the eye never sees.

9. Rather than spectacle(s) and spectator, there are now "only specters" (69/68). Among these specters are ghostings of "the opposite sex," as one still confidently says. Every self-portrait distributes a series of roles "in the heteroportrait, indeed in sexual difference." The sexual difference that was implied in the initial moment of the exhibition, with the daughter of Butades ("more precisely, some drafts*woman*") as the origin of all drawing, and in the epigram or exergue of the catalogue, with Sophie Volland reading in the dark, through our eyes, of Diderot's love, now comes to the fore. We have of course

been hearing it all the while in the two or more voices of this dialogue or polylogue, voices that ruin the chances of the catalogue—which can never be categorical, never masterful, professional, or professorial, inasmuch as the other voice, the voice of the (m)other, will invariably interrupt with jibes about narcissism. Only now that the theme of ruins, ruination, or ruinance has been introduced, with an accompanying invocation of the heteroportrait, does Derrida present the one and only illustration of Narcissus, Cigoli's "Narcissus," number 22 in the exhibition, number 31 in the catalogue.

Derrida's description of the work is entirely elliptical. The catalogue refers simultaneously to the recto and verso of Cigoli's drawing, the *verso* of "Narcissus" portraying the *verso* of a large male figure, presumably Narcissus, standing or falling on the horizontal plane: "Whence the love of ruins. And the fact that the scopic pulsion, voyeurism itself, is always on the lookout for the originary ruin. A narcissistic melancholy, a memory—in mourning—of love itself. How to love anything other than the possibility of ruin? Than an impossible totality? Love is as old as this ageless ruin—at once originary, an infant even, and already old" (72/68–69).

Derrida writes now of the figure of Cupid, not always blindfolded but always causing blindness, the figure ghosted in with a worn pencil at the upper left-hand corner of Cigoli's *recto* drawing. Of Echo, executed with a fine pencil line in the upper right-hand region of the drawing, he says nothing. Indeed, the catalogue as a whole says nothing of Echo. The word *echo* does occur in three places, most often as a verb or participle, and we might interrupt this list of Narcissi to locate these verbal echoes of Echo.

A. Derrida first hears the echoes of philosophy and sophistry in Plato's cave "allegory," the allegory of *Republic* that serves as an "icon" of all blindness and insight in Western art and letters up to and including the back room of "Plato's Pharmacy." Plato draws the picture of mortals chained to the wall of a cave and observing the shadow play on the far wall, taking such shadows to be the things themselves and embracing them as the objects of their endless conversation. Thus mortals lose themselves in "the echoing of voices," in "this infinitely echoing discourse" (22/15).

B. Derrida then introduces echoes that cannot be heard, echoes—this time as nouns—beyond or transcending sound, ultrasonic echoes. He describes an illness of his own, not of his mother: an infected nerve in the left side of his face induces facial paralysis. The most disturbing effect of this facial paralysis is the inability of the left eye to close or to blink, the eye thus being caught in an unseeing stare. His doctors, fearing a stroke, subject the patient to a battery of tests, among them, "the 'Ultrasonic Cervical Assessment' with a transcranial *doppler,* echotomography searching for the 'intraluminal echo'" (38/32), at which point the mildly mocking interlocutor's voice intervenes: "—Things certainly do happen to you, day and night," and the first voice replies, in feigned fragile naiveté, "—You better believe it." Echoes of a mildly chastising lover, perhaps, teasing the little Narcissus who is sick and wants his mummy. Who can say? Texts tell us no more than drawings do. Who demands more, let him mourn.

C. The final use of "echoes" occurs during the account of the blinding of Polyphemus by Odysseus and his men (90/88). Homer's account combines one of the most violent and bloody depictions in literature with one of its most striking puns, playing on the Greek words for *deceit* and *no one.* The cyclops has been "tricked" by "Nobody," and when he merely "echoes" the deceit of Odysseus, crying out to his neighbors that it is a "trick," that "Nobody" is killing him, precisely nobody comes to his aid. For centuries, listeners and readers have echoed laughter over the pun, as blood and gore steam and stream from the ruined eye of the one-eyed giant at the heart of us all.

10. Ruin is enucleation of the cyclops eye. In the solitary staring eye of the self-portrait or the dreamy gaze of the heteroportrait precisely *no thing at all* comes to vision: the ruin "shows *nothing at all* and *with a view to* showing *nothing of the all*" (74/69). The ruin unites memory and mourning: it is itself a monument to the impossible restitution of what never was fully present to us in the first place. "The naked face cannot look itself in the face, *it cannot look at itself in a looking glass,*" notes Derrida, so that the self-portraitist who precisely fixes his eye on the presentation of the eye "attacks his sight right up to the exhaustion of narcissism" (74/69).

11. We are herewith at the *exhaustion* of narcissism, at the very last of Derrida's uses of the words *Narcissus* and *narcissism.* Immediately after this final use will come the brief reference to Félicien Rops's "Woman with Pince-Nez." Derrida's catapolylogue will refer to nothing besides the spectacles that fly across her invisible breast, the removable prosthesis of an enucleated eye. At the exhaustion of narcissism comes a reference to "the shame or modesty" that seems to be a part of Fantin-Latour's self-portraits, their *confessional* character, yet a shame kept at a distance, such distance allowing quite the opposite effect—namely, "histrionics and curiosity, exhibitionism and voyeurism" (74/70). Precisely because the other—the dead one in mourning, the living loved one in love life—remains irreducible and unassimilable, "the ruse of narcissism never comes to an end" (74/70). Derrida cites two strategies of such narcissism: one can either try to capture the other behind closed eyes—one can sneak up on the ecstasy portrayed in Francesco Vanni's "Blessed Pasitea Crogi,"

Fig. 7. Francesco Vanni, "Blessed Pasitea Crogi." Département des Arts Graphiques, Louvre, Paris

Fig. 8.    Gustave Courbet, *The Wounded Man.* Département des Peinture, Orsay, Paris

exposing to visibility the fleshy quality of the eyelids, the raised eyebrows, the slightly flared nostrils, the pursed lips, the image of this woman "who was famous in Florence for her mysticism and her powers of thaumaturgy" (Yseult Séverac, 137/137), leaving intact the pious edification craved by the Siena clergy of the Counter-Reformation; similarly, one can sneak up on the gorgeousness of the beautiful woman's face beneath the beard of Gustave Courbet's self-portrait called *The Wounded Man*[16]—or one can draw into a drawing the artifact that will "compensate for this transcendental ruin of the eye" (74/70), namely, mirrors, monocles, binocles, the pince-nez, telescopes, ultrasonic devices. Normally, the technical prosthesis takes its position "as close as possible to the eye," Derrida stresses. And yet, as we have seen, the recently fallen or but lately pinched device of Rops's "Woman" hovers elsewhere and otherwise, *dilates,* as it were, throughout the sketch.

Here at the end, in lieu of a conclusion, one might well try to follow the pince-nez in its circuitry through the rest of Derrida's *Memoirs of the Blind,* as a *parergon* that makes nakedness manifest by pretending to conceal or veil it (75/72), as something of a mask or supplement to a mask, which normally hides everything but the eyes, the naked eyes of the wearer, or as the detachable yet still threatening, still petrifying head of Medusa (84/73), as the eyelid of the blinded Polyphemus, as a gaping wound (88/87), or as "frontal genitality" (94/92). Indeed, one might try to extend these Echoes of Narcissus and narcissism to Derrida's discussion of the designs of Yahweh, descried only by the farseeing inner eye of Rebecca (100/97–98), to the obscene blinding of Samson after his seduction by Delilah (108–9/106–7), and to the final evocations of the vulnerability of the eye, the weeping eye of Augustine. This lachrymose church father (whom we shall meet once again in Chapter 8) fears light (the feminine *lux*) as the "queen of colors," the radiant queen who entices him "with a tempting and dangerous sweetness" (*Confessions* X, 34, cited at 119–20/118),[17] until the tears of his (m)other Monica lave him and he, in sympathy with the woman who was "a man in woman's clothing," weeps for his unseen father. Finally, in order to end the list, the metonymic prosthesis of sight might lead us to the myopic weeping eyes of Nietzsche, this Dionysos who is a little bit lost somewhere between Thebes and Jerusalem (124/122). Or, behind the closed, blinded, or blindfolded eyes and all prostheses, one might well try to follow Narcissus and Echo to the final lines of the catapolylogue, on the "source-point" or "watering hole" of the eyes weeping, the eyes imploring and deploring, the tears shed by women and by "the Tiresias within us" (129/128). Such tears mark the difference, but also the shared and vulnerable identity, of eyes in the flesh, an identity evoked by the final lines of Andrew Marvell's "Eyes and Tears," to which I alluded in the Introduction:

> Thus let your streams o'erflow your springs,
> Till eyes and tears be the same things:
> And each the other's difference bears;
> These weeping eyes, those seeing tears.
>                                    (130/128–29)

However, such a narcissistic reading as mine, here, stands only as a temptation. No doubt I have compounded Derrida's felony in the eyes of art lovers and art critics, spinning veils of words about images instead of exposing them to the intrepid gaze and calibrating them. Yet sometimes I worry that the best calibrations of the experts are designed to hold images at bay, that they wield amulets of science in order to protect themselves as they disenchant us. It would be terrible if I have compounded that sort of crime. For what I most wanted to see was the way in which Rops's charcoal, "ferocious" but also fine, creates so many palpable textures, or *allows* so many palpable textures of the unseen and unseeing *paper* to come through beneath his busy hand and desirous eye: the velvety hat with feather and netted veil, the lightly smudged coiffure, the resilient cartilage of ear and nose, the metallic earring,[18] the enamel teeth, the glassy lenses of the pince-nez, the flesh of cheek and chin, the mucous tissue of the lips, the hollow of the gorge as dark as her dark and echoing eyes.

*Her* eyes, did I say? Where are the eyes and the spectacles that will allow me to gaze into even one of them?

# PART TWO

---

# Mourning the Work
of Philosophy

# Mourning the Voice

Et quiescente lingua ac silente gutture canto quantum volo.
[And with stilled tongue and silent throat I sing whenever I
like.]
—Augustine, *Confessions* x, 8

. . . at night you came to the bottom of my throat,
you came to touch my name on the tip of my tongue.
—Derrida, *The Post Card from Socrates to Freud and Beyond*

Let us set aside the work of art for a moment in order to take up the question of mourning and affirmation in relation to some of the classic philosophical themes of deconstruction—in the present chapter the themes of logocentrism and the phenomenology of perception, in Chapter 4 those of quasi-transcendentality and the absolute past, and in Chapter 5 those of time, tempor(al)ization, and finitude. Is our relation not only to the work of art but also to the human *voice*, the human *past*, and human *time* in general a relation of affirmative mourning? Derrida's *Voice and Phenomenon* and *Of Grammatology* will serve as our two principal texts in these next three chapters. Allow me now to begin, in my own voice once again, narcissistically, even though Narcissus is in ruins.

In the early 1980s I was asked to participate in a workshop on Jacques Derrida's essay "Differance" (1968). My task was to interpret what Derrida writes there about Freud. Following the trace of *desire* through Derrida's text, desire as constitutive of all signification, I was led back to the books *Voice and*

*Phenomenon* and *Of Grammatology,* both published in 1967. There the thread of desire plunged into a complex weave of the nature of writing and the voice, the repression of writing in the history of metaphysics, and the silence of the voice in the phenomenon by which one hears and understands oneself while speaking—the *s'entendre parler.* Derrida seemed to argue that in and for the history of metaphysics, as desire for presence, speech is privileged and writing repressed.

My initial reply to *Voice and Phenomenon,* a reply that was no doubt based on a misunderstanding, was that in our history the human voice is suppressed every bit as much as writing is repressed: only in the absolute silence of pure autonoesis—thought thinking itself—is the philosopher allowed to raise his or her voice. Similarly, for every Derridian example of repressed writing, I could think of several celebrations of writing in our tradition, from Sacred Scriptures to the Code of Hammurabi to Descartes, nestled before the hearth, meditating perhaps but writing indubitably.

To be sure, *Of Grammatology* complicated my rather too neat separation of voice and writing when it introduced its analyses of phonetic writing, linearity, "protowriting," and "good" and "bad" writing. "Bad" writing, as the tradition reads it, is writing in which the "corporeal integument" of signification, the signifier, obtrudes in such a way that the signified loses its transparency and becomes opaque, inky, worldly, and well-nigh immoral. However, it still seemed that the identical structures of repression were at work in the suppression of the voice, and the title of my reply, "Engorged Philosophy," meant to combat such repression.[1] I found it arresting to associate the gorge—the profound throat, if you will—with other kinds of engorgement: of the penis, lips, clitoris, and other organs with blood; of the esophagus with chyle (those luscious clumps of food and spit); and of the breast with milk. And I became obsessed with the very words lodged in and around the throat: *la gorge,* the anterior/interior part of the neck, home of the larynx and pharynx, that is, the voice box and the place where the nostrils, esophagus, and windpipe converge, the space of the glottis as well as the cleft known as the *rima glottidis.* Yet *la gorge* is also a cleft or hollow in a landscape, as it is in English. And finally, it is the cleavage and, by metonymy, the breasts of a woman. The Germans say *Schlund* when they want to stress the animal cravings of the throat (*der Schlund,* related to *schlingen,* to swallow or gulp) or when they wish to indicate that declivity in the forest that is so dangerous for woodcutters. They say *die Kehle* when it is a matter of the throat's getting split. Again emphasizing the animal in man, they may refer to *der Rachen,* related to both the Nordic *hrāka,* "saliva," and the Greek κράζω, to crow or caw, clearly the origins of the French *cracher*, to clear the throat and expectorate. *Der Rachen,* after a modified Abelian-Freudian inversion, is the beautiful English word *craw.* The upshot of all this was that for a tradition bent on getting the σῆμα out of the σῶμα, that is, on liberating significa- tion from its incarcerating incarnation, the word *engorgement* and the phrase "engorged philosophy" seemed designed to stick . . . in the throat.

Yet it is not simply a matter of words. It is also a matter of a particular kind of experience of the voice and throat. Sartre described one such experience in *La nausée.* There Roquentin invokes the "I think," yet one whose flavor is rather different from the cogito of Descartes's *Meditations.* Roquentin muses in this way: "There is effervescent water in my mouth. I swallow it, it slides down my throat, it caresses me—and there it is again, reborn in my mouth; into all eternity I shall have in my mouth a tiny pool of whitish water—quite discreet—which glides across my tongue. And this pool, it too is me. And the tongue. *Et la gorge, c'est moi.*"[2]

This tiny pool—into all eternity? Sartre's description invites the following questions. If for the tradition there is bad writing and bad talk, are the repres- sion of the former and banishment of the latter nothing other than a denial of the human body as such, a refusal of flesh? If so, how would Derrida's suspicion confront the thought of Maurice Merleau-Ponty? How would deconstruction go to encounter the phenomenology of perception and embodiment? If the scene of writing proves to be in and of the world, as Derrida insists it is,[3] must not deconstruction run headlong into a phenomenology that is *at* the world and a thinking that is interlaced *with* the world?

Three questions:

1. What *status* do the descriptions of the voice have in Derrida's *Voice and Phenomenon?* Are they meant to be, must they be, can they be, "phenomeno- logical" descriptions?

2. Can we elaborate Derrida's descriptions with the aid of Merleau-Ponty's texts in a way that would be fruitful for our reading of both?

3. Might such descriptions and the theme of the engorgement of the voice touch on the apparently remote matters of mourning and affirmation?

## Scribes Describe . . .

Derrida's inquiry into the Husserlian distinction within the sign between expression (*Ausdruck*) and indication (*Anzeichen*) comes to a head, so to speak, in the sixth chapter of *Voice and Phenomenon,* "The Voice that Preserves Silence." Let us read closely a number of its central paragraphs, those on pages 84–90 of the French edition, pages 75–80 of the English translation. They are perhaps the central paragraphs of the book—if such a book may be said to have a center. Their subject is nothing other than voice and phenomenon. Here the voice comes to be heard *phenomenologically*—the latter word resounds repeatedly and affirmatively in these paragraphs. Derrida's initial argument—though I do it an injustice to call it an argument, as though all its terms were known—may be reduced to the following eight steps.

1. There is in Husserlian phenomenology an "unfailing complicity" between idealization and the voice.

2. Because the phenomenological voice does not appear to enter the space of the world, it conducts expression to putative universality and infinity.

3. "The passage to infinity characteristic of the idealization of objects is one with the historical advent of the φωνή."

4. The history of φωνή is also the history of τέχνη, understood as the compulsion to technical mastery: phenomenology claims that within the realm of the *ich kann* it can posit its ideal objects as identical an infinite number of times.

5. Phenomenological ideality must be constituted, expressed, and reiterated in an element that does not impair the presence of its object and the self-presence of its act.

6. "*The name of this element is the voice.*"

7. The speaking subject hears and understands itself speaking—*s'entend parler*—in such a way that its words remain "alive," perdure in a "living present," and never lose themselves in the reaches of a lost time.

8. All nonphonic signifiers, all written signs, by contrast, bar passage to the infinite, inasmuch as they are visible, spatial, "outside," in the world: tokens of mourning, they mourn the voice; themselves dead, they are death as such.

Derrida's demonstration is itself quite intricate, highly technical. Yet it points to a presupposition that is pervasive in our culture. Consider the following lines from Coleridge's "Dejection: An Ode":

> Ah! from the soul itself must issue forth
> A light, a glory, a fair luminous cloud
>   Enveloping the Earth—
> And from the soul itself must there be sent
>   A sweet and potent voice, of its own birth,
> Of all sweet sounds the life and element![4]

And recall William James's eminently sober account of the complicity of idealization and the voice.[5] The context, in chapter 10 of *The Principles of Psychology*, is the "difficulty of apprehending Thought as a purely spiritual activity." James writes:

> In consenting and negating, and in making a mental effort, the movements seem more complex, and I find them harder to describe. The opening and closing of the glottis play a great part in these operations, and, less distinctly, the movements of the soft palate, etc., shutting off the posterior nares from the mouth. My glottis is like a sensitive valve, intercepting my breath instantaneously at every mental hesitation or felt aversion to the objects of my thought, and as quickly opening, to let the air pass through my throat and nose, the moment the repugnance is overcome. The feeling of the movement of this air is, in me, one strong ingredient of the feeling of assent. (PP, 301)

James also notes the way in which strongly felt desires or aversions cause the feeling of centeredness in the head to be displaced downward to the rest of the body. Yet the head and throat of the vertical body retain a certain privilege: it is still the "godly" head of Plato's *Timaeus* (69d–e), with the neck— the sleeve of the voice—serving as the "isthmus and boundary" that separates august Cephalus from the bestial body. James continues:

> In a sense, then, it may be truly said that, in one person at least, *the "Self of selves," when carefully examined, is found to consist mainly of the collection of these peculiar motions in the head or between the head and throat.* I do not for a moment say that this is *all* it consists of, for I fully realize how desperately hard is introspection in this field. But I feel quite sure that these cephalic motions are the portions of my innermost activity of which I am *most distinctly aware*. If the dim portions which I cannot yet define should prove to be like unto these distinct portions in me, and I like other men, *it would follow that our entire feeling of spiritual activity, or what commonly passes by that name, is really a feeling of bodily activities whose exact nature is by most men overlooked.* (PP, 301–2)

James himself appears to shy from the conclusions toward which his own descriptions and analyses draw him (PP, 305). They are conclusions that would cause us to mourn all so-called purely "spiritual" acts or qualities, including the act of assent or affirmation, and the quality of selfhood as such. James would encourage us to ask what sort of affirmation of mourning we have in mind throughout the present book, and he would caution us to avoid any traditional "spiritualization" of affirmation. For even an affirmed mourning remains profoundly committed to the human body, as the site of its tears, its ache, its dull aphasia, its emptiness. At all events, it may be perverse to extend the parallel between *The Principles of Psychology* and *Voice and Phenomenon* any farther. Let me therefore return to my proper theme.

Derrida now proceeds to interrogate what he calls "the phenomenological value of the voice." His series of moves may be summarized in three steps:

1. The transcendental dignity of the phonic signifier rests on a peculiar semblance, one that defines the metaphysics of truth in terms of the opposition between being and "mere" appearance.

2. The ruling semblance—the origin of the fabulous "True World" of which Nietzsche writes in *Twilight of the Idols*—arises from the *phenomenologically given* convergence of expressed signification and expressing act in speech.

3. Such convergence and phenomenological "giving" eventuate because the phenomenal body of the phonetic signifier "seems to fade away at the very moment it is produced," phenomenologically reducing itself to pure transparency and silent, serene ideality.

An unexpressed corollary of this last point is that the famous phenomenological *Epochē,* or reduction (in all its transcendental and eidetic varieties), may be but a bemused repetition of a particular auto-affection (or even *automatism* in Lacan's sense), a repetition that takes itself to be—because it *gives itself out as*—originary and founding. This of course makes the question of the phenomenological status of Derrida's own descriptions, as well as the question of his *access* to the phenomenon under discussion, a burning question—indeed, a conflagration. For Derrida has already quite unobtrusively adopted the gestures and the tone of voice—as though in impersonation—of The Phenomenologist himself: "In any event, the phenomenon of voice, the phenomenological voice, gives itself out in this manner" (VP, 85/76).

How true to life Derrida's impersonation is! Only the slightest demi-semiquaver of a comma, indicating (if not expressing) pure apposition and perfect equivalence, articulates and connects the two phrases "the phenomenon of voice" and "the phenomenological voice." Here indeed is what David Wood has called "the high-grade mimicry of transcendental arguments" in the Derridian strategy.[6] In sober mimicry of The Phenomenologist himself, Derrida continues: "When I speak, it belongs to the phenomenological essence of this operation that I hear/understand myself at the same time that I speak." Let us now interrogate the mime, pump the *mimique.*

"When I speak . . ." Is this the "I" of Husserlian "solitary speech," the "universally operative indication" that Derrida discusses at the beginning of his chapter? Or is the "I" being written (if not spoken) in *Epochē?* Or, on the contrary, does neither the "I" nor the *Epochē* by this time have any life left in them? Is the "I" already here a testamentary "I," hence a figure of mourning rather than a font of evidence or the sphere of interiority or an infrastructure of deconstruction?

". . . it belongs to the phenomenological essence of this operation . . ." Eidetic essence? Has "this operation" been subjected to eidetic variation? Has sufficient effort gone into the task of breaking up the monolithic demonstrative pronoun *this?* Or, on the contrary, are we here in a domain (the sphere of immanence?) that founds the very possibility of eidetic variation yet resists absolutely all such variation, a domain whose self-giving is primordial, albeit illusory? In that case, would not all of Derrida's descriptions of the voice be in a parlous state?

". . . that I hear/understand myself at the same time that I speak." Yet if the voice of The Phenomenologist preserves silence, in what sense does it ever come to speak at all? Does the ear of The Phenomenologist ever hear anything like a melody or a tone? Does it ever hear its own voice? Or, on the contrary, does it not exercise a mathematically trained yet woefully impoverished imagination and then *write?*

To be sure, it is not The Phenomenologist's voice as such that Derrida has in mind. "Such is the essence or normative quality of speech [*parole*]. It is implied in the very structure of speech that the speaker hears himself: both that he perceives the sensible form of the phonemes and that he understands his own expressive intention" (VP, 87/78). Yet this subtle shift from *voix* to *parole,* to the very structure of speech, should give us pause: if the phenomenological voice guards silence, it certainly never breaks into speech. Even if Derrida is granted full liberty to invoke the "essence" and "very structure" of speech (but invoked how? eidetically? apodictically? adequately?), it is uncertain whether and in what way these Husserlian lucubrations might engage speech. Derrida is therefore right to continue, "Now, to account for the phenomenological power of the voice, we shall have to specify the concept of pure auto-affection precisely and to describe what in it makes it open to universality" (VP, 88/79; cf. G, 405 ff.).

Auto-affection is the dissimulating reduction of "even the inward surface of one's own body," writes Derrida, going down the throat of both the pragmatics and the phenomenology of the *corps propre,* which, as we shall see, he will claim to have eschewed. This "inward surface" is of course the gorge, the throat that our tradition has been able to suppress and ignore. Auto-affection appears to dispense with the body image and space in general, achieving an illusory self-proximity. More than proximity, we might add: perfect superposition, *volle Deckung,* is what voice and phenomenon appear to undergo. Such self-proximity, more a proprietary holding than a mere propinquity, has various names in philosophy: transcendental subjectivity, the *für-sich* (better, the *bei-sich*), consciousness, self-consciousness, the sphere of immanence, attunement to being. Not even spoken dialogue can shatter the crystalline purity of this monologue. For to speak to another is to make him or her "repeat immediately in himself or herself the *s'entendre parler* in the very form in which I produced it," and such tacit reproduction "gives itself out as the phenomenon of a mastery or a limitless power over the signifier." After describing the sovereign mastery of speech, which bestows on me my interiority and allows me to box the ears of all the others I address, box them and take them home with me, Derrida brings these paragraphs to dramatic peripety and denouement in one brief sentence: "This proximity is broken when, instead of hearing myself speak, I see myself write or gesture" (VP, 90/80). *Incipit scriptio. Incipit tragœdia.*

It is no doubt unfair of me to truncate Derrida's argument at this point. For the crucial demonstration—the generation of space, or "spacing," the effraction and engorgement of any pure "inside" with the protowriting of traces, the traces themselves proliferating by the fission of the living present in the process Derrida calls *différance*—occurs only now, in the next few pages of chapter 6 of *Voice and Phenomenon.* It is a devastating demonstration indeed, bringing to bear both the Hegelian dialectical and the Heideggerian ecstatic analyses of time on the Husserlian philosophy of meaning. Yet I will stop now, in order to recapitulate the substance of Derrida's descriptions and to suggest how the resonance of another phenomenological voice, that of Maurice Merleau-Ponty, might alter the course of Derrida's demonstration while conducting it to the same end. For "the irreducible openness in the inside," and "the eye and world within speech" (VP, 96/86), emerge in the colloquy of both thinkers, in which neither gets his ears boxed.


## . . . and Phenomenologists Write

It is a curious colloquy, to be sure, inasmuch as Derrida so seldom mentions Merleau-Ponty.[7] Yet it would be wrong to imagine him being indifferent to one of the most important things that happened to phenomenology in France. In a sense, we have Derrida's reply to the *Phenomenology of Perception* and "The Philosopher and His Shadow"; but where is the response to *Eye and Mind* or *The Visible and the Invisible*? That response is no doubt taking its own time, but it is proceeding apace: we have already seen (in Derrida's *Memoirs of the Blind*) the most affirmative response so far. For the moment, we shall restrict ourselves to the earlier references to Merleau-Ponty in Derrida's works.

Derrida explicitly denies that "the phenomenology of one's own body" will enable us to comprehend fully the movement of the idealization that concerns him (VP, 84/75); at the very end of *Voice and Phenomenon* he repudiates phenomenology as such, which, he writes, "is always phenomenology of perception" (VP, 117/104). The first phrase clearly refers to Merleau-Ponty; the second, too, appears to do so. Yet appearances, even at the end of metaphysics, can be deceptive. For the "perception" Derrida means, if I understand him well, is not the object of Merleau-Ponty's philosophy of ambiguity; it is rather the source of Husserl's confidence in a proximity to the *Urquelle* of *Evidenz* in the "living present," the latter conceived ultimately as the *Quellpunkt* for internal time consciousness and for all the contents of consciousness.[8] For the principal thrust of Merleau-Ponty's phenomenology—stressing description rather than reflexive analysis, the always-already-there character of the world, the impossibility of complete reduction, the merely apparent independence of eidetic essences, and the "infinite meditation" or interrogation that can never be certain where it is headed—is to unsettle all the mechanisms and presuppositions of Husserlian phenomenology. As for the first phrase, which rejects all phenomenology of the lived body, there is in *Voice and Phenomenon* an "I" that, whether within reduction or outside of it, whether in mimicry or not, whether testamentary or not, offers a compelling description—a scription, no doubt, but one that is *about* something, hence a *de*-scription—of what happens when the phenomenological "I" raises its voice. When that "I" speaks, it invokes an experience—one experience, a sharply profiled, if terribly elusive, experience—of mortal speech. If the "I" were not to speak, if there were no experience of any kind, if there were no phenomenological voice-giving-itself-out-as, if there were no simulacrum of giving at all, Derrida would have nothing to write home about. Concerning that experience, Merleau-Ponty might prompt questions such as the following, in reply to the eight points elaborated in section one of this chapter, "Scribes Describe . . ."

1. Must the voice function in unfailing complicity with idealization? Or might the voice itself, especially if it is engorged by, say, a Jacques Derrida or

a Maurice Merleau-Ponty, hear the dull reverberations—the *glas*, or death knell—of all its supposedly "pure ideas"?

2. Can the speaking voice—leaving the phenomenological voice to enjoy its chronic laryngitis—ever refrain from plunging into the space of the world? Is not the space of motility, the motility of James's glottis, tongue, teeth, lips, and lungs, inevitably a space in the world, a space of embodied situation rather than location? Are not the presumed infinity and universality of thought also historical *sedimentations* of speech, as well as any given speech's dissimulating giving? Is this not the very sense of what Derrida calls protowriting—that it applies to *all* signification, whether written or spoken, whether disgorged to the outside or preserved "inside," within the sleeve of the gorge?

3. Is it phonality as such that is decisive for the tradition of spiritualism and intellectualism, or is it not rather the perceptual faith of an anonymous visibility, along with the *disponibilité*—the being at my disposition, at my disposal—of acquired speech and the hypocritical sentiment of eternity, that conjure the putative transparency of thought?

4. Need phonality and phonetic writing always and everywhere express themselves as technical mastery? What about the writer of fiction or lyric poetry, who never knows what she or he will write until it is written? What of the proverbial orator or lover who cannot wait to hear what he or she will have had to say?

5. Does not Husserl's initial, pristine notion of intentionality subvert the intent of both the reductions and all genetic phenomenology, so that phenomenological consciousness, far from being the pure self-presence of the *ich kann*, is cast forth again and again into the elemental, primordial, and irreducible medium of an already constituted *Lebenswelt*?

6. Is it not precisely the voice-in-communication that introduces alterity into the speaking subject, allowing the speaker to deform acquired speech in order to say something new, although never allowing one to know for certain whether one is speaking or listening to language?

7. Are not my words—if I am speaking here and now—so alive that they leap into the space of the world, drawing me out of myself in their wake and thus making me an "allocutor," someone who speaks and is *spoken to*, and one who therefore is never perfectly coincident in time and space?

8. Is it not the nonacoustic signifier, preeminently the *written* sign, that grants access to a monumentalized, scripturalized, immortalized infinite? Is not the most intriguing possibility concerning Derrida's analysis of the voice the fact that it never speaks, but only writes phenomenological or deconstructive tracts? Is there not a sense—admittedly, a very limited and perhaps

quite naive sense—in which Derrida is so entirely right because he is so completely wrong? So that the result would be, not a contradiction or a confusion in his views, but an *ambiguity?*

With regard to Derrida's remarks on "the phenomenological value of the voice," Merleau-Ponty would perhaps intervene only at step 3, where the phonetic signifier "seems to fade away at the very moment it is produced," thus allowing a kind of frictionless ascent into the realm of the signified. Here Merleau-Ponty would surely agree that such ascent is possible, although he would dispute its inevitability. However, let me now give him the opportunity to comment for himself and in detail.

Both in the *Phenomenology of Perception* and in the later writings, Merleau-Ponty emphasizes the rootedness of speech and writing in the spatiality of the gesturing body, one's own body, alive. Talking and writing alike can be described in terms of motility, kinesthetic structures, and the duly "deconstructed" body schema or body image. Is there not in Derrida's descriptions— in spite of his demur in *Voice and Phenomenon,* and in spite of his rejection in *Of Grammatology* of what he calls "transcendental kinesthetics"—a residual genetic claim, a claim that spatialization as such is a matter of *écriture* or, at least, of an *archi-écriture?* Precisely that *arché*ological claim should give us pause, in the way that Foucault's archeology of reason, madness, and power gave Derrida pause. If a genetic phenomenological residuum is found here, can we not at least try to dissolve it in a structural (if not structuralist) account of body space? Would writing, defined as the compromise transaction of hand and eye (G, 409/289), derive its irreversibility from the temporalizing linearity of phonation? Or would writing be the gesture that is defined in the first place as a *prise* on the world of paper, parchment, or stone, a gesture that contains all its movements globally and is prefigured in the two-handed, oriented, bilateral body-in-the-world?[9]

However, let me hasten to the second-order sense of the body in Merleau-Ponty's project, according to which the signifier itself is flesh. In "On the Phenomenology of Language," Merleau-Ponty discusses the "quasi-corporeity of the signifier."[10] Here, as everywhere, he acknowledges the diacritical and differential nature of signification; precisely this "action at a distance" in language makes signification "an eminent case of corporeal intentionality" (S, 110–11). Just as the spatiality of my body is neither a location in geometric space nor a mental representation, so too speech and writing are neither physical causalities nor pure ideas. They have a gestural sense. Such sense Merleau-Ponty himself defines as a *trace,* that is, a meaning that is never wholly transparent or fully present to us. Yet for Merleau-Ponty the traces of speech and writing diverge in directions quite opposed to those sighted by Derrida.

In the *Phenomenology* (especially the chapters "The Body as Expression, and Speech" and "The Cogito"), Merleau-Ponty accounts for the intellectualist tradition of an ostensibly supratemporal, atemporalizing idealization in terms of acquired or sedimented expression. The *disponibilité* of achieved expression—*disponibilité* being the very word Derrida employs to express such mastery—creates the illusion of a free-floating ideality. Although Merleau-Ponty does refer to examples of spoken words,[11] his analyses of sedimentation usually involve the written word, words on paper, which the reading eyes seem to follow yet actually see *through* to the things signified. As we read Descartes's second *Meditation,* we glide across the printed lines of the particular musty artifact we hold in our hands up to the ozone layer of the cogito. Derrida's eyes follow the traces of these very lines, but he begins to hear Descartes whispering off the page, in a kind of *proto-parole.* Precisely as a result of his insatiable reading, Derrida quits the eye and hand, and ultimately even the ear. He goes for the throat.

Both Merleau-Ponty and Derrida focus on the temporal character of expression, especially oral expression, although Derrida has much more to say than Merleau-Ponty does about how the time of the voice unfolds in and as the space of writing. And both thinkers celebrate the mysterious power of language to deform itself in order to say something new, Derrida in the dissemination of possible meanings or *"blancs"* in a text, Merleau-Ponty in the voices of silence—especially in the "musical ideas" of the novelist and poet.

In the manuscript on which Merleau-Ponty was working when he collapsed in 1961, *The Visible and the Invisible,* we find a remarkable anticipation—with a difference—of Derrida's treatment of the voice. That book was originally one part of a two-pronged project. Under the title *The Origin of Truth,* it was to have shown how a phenomenology of perception would proceed to the cultural and intellectual world, to the realm of ideas. Simultaneously, a work entitled *Introduction to the Prose of the World* was to show how all ideas, whether musical, poetic, philosophical, or mathematical, are forms of embodied expression: language would be not the mere clothing but the very flesh of thought. The latter work was abandoned, though its thesis never was; and the "origin of truth" became the fragment we possess today as *The Visible and the Invisible.*[12]

The crucial chapter of *The Visible and the Invisible* is entitled "The Intertwining—the Chiasm." If the chiasm is Merleau-Ponty's answer to the question of "the origin of truth," Derrida's reply to it can be readily imagined. Yet one should not be too quick to assume that for Merleau-Ponty origin means complete presence. If he closes his chapter with a reference to "ultimate truth," it is not in order to bathe that chapter in pure light but to allow it to return to an inexpungible obscurity and essential ambiguity. Merleau-Ponty's "ultimate truth" is given the title *reversibility*. It is not dialectical reversal or speculative synthesis of any kind, but a "mystery as familiar as it is inexplicable" (VI, 172/130). The reversibility by which my look seems both to strip and to envelop the things seen, "clothing the world with its own flesh" (VI, 173/131); by which vision seems sovereign yet formed at the heart of the things we see; by which tactility is touched in turn by the things it went out to manipulate, the hands themselves proving to be as tangible as the eyes are visible—such reversibility is no intellectualist sleight-of-hand. The word *reversibility* designates not a transparency but the thickness of the body and the depths of the world. For Merleau-Ponty—who throughout the 1950s was reading Heidegger, as was Derrida—reversibility is a paradox of being, not of man: "the body pertains to the order of things, as the world is universal flesh" (VI, 181/137).

After discussing the reversibility of vision (the seeing/seen, the sensing/sensible), Merleau-Ponty proceeds to the question of expression, but not before developing his notion of intercorporeity, his astonishing description of the patient and silent labor of desire—lovemaking as the paradox of expression. Only then does the phenomenological voice come to speak in his text. Likewise, in *Signs,* which continues on the path opened up by the chapter "Others and the Human World" in the *Phenomenology,* Merleau-Ponty interprets Husserl's insistence that transcendental subjectivity is an intersubjectivity in such a way that intercorporeity invades and permeates the once sacrosanct sphere of immanence. As Merleau-Ponty extends his analysis of reversibility beyond the circle of visibility and intercorporeity, he invokes the movements of the human countenance, expressive gestures, "and, above all, these strange movements of the throat and mouth" that are called the voice. Merleau-Ponty begins by echoing Hegel,[13] for whom sound [*Klang*] constitutes the first reverberation of subjectivity in nature, and then refers to specifically human sounds:

> Like crystal, metal, and many other substances, I am a sonorous being. Yet the vibration of me [*à moi*] I hear from within; as Malraux says, I hear with my throat [*je m'entends avec ma gorge*]. It is a matter in which, as he also says, I am incomparable; my voice adheres to the mass of my life as no one else's voice does. Yet if I am close enough to someone talking to hear his or her breath, to hear the effervescence or the fatigue, I attend in them, almost as I do in myself, the terrifying [*effrayante*]

birth of vociferation. Just as there is a reflexivity of touch, of the view and of the system tactility/vision, so is there also a reflexivity of the movements of phonation and hearing: they have their sonorous inscription, the vociferations have in me their motor echo. This new reversibility and the emergence of the flesh as expression are the point of insertion of speaking and thinking in the world of silence. (VI, 190/144–45)

A marginal note asks whether this reversibility of expression is new at all, or whether the perceived world is not always bubbling with speech and thought: the very notion of passage from a silent to a talking world will have to be overcome, or at least qualified. And there are even more severe problems with the description than this one. I shall proceed to them directly, after repeating one phrase from the description, in order that it may exercise its full impact on the project we associate with Derrida. Merleau-Ponty writes that a reversibility or reflexivity "of the movements of phonation and hearing" obtains, and he accounts for that reversibility in this way: such movements "have their sonorous inscription, the vociferations have in me their motor echo." If something like a Merleau-Ponty/Derrida colloquy is to develop, might it not hinge on the question of the relation of sonorous inscription to archaic writing? And would not such a colloquy link phenomenology and deconstruction alike to an engorged philosophy, a philosophy of Echo?

## The Gorge

Merleau-Ponty is not satisfied to have expanded my hearing of my own speech *avec ma gorge* to hearing another speaker who is close to me; he introduces into his account a kind of divergence (*écart*) that enables me to hear myself from the outside, as it were, in the world. Along with my "heard voice" there is, he says, "my articulated voice" (VI, 194–95/148). By that he appears to mean something different from what Derrida and Rousseau call the consonantal, algebraic voice (G, 443–44/315–16). From the very outset of speech, according to Merleau-Ponty, and as we have already heard, I am for myself not only a locutor but also an allocutor, someone speaking and spoken to, even if I am only talking to myself. "To the extent that what I say has meaning, I am for myself, when I speak, another 'other'; and to the extent that I understand [*comprends*], I no longer know who is talking and who is listening" (S, 121). Merleau-Ponty's remark is quite close to that of Derrida on the testamentary ego: for both thinkers, an alterity haunts meaning, and pure signification implies something like loss and mourning. Only through such an interrupted intentionality or deflected directionality can there be a delocutor, that is, the speech (of) which one is speaking. If we think of the figures on the Cozumal-huapa stelae in the Dahlem Museum in Berlin, figures whose discourses with one another are portrayed by coiling ribbons of speech flowing from the mouth of each to the mouth (not the ears) of the other, then we must understand that both figures of the discourse embody and enact together what we call language. The articulated-reticulated bands go from gorge to gorge, through the medium of the world.

It is important to note here, if only in a preliminary way, the further reverberations of this *Klang*, this phonation, as they pass from Hegel to Merleau-Ponty and on to Derrida. One might say that the "divergence" that Merleau-Ponty identifies at the heart of phonation sounds the death knell—the *glas*—of pure idealization and of absolute knowing. Thus Merleau-Ponty's analyses of the gorge in *The Visible and the Invisible* are linked not only to Derrida's reading of Husserl in *Voice and Phenomenon* but also to his readings of Hegel and Genet in *Glas*, which we shall examine in Chapter 7. Reversibility in Merleau-Ponty is echoed in the glutinous remnants or residues of phonation—the glottal *gl* of *Glas*. And this would imply that reversibility, far from being victorious, far from being an expression of a militant phenomenology of perception, is itself an affirmative—and embodied—expression of mourning.

To be sure, such reversibility, which is also a kind of doubling, is in danger of working too well—the intellectualist danger par excellence. My speech, says Merleau-Ponty, "offers itself and all speech to a universal Speech" (VI, 202/154). What would this articulated voice be, which, while not dead, is outside of me as a second-order hearing? What makes this description so problematic—crying out, as it were, for deconstruction—is the fact that Merleau-Ponty at times seems to suppress the *effrayante* birth of voice—the *frayage* or breaching of the gap, the gap one might be tempted to call the *Gorgo*—in order to ascend to a "sublimated" and more highly rarefied, "subtle," and "transparent" form of flesh. To incarnate this second-order reversibility of expression, Merleau-Ponty even conjures a quasi-Coleridgean "glorified body," so that at the very moment when he wants to emphasize the fact that invisibility is *of* the visible, and speech and thought *of* the world, his writing slips into an all-too-familiar metaphysical register. Similarly, in *Signs* (S, 100–101, 120), Merleau-Ponty persists in the notion of truth as "the presence of all presents," affirming the Husserlian fabulation of "living presence" as the *fons et origo* of all meaning, even though his own analyses of signification and human temporality ought to have convinced him that such presence occludes, rather than discloses, meaning.

However, Merleau-Ponty himself always and everywhere resists the inclination to ascend. At the end of his chapter on the chiasm, he plays on the word *entendre*, so central to Derrida's descriptions in *Voice and Phenomenon*. To understand *is* to hear—with the ears, or within the gorge, of the living body. The ambiguous world of perception adheres to speech and ideality, so that the putative progression *voir, parler, penser* is itself reversible: it returns all high-altitude thinkers to the flesh of the visible.

In Merleau-Ponty's reversible progression, *voir, parler, penser,* Derrida would deconstruct the first term, which is also the last term, fearing that if all phenomenology is phenomenology of perception, it will take visibility as its *Urquelle* of evidence. In Derrida's view, the second or mediating term, *parler,* is what usually occasions the dreamy ascent to the third, *penser,* which is therefore all but unmentionable in Derrida's vocabulary. Fearing that for Merleau-Ponty the intertwining works too well, Derrida seems determined not to allow it to work at all: he will not let us look at the world, it seems, but only at the World Book.

And yet, the scene of writing is *of the world;* the play of writing is *the play of history.* If the philosopher cannot quit the Hegelian gallery of spirit's heroes, a gallery that is in fact a labyrinth, he or she can surely learn that one's own maze and the world are not necessarily coterminous. Phenomenologists and scriveners alike must learn amazement. Foucault accused Derrida of *la petite pédagogie,* with all the little scholars rapt to His Master's Voice. If we want to say that Foucault's accusation is unfair, as I am convinced it is, then we must insist on the worldly engagement—and engorgement—of deconstruction. We must insist on the phenomenological and even ontological weight, the *frontal-ontological* import, as it were, of contemporary thought.[14]

## The Keen

What of this voice, then, and what of the invaginated site of the metaphysics of *Sein und Schein?* (Invagination, incidentally, is Merleau-Ponty's word, along with the words *écart, déhiscence, différence,* and *inscription.*) Is the voice the secret of all idealization? Or is Merleau-Ponty right to ask (VI, 211), "The proposal to demand of experience itself its secret—is this not already an idealist outlook on things?"

If it is not *the* secret of experience, and if deconstruction too has made the intimacy of all "experience" suspect, the voice nonetheless remains one of the obsessions of an engorged philosophy. The flesh of the voice heard and understood remains *effrayante*, more Gorgo than Gorgeous, for both Merleau-Ponty and Derrida, and also for us. Why, after all, is the threat of mutism—for example, as the result of throat surgery—literally a knife at the throat, a total threat, a shadow of what Freud calls *Kastrationsangst?* Laryngitis, the burlesque of mutism, is comic in the way that jokes about circumcision are comic. Even the alienation of my voice from me in a tape recording evokes embarrassment, rage, and something like helpless shame at the public exposure of my sphere of immanence ("Oh, but you *do* sound that way!" the others assure me, these idiots who have no call to be between my ears), a rage and shame that would be appropriate to the full frontal exposure of me, naked to ridicule.

And the gorge itself, this "isthmus" with its "sensitive valve"? How explain the burning resentment, the fury I feel at the onset of a simple sore throat? In many languages, a sore throat has the name *angina,* related to the word *Angst,* as though the gorge were the very heart of me. And when the word *angina* is pronounced in many Western tongues, it reminds the speaker of yet another flute or fold, and the topic and *topos* of engorgement becomes more involuted than one would have thought. This sleeved site, so susceptible, so vulnerable, is the suppressed site of metaphysics from Plato through Hegel. It is also the site of phenomenology and deconstruction alike, a site that by now is no stranger to mourning—to ululation and the keen.

Of course, the keen can be so high-pitched that it is all but inaudible to the human ear. Such is the keen of Oedipus, banished from the catapolylogue of the Louvre exhibition but returning now in mournful triumph to conclude this chapter. Nietzsche, in an early text written during his years as a professor of classical philology at Basel, evokes the voice of mourning in and as the figure of Oedipus. Under the heading "Oedipus," and the subheading "Talks of the Last Philosopher with Himself: A Fragment from the History of Posterity," Nietzsche writes:

> I call myself the last philosopher because I am the last human being. No one talks to me other than myself, and my voice comes to me as the voice of a dying man. With you, beloved voice, with you, the last vaporous remembrance of all human happiness, let me tarry an hour longer. With your help I shall deceive myself about my loneliness; I shall lie my way back into society and love. For my heart refuses to

believe that love is dead, cannot bear the terror of the loneliest loneliness: it compels me to talk, as though I were two.

Do I hear you still, my voice? You whisper as you curse? And yet your curse should cause the bowels of this world to burst! Yet the world lives on, gazing at me all the more brilliantly and coldly with its pitiless stars; lives on, as brutish and as blind as it ever was; and only one dies—the human being. And yet! I hear you still, beloved voice! Another besides me dies, another besides me, the last human being in the universe: the last sigh, *your* sigh, dies with me—the prolonged *Woe! Woe!* sighed about me, the last of the men of woe, Oedipus. (7:460–61)

# 4

# Mourning
# Ultratranscendence

I "worked" this morning, but you now know what I
understand by that: mourning—mourning me, the us in me.
—Derrida, *The Post Card from Socrates to Freud and Beyond*

After posing the question of the *phenomenological status* of some of Derrida's
descriptions, it seems natural enough to ask about their *transcendental stature*.
Derrida himself has put—and even pushed—this question for decades now,
and many commentators have taken it up, Geoffrey Bennington most recently
adding his analysis to those of Irene Harvey, John Llewelyn, and Rodolphe
Gasché.[1] In the current chapter, I do not wish to engage directly the issue of
the "quasi-transcendental" quality of Derrida's (infra)structures and decon-
structions, or to add anything to what I have elsewhere called the "queasy-
transcendentality" of Derrida's project;[2] rather, I wish to launch several rafts of
questions concerning the transcendental as such, if one can say so, questions
arising from three specific passages in *Of Grammatology*. Whether they will
advance the current philosophical discussion I cannot say. What I am searching
for is greater clarity concerning the necessity—in Derrida's view—of *passage*
to what lies beyond all determinations within the empirical, mundane realm;
what I want to ask is how such a *beyond*—let us agree to call it the domain of
*ultratranscendence*—relates in Derrida's oeuvre to the theme of the *absolute past*,
the past that never was present. For in such a relation I see the work of mourning and affirmation, inasmuch as the effect of the absolute past is to make

successful passage to the ultratranscendental realm impossible. In both cases, however—that is to say, in both mourning and transcendental philosophy—Derrida insists that we attempt the impossible.

The three passages I have in mind, and the rafts of questions I wish to launch, will move in the direction of a laconic and even mournful phrase from the final page of the "theoretical matrix" that constitutes the first part of the *Grammatology*. "To think—that is what we already know we have not yet begun to do [*Penser, c'est ce que nous savons déjà n'avoir pas encore commencé à faire*]" (G, 142/93). The declaration is riven by contrary temporal indications, the "already" and the "not yet" dividing between them the spoils of both thought and knowledge: a kind of perfect or perfection is there, mirrored in the *savoir déjà* that seems to grant a priori status to a claim of knowledge; yet that mirroring is marred by a perfect-tense imperfection, to wit, our *n'avoir pas encore commencé*. At this point in the theoretical matrix, one might suppose, the tain of the mirror is scratched away, so that one can see through to the other side—but to an other side that has never yet been descried or deciphered, much less occupied and surveyed. The third term of Merleau-Ponty's progression, *voir, parler, penser,* is rare in Derrida's vocabulary precisely because the effort of ultratranscendal passage is painful.

The second of the three chapters in the first part of the *Grammatology*, entitled "Linguistics and Grammatology," contains the passages that I want to read and interrogate here. The context, program, or plan of Derrida's chapter is too complex to summarize; yet his own words at the end of the chapter help us to recall what that chapter was to have accomplished:

> It is thus the idea of the sign that would have to be deconstructed through a meditation upon writing that would merge, as it must, with an undoing [*sollicitation*] of onto-theology, faithfully repeating it in its *totality* and *making it insecure* in its most assured evidences. One is with all necessity led to this from the moment the trace affects the totality of the sign in both its faces. That the signified is originarily and essentially (and not only for a finite and created spirit) trace, that it is *always already in the position of the signifier,* is the apparently innocent proposition within which the metaphysics of the logos, of presence and consciousness, must reflect writing as its death and its resource. (G, 107–8/73)

Even though this passage is reproduced here only in order that we may find our feet, one should not be blind to its strangeness—its decidedly mournful character. A meditation upon writing is called for that would both *repeat* and *deconstruct* the metaphysics of presence in its totality, being *reflected by* that totality "as its death and its resource." It is as though the meditation on writing would have both to *affirm* and to *mourn* its own position vis-à-vis the tradition as a whole. The trace would reveal itself to such a meditation as necessarily and primordially inscribed in the signified, in what used to be deemed pure meaning, so that every signified takes on the flesh of signifiers, and not merely for the inspection of finite creatures. Even if God were to signify "Light!" the signification would bear traces of chiaroscuro. The onto-theology that interprets such significations would have to be solicited in a double sense: incessantly brought to witness, the onto-theological tradition would also have to be radically and totally dismantled—indeed, *faithfully* deconstructed. Curious faith! If writing is both the death and the resource of the monstrous meditations to come, then structures of mourning assuredly undergird its affirmations. If Derrida's more recent work thematizes mourning and affirmation with ever greater insistence, there can be no doubt that these things were intertwined from the start. However, we are going too far too fast.

The chapter "Linguistics and Grammatology" begins with a discussion of the domain of linguistics as a field of science. It soon focuses on *phonology* as the scientific center of linguistics—a center, to be sure, that is repeatedly decentered in the debates surrounding the work of Saussure and Hjelmslev. If writing and grammatology appear to be the "outside" of speech and phonology, that outside, through "figuration" and "institution," soon contaminates the entire domain of the science. If writing is the usurper in the unhappy kingdom of phonology, that usurper was always at home there, always necessary, from the beginning. The scandal was from the origin, if origin there ever was.

Yet that is precisely the difficulty to which discussions of transcendental a priori structures always return: how can one invoke "the origin" without instigating yet another scandal—or, as Schelling said in another context, without pushing the difficulty one step farther down the line without resolving it?[3] No doubt, from within the discourse of the science of linguistics Derrida can reply to Saussure: "Before being or not being 'noted,' 'represented,' 'figured' in a graphics, the linguistic sign implies an originary writing" (G, 77/52). However, can he elevate the "originary" writing to an ἀρχή without causing the trace and differance to petrify?

This question has been put so often, and often as crudely as I have posed it here and now, that I want to set it aside. Wanting to do so is insufficient, however, and the question returns to haunt. Indeed, the second and third subsections of Derrida's chapter, entitled "The Outside Is the Inside" and "The Jointure Out-of-Joint [*La brisure*]," may be read as Derrida's own responses to this haunting. For these two subsections offer a series of strategies for advancing less crude formulations of the question of origins. These strategies and moves, all of them in pursuit of the trace, pass through three domains—not scientific fields but regions of interrogation that are nonetheless delineated clearly and repeatedly in the text.[4]

1. The structure of our relations with the "other," with special emphasis on what metaphysical cosmology defines as inanimate being, is the first domain of interrogation with regard to the trace. Long before such texts as *Of Spirit* or "Interpreting Signatures," Derrida had been asking about the regions of beings that are summarily determined as inanimate, animate, or conscious—in short, the regions of death, life, and *lifedeath*.[5]

2. The second domain of interrogation concerning the trace comprises the movement of tempor(al)ization as (a repressed yet irrepressible) spatialization of time. Elsewhere this movement of tempor(al)ization, that is, of temporal unfolding *and* deferral, will be named first, first of all, in Derrida's meditation on the trace.

3. Language as writing—in both the current and the arcane, archaic, deconstructive senses, language as *écriture* and *archi-écriture*—is the third and last domain.

One might venture a preliminary question or two in response to the mere designation of these domains marked by the trace. Does not the sheer juxtaposition or listing of these areas—alterity, life, and lifedeath; tempor(al)ization; and language—compel what one would have to call the "transcendental move" toward conditions of possibility? What lies behind such a compulsion—mere inherited, historical habit, or the force of "the things themselves"? Why—and whence—these three domains, and no others?

The selfsame "possibility" runs through them, according to Derrida; the selfsame possibility opens them and embraces them, "at once," *à la fois,* in an "irreducible arche-synthesis" (G, 88/60). Such a synthesis (the very word that commands all transcendental, a priori analyses) unites the structures of "archewriting," time, and life to the "movement of *différance.*" We have, Derrida insists here, as he did in *Voice and Phenomenon,* an "experience" of this opening, embrace, and synthesis. It is not an experience that stands in relation to a presence, but is nevertheless an experience as "lived," presumably in "time." It is an ultratranscendental experience, if such a thing may be said. What avenue can grant us passage to the irreducible arche-synthesis of life and alterity, time and space, speech and writing?

## Ultratranscendental Passage

Let us now begin to read *Of Grammatology*. The context is "the case of experience as arche-writing," experience not of, but as, arche-writing. It is as though "experience" and "arche-writing" were set in parentheses or brackets rather than quotation marks. Derrida continues:

> The parenthesizing of regions of experience or of the totality of natural experience must discover a field of transcendental experience. This experience is only accessible in so far as, after having, like Hjelmslev, isolated the specificity of the linguistic system and excluded all the extrinsic sciences and metaphysical speculations, one asks the question of the transcendental origin of the system itself, as a system of the objects of a science, and, correlatively, of the theoretical system which studies it: here of the objective and "deductive" system which glossematics wishes to be. Without that, the decisive progress accomplished by a formalism respectful of the originality of its object, of "the immanent system of its objects," is plagued by a scientistic objectivism, that is to say, by another unperceived or unconfessed metaphysics. . . . It is to escape falling back into this naive objectivism that I refer here to a transcendentality that I elsewhere put into question. It is because I believe that there is a hither side and a yon side [*un en-deçà et un au-delà*] of transcendental criticism. To see to it that the yon side does not return to the hither side is to recognize in the contortion the necessity of a *pathway* [*d'un* parcours]. That pathway must leave a track [*un sillage*] in the text. Without that track, abandoned to the simple content of its conclusions, the ultra-transcendental text will so closely resemble the precritical text as to be indistinguishable from it. Today we must form and meditate upon the law of this resemblance. What I am here calling the erasure of concepts ought to mark the places of that meditation to come. For example, the value of the transcendental arche [*archie*] must make its necessity felt before letting itself be erased. The concept of arche-trace must comply with [*faire droit à*] both that necessity and that erasure. It is in fact contradictory and not acceptable within the logic of identity. The trace is not merely the disappearance of origin. Here—within the discourse that we are sustaining and according to the pathway that we are following—it means that the origin did not even disappear, that it was never constituted except reciprocally by a nonorigin, the trace, which thus becomes the origin of the origin.

From then on, to wrench the concept of the trace from the classical scheme, which would derive it from a presence or from an originary nontrace and which would make of it an empirical mark, one must indeed speak of an originary trace or arche-trace. Yet we know that the concept destroys its name and that, if all begins with the trace, there is above all no originary trace. (G, 89–90/61)

So many questions cry out to be formulated. Let us be satisfied with two meager ones. First, is not the project of bracketing (parenthesizing?) both the regional sciences and all metaphysical speculation the very project of Husserlian phenomenology? And yet, second, is not the promise of such a delimitation a promise that is fulfilled, whether in Husserl or in Derrida, only when *nothing hangs on it?*

The transcendental passage or pathway, the *parcours,* is itself difficult to conceive, much less to traverse—unless one collapses back into the ready-made structures of all the transcendental idealisms from Kant onward that a "tradition" apparently places at our disposal. Further, such passage would leave a mark in its wake. Without such a (permanent?) wake, the hither and yon of transcendental passage would be indistinguishable. *With* such a mark, the advance to an ultratranscendence succeeds, and an orderly recursion to the "empirical" becomes possible. The *temporality* of the ultratranscendental pathway or passage and return remains problematic, as does the *priority* of the archaic necessity that causes itself to be felt before letting itself be erased. The *alterity* that is descried in such passage calls out to be remembered, even as it submits to a certain obliteration. And the *language* of such a voyage to the beyond, the spume of the wake, as it were, remains deceptively familiar. One has to exercise a particular vigilance in order not to let the *parcours* of ultra-transcendental experience collapse back into similar traditional strategies—which are not so much at our disposal as chained to our wrists and ankles.

It is difficult to see how one can prevent the ultratranscendental *Er-fahrung* (for is not such *passage* what Hegel meant by a science of the experience of consciousness as *appearing* consciousness?) from becoming the restoration or restitution promised by the "concrete concept," as Hegel describes it in the preface to the second edition of the *Encyclopedia of Philosophical Sciences:* "It is the most difficult path, but the only one that can be of interest and value to spirit once it has struck out on the path of thought. . . . Spirit soon discovers that method alone can bind up its thoughts, leading it to the matter [*zur Sache*] and preserving it there. Such an advance [*Fortführen*] proves to be nothing other than the restoration [*Wiederherstellung*] of that absolute import beyond which spirit initially strove and to which it exposed itself; but it is a restoration in the ownmost and freest element of spirit."[6]

Or is Derrida's ultratranscendental experience closer to Heidegger's *veritas transcendentalis*, that is, more reminiscent of a fundamental, universal, phenomenological, and hermeneutical ontology of Dasein, "which as an analysis of *existence* has fastened the end of the guideline of all philosophical inquiry at the point from which it *arises* and to which it *returns*"?[7] Or, finally, is ultratranscendental passage the heady experience that Kant recounts in the foreword to the first edition of the *Critique of Pure Reason?* Kant exults as follows:

> I have entered upon this path [of a critique of pure reason that is independent of all experience] . . . and flatter myself that in following it I have found a way of guarding against all those errors which have hitherto set reason, in its non-empirical employment, at variance with itself. I have not evaded its questions by pleading the insufficiency of human reason. On the contrary, I have specified these questions exhaustively, according to principles; and after locating the point at which, through misunderstanding, reason comes into conflict with itself, I have solved them to its complete satisfaction. . . . In this inquiry I have made completeness my chief aim, and I venture to assert that there is not a single metaphysical problem which has not been solved, or for the solution of which the key at least has not been supplied. . . . I have to deal with nothing except reason itself and its pure thinking; and to obtain complete knowledge of these, there is no need to go far afield, since I come upon them in my own self. . . . In this field nothing can escape us.[8]

What would it be like to traverse the ultratranscendental domain with such confidence? Dreams and delusions of either Husserl's "rigorous science" or Hegel's methodological restitution or Heidegger's circular guideline or Kant's flawless inventory cannot be allowed to undergird and thus subvert the Derridian passage—the *parcours* beyond the empirical realm—toward ultratranscendence. Derrida walks—or limps—in or at the wake (Finn, again) of his predecessors, mourning the loss of the confidence they possessed. The *non plus ultra* of ultratranscendence, like Merleau-Ponty's reversibility, is not a perfection but an imperfection, an experience of withdrawal and default. The necessity that drives Derrida's thinking of the trace to the yon side of transcendental experience is not victorious; however confident its gesture seems to be, the ultratranscendental experience is fraught. It is caught at the moment when the beautiful, having deigned not to destroy us (as Rilke says), begins to slip away, and no successful pursuit is possible. For what would it be like to run with concepts that destroy their own names? What would it be like—to alter Homer's refrain—to ply broken knees?

## The To-Appear of Appearing

Derrida now proceeds to a discussion of the "acoustic image" or "psychic imprint" that is so crucial for phonology and linguistics in general. Here an essential Husserlian corrective is introduced, an indispensable phenomenological reduction that will "save" a number of "essential distinctions." The major distinctions with regard to the acoustic image or psychic imprint are those between the mundane and the lived, and, less familiarly, between the appearing sound and the differential to-appear of the sound, *l'apparaître du son*. Here too one cannot proceed by election: here too passage to the ultratranscendental—this time by transcendental reduction of the mundane—is intrinsically necessary.

> [I]t should be recognized that it is in the specific zone of this imprint and this trace, in the temporalization of a *lived experience* [*d'un* vécu] which is neither *in* the world nor in "another world," which is not more sonorous than luminous, not more *in* time than *in* space, that differences appear among the elements, or rather produce them, make them emerge as such and constitute the *texts*, the chains, and the systems of traces. These chains and systems cannot be outlined except in the fabric of this trace or imprint. The unheard difference between the appearing and the to-appear [*l'apparaissant et l'apparaître*] (between the "world" and "lived experience") is the condition of all other differences, of all other traces, and *it is already a trace.* This last concept is thus absolutely and by rights "anterior" to all *physiological* problematics concerning the nature of the engram, or *metaphysical* problematics concerning the meaning of absolute presence, the trace of which is thus opened to deciphering. *The trace is in fact the absolute origin of sense in general. Which amounts to saying once again that there is no absolute origin of sense in general. The trace is the differance* that opens the to-appear and signification. (G, 95/65)

Again, a whole range of questions crowds to the fore. Why or how is the Husserlian reduction itself here immune to the *différance* that we saw undermining it, "soliciting" it, or at least putting it into question in the preceding chapter, which was itself devoted to voice and speech, hence phonology? How does the appeal to "lived experience" here survive the analyses—in *Voice and Phenomenon*, "Differance," and elsewhere—of the fission that occurs in *and to* the "living present"? It is clear that no scientistic or empiricist appeal to the mundane will be equal to the question of the genesis or constitution of aural (or any) experience. Yet how does the "unheard" or "unheard-of" difference within the acoustic image come to be heard or seen through "reduction"? There seems to be some sort of surreptitious appeal here to the distinction between *Seiendes* and *Sein*, if not between *Schein* and *Sein*, in the "essential distinction" between the mundane appearing (*l'apparaissant*) and the phenomenological to-appear (*l'apparaître*) within the psychic imprint. That distinction is proclaimed the anterior condition, the quasi-transcendental condition of possibility, of all other differences. Yet what is the force of the italicized phrase, "and *it is already a trace*"?

The trace structure, the fission of differance, seems to undercut the very condition—the a priori, anterior condition—that is marked by the distinction between the appearing sound (in the "world") and the to-appear of ("lived," experienced, psychically imprinted, differentiated) sounds of sense. Can such undercutting be prevented by the ultratranscendental *parcours*?

What is it like to be able to think back to what is absolutely anterior? Or to pretend to be able to think—or to hear—back? Or to have to pretend to be able? What would it be like to scurry *backward* with shattered knees?

## Jointures Out of Joint

For Descartes, knees are *hinges* in a fresh cadaver, and like the parts of any other dependable machine, they must be always still able to work. Derrida's knees belong to a living body, one that can and does suffer wear and tear. It is to the unhinged hinge, the joint or jointure out of joint, or the breach, *la brisure*, that we must now turn. The third passage on ultratranscendental passage in Derrida's *Of Grammatology* reads as follows:

> Origin of the experience of space and time, this writing of difference, this fabric of the trace, permits the difference between space and time to be articulated, to appear as such [*d'apparaître comme telle*], in the unity of an experience (of a "same" lived out of a "same" body proper

[*corps propre*]). This articulation therefore permits a graphic ("visual" or "tactile," "spatial") chain to be adapted, on occasion in a linear fashion, to a spoken ("phonic," "temporal") chain. It is from the primary possibility of this articulation that one must begin. Difference is articulation. (G, 96/65–66)

Allow me to interrupt and recapitulate thus far. Difference is here declared the articulation of the experience of space and time, two of the themes most intimately tied to the tradition of transcendental analysis. Further, even though quotation marks, or "scare quotes," unhinge the hinge, the condition of possibility extends nonetheless to an experience of the human body as the "same" and as "one's own," the body, one might say, as the site of an engorged philosophy—regardless of Derrida's reservations, cited in the foregoing chapter, concerning the possibility of a phenomenology of embodiment and of *le corps propre*. Finally, the articulation of space and time in a lived body enables a graphic chain to be forged or linked to a phonic chain, arche-writing to speech. Derrida now connects the notion of the "psychic imprint" or "acoustic image" with what one might have to call *arche-articulation* and, after discovering a novel kind of "passivity" in articulation, is led as though by the force of the things themselves to the utterly strange notion of an *absolute past*. Here the fate of ultratranscendence is decided. The third passage continues:

> The idea of the "psychic imprint" therefore communicates essentially with the idea of articulation. Without the difference between the sensory appearing [*apparaissant*] and its lived to-appear [*apparaître vécu*] ("psychic imprint"), the temporalizing synthesis, which permits differences to appear in a chain of significations, would not know how to do its work. That the "imprint" is irreducible means also that speech is originarily passive, but in a sense of passivity that all intramundane metaphors would only betray. This passivity is also the relationship to a past, to an always-already-there that no reactivation of the origin could fully master and awaken to presence. This impossibility of reanimating absolutely the manifest evidence of an originary presence refers us therefore to an absolute past. That is what authorized us to call *trace* that which does not let itself be summed up in the simplicity of a present. It could in fact have been objected that, in the undecomposable synthesis of temporalization, protention is as indispensable as retention. And these two dimensions are not adjoined one to another, but the one implies the other in a strange fashion. To be sure, what is anticipated

in protention does not sever the present any less from its self-identity than does that which is retained in the trace. But if anticipation were privileged, one would risk effacing the irreducibility of the always-already-there and the fundamental passivity that is called time. On the other hand, if the trace refers to an absolute past, it is because it obliges us to think a past that can no longer be understood in the form of a modified presence, as a past present. Since "past" has always signified past present, the absolute past that is retained in the trace no longer rigorously merits the name "past." Another name to erase, especially since the strange movement of the trace proclaims as much as it recalls: differance defers-differs [*diffère*]. (G, 96–97/66)

Whereas earlier it was the "arche-synthesis" that announced itself as "irreducible," it is now the psychic imprint itself that is "irreducible." Whereas earlier we dreamed of a successful reduction, a quasi-phenomenological reduction that would be essential to transcendental synthesis, we are now confronted with an imprint that will *not* be reduced. It is perhaps only now that the impact of the *necessary* but *impossible* ultratranscendental passage is felt, only now that the inevitable erasure and not always orderly retreat hither can commence: the effect of passage to the yon side of transcendental experience, its wake or track or trace all but effaced in the return to the hither side, opens upon a disconcerting absolute. Whereas the *synthesis* may have promised something like passage to an absolute of knowing, an absolute of philosophy, the *imprint* enjoins the inevitable return to passivity, to a past that has never been present, a past that is past all passing, and hence passing strange.

Ultratranscendental passage now confronts an *impossibility* rather than a (condition of) possibility. That impossibility announces itself in the essential "originary passivity" of speech, a passivity that sends shock waves through the very sense of "originary." What is now irreducible is the "always-already-there," the fundamental passivity of what are called *alterity, time,* and *language.* Only against the backdrop of such surpassing passivity does the word *trace* make any sense: the trace is that which never was, is, or will be fully present to the world, to itself, or to us. Thus the trace does not retain a present that is (now) past, transforming it into a past that is now (and forever) present; rather, the trace casts the fleeting shadow of tempor(al)ization "as such," if one may say so. The parentheses within the word *tempor(al)ization* betray the delay or failure of perfect coincidence in the unfolding of the trace as time. The trace inscribes, somewhat after the manner of the daughter of Butades, a shadow or echo of what is ineluctably passing. The trace thus marks its own passage to the transmundane and ultratranscendental, yet always reverts to this side of the absolute past. No hinge but that turns on itself; no knee but that buckles.


## The Limp

Ultratranscendence is inhospitable. It is no domain in which we can take up residence. What a confrontation with the absolute past enjoins is our lame return to the hither side of transcendental experience. The transcendental *parcours* has as its sole necessity *our* need to learn what is at stake in the trace, which is something like a condition of *impossibility.* As I have tried to indicate in more detail elsewhere, the trace guides us back to the slippery slope that we who are forever *on the verge* will never be able to quit.[9]

One might take the *parcours* to be David Wood's "high-grade mimicry" of the transcendental move—deconstruction talking through Leopold Bloom's (*alias* Henry Flower's) "high-grade hat." Or one might take it to be, in Geoff Bennington's words, "a disappointed transcendental ambition" (JD, 268). Yet Bennington himself correctly sees that Derrida's ambition is to challenge "the transcendental privilege" as such, and therefore to put into question what Derrida himself calls the ultratranscendental. Bennington writes: "If Derrida undeniably contests the transcendental privilege, and this is the very object of deconstruction (cf. *Glas,* 156), this is not in the name of the 'positivities' recognized by the human sciences, which fall constitutively short of transcendental questioning . . . , but in the name . . . if not of an ultra-transcendental, then at least of a passage through the transcendental (cf. *Of Grammatology,* 60–62)" (JD, 271). It is the function of the ultratranscendental passage to put into question "the very structure of transcendence," pulling it back down to a domain that transcendental philosophy would want to identify as "empirical" but that is the site of philosophy's contamination and ultimate demise: "This analysis does not ruin the transcendental by bringing it back down to a harsh reality of death, but contaminates it with the contact of what it attempted to keep at bay, whereas it lived only on the basis of that keeping at bay" (JD, 277–78).

It thus becomes somewhat clearer why both Derrida and Gasché prefer to speak of "*quasi*-transcendentality," and why Gasché refers to the five principal levers of deconstruction—the arche-trace, differance, supplementarity, iterability, and the re-mark—as *infrastructures.* That the play of such infrastructures is here below (*infra*) suggests that no matter how ultratranscendent their employment may be, they remain embedded in specific texts, specific worlds, and specific histories—none of which ever escapes the absoluteness of an absolute past. (One thinks of Schelling, between 1810 and 1815, writing, rewriting, recasting, and then retracting the first and only part of his never-published tripartite masterwork, *The Ages of the World;* that first part, which swallowed the whole, was called, in each of its many versions, *Die Vergangenheit,* "the past," "the bygone."[10]) Thus Gasché speaks of the infrastructures as forming "a system beyond being," ἐπέκεινα τῆς οὐσίας, not because they provide transcendental a priori concepts and not because they pertain to what Heidegger calls "the altogether earliest," *das Früheste schlechthin,*[11] but because the transcendental *parcours* finds and uses them as way stations. While Gasché wishes to systematize the infrastructures to the greatest possible degree, his own pathway or passage wrings from him the concession that "the infrastructures are not *strictu sensu* transcendentals or conditions of possibilities" and that "no system is ultimately possible on the level of the infrastructures" (TM, 224). "Purification" and "idealization" of the infrastructures are impossible "because the specific sort of synthesis that they achieve is context-bound" (200). Thus the play of the infrastructures may give rise to "an illusion of perfection," whereas their inscription on the marred tain of the mirror remains "incapable of reflecting, of sublating its limits" (238). Indeed, the apparent innocence of the phrase "context-bound," like that of "the trace," loses its innocence in the mournful experience of the absolute past, in which, as Descartes would affirm, everything that we yearn for is *tellement perdu.*

Ultratranscendental passage does not guide us to a realm beyond lifedeath, beyond the inextricable interlacing of inanimate and animate, the bestial and the human, the daimonic and the divine. Nor does it merely leave us on this side of those distinctions so beloved of metaphysics and morals. Ultratranscendental passage causes the terrain of those distinctions to shift and slide; it grants entry to the realm one might have to call—at least from the point of view of Derrida's *first* domain of the trace, that of life and alterity—*daimon life.*

Ultratranscendental passage does not expose for our inspection the mysteries of Derrida's *second* domain, tempor(al)ization and spatialization. Yet it allows us to see how those mysteries are bound up with the engorged voice that hears and (mis)understands itself while speaking and with the hands that weave lines of writing.

Ultratranscendental passage does not substitute *language* (the *third* domain) for the self or the transcendental subject. It does not erect language as the glorified body or monument of transcendence. It grants language new possibilities of analysis, but founds those exciting new possibilities on an experience of *impossibility*, an experience of passage, passivity, and a pastness that is to be both affirmed and mourned.

Ultratranscendental passage leaves us on the verge of what Nietzsche calls the *Es war*, the "It was," of time (*Thus Spoke Zarathustra*, "On Redemption," 4:180). It forces us to recognize the preeminence of the *imperfect* over every *perfect* tense, including Derrida's beloved *future anterior*, or *future perfect*, which, as we shall soon see, fails to provide a perfect future. It forces us to acknowledge the happenstance that at the end of my every project I discover what I badly needed to know before I began—what *Beyond Good and Evil* calls *das ewige leidige Zu-spät*, the eternally wretched and wrenching "Too late!" (5:229). As we shall see in the following chapter, Heidegger, writing perhaps on the trail of Nietzsche, insists in "Who Is Nietzsche's Zarathustra?" that the essence of time is *Vergehen*, "passing," or "transience"; in his *Contributions to Philosophy* he writes of the temporality and historicity of the gods themselves as *Vorbeigang*, which is both a passing by and a passing away, a becoming bygone, the divine itinerary of an imperfect(ion).[12]

However, when Derrida compels us to return from an ultratranscendental experience of the absolute past, and to climb back down from the realm of the sky gods to the mundane earth, what imperfect world does he invite us to inhabit? If we are to dwell in neither the heaven of arche-synthesis nor the hell of a complacent objectivism or a smug scientism, would not the imperfect world of Derrida's thought best be designated as an *arche-limbo*? However, in such a limbo, could one ever achieve ecstasy or affirmation?

# 5

# Mourning the Perfect Future

I truly believe that I am singing someone who is dead,
someone I did not know. I do not sing for the dead
(that is the truth, according to Genet), I am singing a
death, singing *for* a man or a woman already dead.
Except that, because the gender and the number are
inaccessible to me, I could play with the plural.
And multiply the examples or the working hypotheses,
the hypotheses of mourning.
—Derrida, *The Post Card from Socrates to Freud and Beyond*

Let me extend for a few pages more a reflection on *time* and *tempor(al)ization* in Derrida. To be sure, "in Derrida" always means in Derrida *and Kant*, in Derrida *and Husserl*, in Derrida *and Heidegger*. In the present chapter I focus on the last-named conjunction. As we have just seen, time and tempor(al)-ization constitute a privileged domain in and for a transcendental philosophy and a phenomenology of the trace, and especially for Heidegger's fundamental ontology and thinking of being. My own reflection on the work of mourning, art, and affirmation in Derrida's thought must at least remain sensitive to the temporal flow of such labors. Further, it must remain sensitive to *finitude*, with which Heidegger is so directly concerned and to which Derrida, however much he shuns direct discussion of it, is no stranger.

I focus on Heidegger's analysis of ecstatic temporality in *Being and Time*, in which the temporal ecstases of the *future* and of *having-been* (the future and the perfect) vie for primacy. To that analysis I counterpose Derrida's account of tempor(al)ization as spatialization and deferral, an account in which neither the future nor the perfect but the *future anterior* or *future perfect* and—I argue—the *imperfect* share something like primacy. Finally, I seek the imperfect(ion) of time in one of Heidegger's and Derrida's most beloved accursed poets, Georg Trakl.

I therefore say not a word in the present chapter about an entire array of questions and topics evoked by the conjunction of the names *Derrida* and *Heidegger*. Not a word about the end of metaphysics as the closure or eschatology of being, not a word about the metaphysics of presence; not a word about the essence of truth, whether as correctness, unveiling, historic unfolding, or dissimulation; not a word about representation and the destiny or sending of being; or about the redrawing of metaphor and metaphysics, or about *Ereignis* and abyss, proximity and undistancing; not even to ask whether we are at all understanding the relation of questioner and questioned when we take it as one of proximity rather than of distance and evasion. Not a word about two of the three topics this chapter was originally to have introduced—nothing about either the vaunted neutrality of the "who?" of Dasein or the troublesome distinction between the proper and the inappropriate, *Eigentlichkeit* and *Uneigentlichkeit*, in *Being and Time*.

Not a word about these things? Well, then, what?


## The Ecstatic Perfect

To begin with, a few remarks concerning Heidegger's analysis of ecstatic temporality and the finitude of time—an analysis that seems to me crucial for deconstruction. Heidegger's ecstatic analysis makes all the difference for deconstruction, insofar as deconstruction experiences differance and the trace—at least in part—precisely in terms of tempor(al)ization. However much in Heidegger's own view the ecstatic analysis of temporality elaborated in *Being and Time* may have failed, that analysis, one may say, is perfect. Or at least *of* the perfect.

In section 18 of *Being and Time* Heidegger writes that in our everyday concerns with things that are at hand or on hand, in our manipulations of the handiest sorts of things, we have always already let the things have their application or involvement (*Bewandtnis*) in the world. The fact that we have always already done so—as though impelled to do so by some sort of psychic imprint working its effects out of an absolute past—characterizes the perdurant manner of being of Dasein itself. We always have already let something go, released it, and let it become involved (*bewenden lassen*) in a structural totality of meaningful relations, with a view to the whole of our involvements in the world. Heidegger writes: "Das auf Bewandtnis hin freigebende Je-schon-haben-bewenden-lassen ist ein *apriorisches Perfekt*, das die Seinsart des Daseins selbst charakterisiert [Always-already-having-let-something-be-involved, which liberates a thing for its involvements, is an *a priori perfect* that characterizes the manner of being of Dasein itself]" (SZ, section 18). The Gesamtausgabe edition of *Sein und Zeit* adduces the following "marginal note" after the expression *apriorisches Perfekt*:

> In the same paragraph there is mention of an "anterior release" ["*vorgängigen Freigabe*"]—namely (stated in a general way), of being [*Sein*], for the possible openness [*Offenbarkeit*] of beings. "Anterior" in this ontological sense means the Latin a priori, the Greek *proteron tei physei* (Aristotle, *Physics* A 1; even more strikingly in *Metaphysics* E 1025b 29: *to ti en einai*, "that which already was—being," "that which in each case already ahead of time unfolds essentially [*das jeweils schon voraus Wesende*]," the has-been [*das Gewesen*], the perfect). The Greek verb *einai* knows no perfect form; it is designated here in the *en einai*. Not some bygone ontic thing [*ein ontisch Vergangenes*], but that which in each case is earlier, that back to which we are directed with the question concerning beings as such; instead of a priori perfect it could also say ontological or transcendental perfect (cf. Kant's doctrine of the Schematism).

Heidegger's is a spacious margin—for it contains a large portion of the history of metaphysics up to and including *Being and Time*.

The crucial words with respect to the a priori perfect are the prepositions *auf* and *hin*: Heidegger aims to define the *Woraufhin*, that is, "that toward which and upon which" every human involvement is projected. In the 1925 lectures on time, the 1927 *Basic Problems of Phenomenology*, and the 1928 Leibniz logic course, he designates the *Woraufhin* as "presence," *Praesenz*. (A highly complex *Praesenz*, it must be said, one that is ostensibly nonecstatic and yet in some bewildering way includes *Absenz*.) Strikingly, in *Being and Time* Heidegger does not at all identify the toward-which and upon-which of liberation as "presence," nor does he there employ the otherwise omnipresent phenomenological vocabulary of the "horizon." There the *Woraufhin* is called simply "world," although by it Heidegger means nothing mundane. One must sympathize with Heidegger's reluctance to invoke *Praesenz*. For what would it mean for an existential analysis of Dasein, committed as it is to the primacy of the *future*, the future being the privileged ecstasis of the *finitude* of time, to assert that the a priori perfect is *presence?* It would at least imply that the relationship of division II to division I of *Being and Time* is not merely one of recovery, reprise, or repetition; it might even suggest that division I's preparatory analysis of everydayness (of beings that are either handy or at hand, where presence handily prevails) does not and cannot prepare the way for division II's fundamental-ontological analysis of Dasein proper in its finitude (for which, to repeat, the *future* is said to be the ecstasis from which the other temporal ecstases spring).

However, I am not at all certain that the a priori perfect corresponds to what division II calls *Gewesenheit*, "having-been." I will not repeat here what I have tried to say elsewhere in some detail about ecstatic temporality,[1] but will merely note that for the project of fundamental ontology everything depends on the question whether the ecstases of time (future, having-been, and present) are "equally original," *gleichursprünglich*, or whether they are structured by some order of implication, priority, or ontological founding.

Heidegger is by no means embarrassed by the notion of "equal originality." Indeed, he criticizes the "unbridled tendency" of traditional ontologies to seek for every element a "simple 'primal ground' [*einen einfachen 'Urgrund'*]" (SZ, 131). He does not so much surrender the notion of equiprimordiality— by which future, having-been, and present would encompass *and* release one another in a ring dance of changes and exchanges—as vacillate on the question of the locus, site, or horizon of temporalization as such. He vacillates, as it were, on the very *space* of temporalization, and it would not be too much to say that Derridian deconstruction is born of that vacillation.

Because traditional ontologies understand being as presence and beings as being at hand, *Vorhandenheit*, and because such interpretations of being and beings seek to guarantee for humankind, or parts of it, a perfect future, that is, a future defined in terms of permanence of presence, Augustine's *nunc stans*, Heidegger stresses the primacy of the *future* in Dasein as possibility-being. For among the most possible of possibilities, from the beginning, is our coming to an end, hence our being *toward* the end.

Yet the following quotations from *Being and Time* indicate that in fundamental ontology no particular ecstasis, not even the future, can claim genuine primacy, in terms of a grounding function, over the others: "The phenomena of the toward . . . , back onto . . . , and by . . . , reveal temporality as the ἐκστατικόν as such. Temporality is the original 'outside itself' in and for itself. We therefore call the designated phenomena of future, having-been, and present the ecstases of temporality. Temporality is not, prior to that, a being that merely steps outside itself; rather, its essence is temporalization in the unity of the ecstases" (SZ, 329). Later (SZ, 350), Heidegger writes, and italicizes, as follows: "*Temporality temporalizes completely in each ecstasis. That is to say, the totality of the structural whole of existence, facticity, and falling*—and thus *the unity of the structure of care*—*is grounded in the ecstatic unity of any given full temporalization of temporality.*"

For the first of these two passages, it is the unity of the three ecstases, their shared, encompassing horizon, that serves as the ground; for the second it is each ecstasis "in itself," as it were, that embraces the whole. The Marburg lectures of 1927 and 1928 remain on the lookout for the ultimate horizon of the temporalization of time, the "in and for itself" of the original "outside itself," the ἐκστατικόν. Heidegger's most telling depiction of temporalization in those lectures, as in *Being and Time,* is captured in the word "rapture," *raptus, Entrückung.* The transports or raptures of time, including the μεταβολή that Aristotle espies at the heart of the "now," are discussed in *Being and Time* and, much more fully, in the subsequent lecture courses. In both cases they are taken to be the proper site of the fulgurations and the finitude of time.

## Ecstatic Unity as Radical Displacement

Yet the ecstatic unity that traces itself in and as radical displacement, *Entrückung,* the sudden transports or raptures of temporality that constitute the very metabolism of time, provide nothing like a fundament. They prove to be far more destructive of fundamental ontology than any *Destruktion* Heidegger may have envisaged for traditional ontology. Heidegger's analysis of the gathering of the ecstases into a unity, ground, or order of implication— with the ecstasis of having-been springing from the future and releasing the present—is endlessly complicated and ultimately frustrated. While he retains the word *Entrückung* in his later writings, it is no longer in service to the ecstatic analysis of temporality. As early as 1928 he concedes the following: "The totality of the *Entrückungen* is not, as it were, centered in something that itself would be raptureless, nonecstatically at hand as a collective center for the instauration of, and point of departure for, the ecstases. Rather, the unity of the ecstases is itself ecstatic."[2]

Was Heidegger correct in saying in 1961 (in the Todtnauberg Seminar on "Time and Being") that his earlier, abandoned analysis of ecstatic temporality was unable to reach what is most proper to time, *das Eigenste der Zeit,* albeit correct in a way he himself may never have envisaged?[3] For if the unity of the temporal ecstases or of any given ecstasis is "itself" ecstatic, hence radically displaced to an incorrigible eccentricity, subjected to centrifugal dispersion without any possible frame, enframing, or containment, what is left of Dilthey's concatenation of life (*Zusammenhang des Lebens*), of the "substance" of "existence," of the "stability" (*Ständigkeit*) of Dasein, stretched between birth and death? What is left of the *Augenblick,* the moment of vision, the blink of an eye that would carry a resolutely open and appropriate Dasein into a perfect future? What is left of the appropriate, "authentic" self of selfhood, the *Da-* of Dasein, the clearing and the truth of being "itself"?

Did the ecstatic analysis fail, or did it succeed smashingly well? That is the question I would love to see Derridian deconstruction—or, dare I say, *Derrida himself*—pursue with energy and persistence.

For if ecstatic displacement—*Entrückung,* μεταβολή, *raptus*—is a movement of excess and dehiscence, readers will hardly be surprised to hear in it anticipations or echoes of another discourse, in phrases such as "the possibility of the trace," "the play of the world," "differance," "the irreducible arche-synthesis," "the absolute past" (as an) "always-already-there" (which is just perfect), and finally, *le temps mort,* "dead time" (which is somewhat less than perfect: see G, 69, 73, 77, 88, 97, and 99). Nor will it surprise my readers that I wish to insert the Heideggerian analysis of ecstatic temporality into the *Grammatology,* precisely between pages 95 and 96, which are two of the three pages that occupied us in the preceding chapter. These pages conclude the section on the outside/inside and open that hinged wound entitled *la brisure.* They appear recto-verso on a single sheet of the book, however, so that I would have to slit that sheet from the outer margin to the spine in order to make the graft.

Why go to all that trouble? Why the violation? Because deconstruction of the Husserlian "living present" will not of itself—not even with the help of the Freudian economy of lifedeath, or even with the invocation of an absolute past that adheres to the psychic imprint—suffice to rescue deconstruction from its queasy ultratranscendental arche-limbo. Or, if one does not want to presume to "rescue" deconstruction, one may still be inclined to grant it what Beckett called "an agreeable addition to *company.*" Heidegger's ecstatic analysis of time would provide such company.

Can Heidegger's ecstatic analysis do what no other *Destruktion* can do for deconstruction? Is it privileged? Perhaps it is, at least for an ultratranscendental pathway or passage, precisely because it succeeds beyond Heidegger's own expectations, by some strange sort of ecstatic dissemination subverting the very fundament of fundamental ontology. Perhaps Heidegger's discovery of a resurgent *perfect*, where he expected the *future* to prevail, contains the seed of something like an absolute past, a past that will not be reduced to or derived from any other ecstasis of time, a past that is more abyss of imperfection than ground, and hence most appropriate to mortal existence? Perhaps we should try to recover Heidegger's analysis, and elaborate it once again, in detail, in the light of deconstruction? Not here and now, to be sure, inasmuch as the recovery would be arduous and time-consuming, but in some ecstatic future?

The only point I would like to make at this juncture, and to make as simply and as lucidly as possible, without footnotes, is that Derrida has never to my knowledge taken up in any real detail Heidegger's analysis of ecstatic temporality. Yet ecstatic temporality—with its raptures and its discontinuities, interruptions and ruptures—may be the single most important aspect of Heideggerian thought for deconstruction. Derrida has no doubt tended to do to Heidegger what I am doing here to him: he has been inclined to write about those aspects of Heidegger's thought that seem most problematic to him—Heidegger's apparent confidence that *questioning* guarantees him a certain proximity to being, his apparent self-assurance that an abyss of essence separates human existence from other forms of life, his apparent conviction that Germany, in Europe's heartland, has inherited the mantle of Greece and thus will have to rescue a wayward Europe and a hopeless America. And it has been essential that Derrida expose these moments of greatest self-assurance— these staggering weaknesses—of Heidegger's thought, expose them relentlessly, without succumbing to the temptation of banishing him or burning his books. All I mean to insist on here is that what Derrida calls the *via rupta* of the trace, the trace of *différance*, the trace of a passage that one tries to follow to the ultratranscendental realm only to find oneself confronting an absolute past, is somehow anticipated in the most radical moment of Heidegger's existential analysis—the moment of ecstatic temporality, the moment of *Entrückung, raptus,* μεταβολή. We will return to this moment in Chapter 8, though only briefly. Perhaps some day I will be able to follow the *via rupta* of Derridian differance and trace with greater persistence, follow it ecstatically—although it would be far better for us all if Derrida himself were to follow it and to chart for us its crazy course.

## The Future of Ecstatic Having-Been

Allow me instead a brief remark on the "later" Heidegger, for whom what-has-been, *das Gewesene*, becomes increasingly significant, increasingly Heidegger's own future. One example among the many possible: commenting on the final line of Georg Trakl's poem "Jahr" (Year), in which something is said of *das Ende* ("the end"), Heidegger writes: "Here the end is not what follows inception; it is not evanescence of the inception. The end, precisely as the end of the decomposing race [*Geschlecht*], precedes the inception of the unborn race. However, as the earlier dawn, inception has already outstripped the end."[4]

"Outstripped" translates the word *überholt*. In *Being and Time* Heidegger had defined the death of Dasein in terms of death's never being outstripped: essential to the existential conception of death is *die Unüberholbarkeit des Todes*. Now, in the essay on Trakl, it seems as though something quite early—the "inception" of the as yet unborn *Geschlecht*—is going to be outstripped. As Heidegger unfolds the romance of the dawn, he seems to be guided by the vision of a perfect future, from which mourning will have been banished: "This dawn preserves the still veiled original unfolding [*das Wesen*] of time. . . . Yet true time is the advent of what has been [*Ankunft des Gewesenen*]. The latter is not the bygone but the gathering of what essentially unfolds, a gathering that precedes all advent. For the advent, as such a gathering, always safeguards within itself what is earlier."

*Das Ge-wesene*, what-has-been, advenes as "true time," as the gathering and safeguarding of the earlier, the gathering and essential unfolding of essence. What can that mean? Will all mortal passage, transience, and even death itself—all the sundry appurtenances of the absolute past—be outstripped? It sounds as though Heidegger is trying to provide some sort of solace to a race in disarray, as though to say, "Some of you have been worried about the future. Do not worry about the future. The future will always already in each case have been absolutely perfect."

Yet the essence of what-has-been, as gathered, as *das Ge-wesene* (presuming that the *Ge-* is to gather all the variants of *Wesen* in the way *Ge-birge* gathers the solitary mountain crags), is haunted by that other kind of *Wesen* to which Georg Trakl is so sensitive: *ver-wesen*, literally, "decomposition," the *ver-* of what is ineluctably bygone, *ver-gangen*, "bygone." *Ver-wesen* invokes the disessencing of decay, decomposition, and wasting away, which very early in the history of metaphysics was called φθορά, "corruption."

I am moving far too quickly, I know, and toward an uncertain future. Looking forward to the hand of man according to Heidegger,[5] remembering the radical displacements, disseminations, and dispersions of ecstasis, dwelling still on *Entrückung* or rapture as the fulguration and finitude of time, I want to read two sets of lines by Georg Trakl in which this troubling word *verwesen* appears. For *ver-wesen* is not so much corruption in any traditional sense, I will suggest, as the *mourning of essence*. I will, as I mentioned above, return to the matter of ecstatic displacement in a later chapter, the eighth, looking for a certain Augustinian sense of *raptus*, μεταβολή, or *Entrückung*. For Augustine, as for Trakl, the raptures of time have everything to do with mourning. For Augustine, as for Trakl, mourning in turn is bound up with concupiscence and sensuality—with the (m)other to whom one is always still clinging. However, for the moment, let me set Augustine aside, in order to present, by way of Trakl's hands, the mourning of essence.

## The Ecstatic Imperfect(ion) of Trakl's Hands

First, from the later version of "De Profundis":

> Bei der Heimkehr
> Fanden die Hirten den süßen Leib
> Verwest im Dornenbusch.[6]

> Turning homeward
> The shepherds found the sweet body
> Decomposed in the briar.

Second, from "*Traum und Umnachtung*" (Dream and delusion), section 1:

> er besah . . . die Leichen, die grünen Flecken der Verwesung auf ihren schönen Händen. (80)

> he gazed on . . . the corpses, the green spots of decay on their beautiful hands.

Surely, there is nothing handy about these hands now, if indeed there ever was. If *das Ge-wesene* is the all-gathering, all-composing hand of time, *ver-sammelnd*, how will that finite, beflecked, and bygone hand envisaged by Trakl gather the decomposition and wastage, *die Ver-wesung*, that lays waste to all that lives in time? Surely no mere manipulation of time will suffice, not even the machinations of perfected technical representation, not even the *Ge-* of *Gestell*. Or does Heidegger mean to invoke the sheer force of will, will as will to power, when it comes to gathering and safeguarding what-has-been? Surely not.

Zarathustra descries the origin of all revenge, "the will's gnashing of teeth and loneliest grief," in the "It was," the imperfect(ion), of time: "This, yes, this alone is *revenge* itself: the will's ill will toward time and its 'It was'" (4:179–80). In the lecture "Who Is Nietzsche's Zarathustra?" Heidegger invokes this ill will. He insists that the *Es war,* the imperfect, far from being superfluous for gathered time, is nothing less than "the fundamental trait of time in its proper and entire unfolding as time [*der Grundzug der Zeit in ihrem ganzen und eigentlichen Zeitwesen.*]"[7] *Ganz* and *eigentlich,* the two watchwords of the second division of *Being and Time,* here apply to time as such, *not* as the *perfect* having-been of a gathering, *not* as the *perfection* of a successfully recuperated time, but as *imperfect:* "Yet how do matters stand with time 'as such' [*mit der Zeit*]? They stand in this way: time goes. And it goes by passing [*sie geht, indem sie vergeht*]. Whatever of time is to come never comes to stay but only to go. Where to? Into passing [*Ins Vergehen*]."

If the essential unfolding of time "itself" and "as such" is *Vergehen,* passing away or "transience," my own reflections on the a priori perfect and the perfect future, insofar as they are directed toward a Derridian encounter with ecstatic temporality, should in the end become—not apocalyptic, and not apoplectic, but ecstatically somber, affirmatively mournful, and tensed by the imperfect.

Not without a certain anxiety, not without risk of violence, I present the following extracts from section 3 of that same prose poem, "Traum und Umnachtung." My intention is to let certain words ring out, namely, the words "race," "generation," "curse," "dispersion," "hand," and "foot," inasmuch as each of these words—essential to Derrida's confrontations with Heidegger over the years—sounds a knell. Each betrays the "It was" of time, not in order to oppose it by some ill will or to subject it to some project of revenge, but in order to acknowledge the imperfect(ion) of time for the work of an always unsuccessful—and thus *possibly* faithful—mourning. By the time the knell fades, I will have ended, if I have not already done so.

O des verfluchten Geschlechts! Wenn in befleckten Zimmern jegliches Schicksal vollendet ist, tritt mit modernden Schritten der Tod in das Haus. . . . O, die dämmernden Frühlingswege des Sinnenden. . . . Frei ergrünt der Bach, wo silbern wandelt sein Fuß, und ein sagender Baum

rauscht über dem umnachteten Haupt ihm. Also hebt er mit schmäch-
tiger Hand die Schlange, und in feurigen Tränen schmolz ihm das Herz
hin. . . . O die strahlenden Engel, die der purpurne Nachtwind
zerstreute. . . . Weh der gebeugten Erscheinung der Frauen. Unter
erstarrten Händen verfielen Frucht und Gerät dem entsetzten
Geschlecht. . . . O die Wollust des Todes. O ihr Kinder eines dunklen
Geschlechts. . . . O, der Nächtlichen; o, der Verfluchten. (82)

O of the accursed race! When in maculate rooms every destiny is
consummated, death steps into the house with musty footfall. . . . O,
the vernal twilight paths of the one in reverie. . . . Freely the brook feeds
the greenery, where his silvery foot strays, and a tree speaks, rustling
above his benighted head. And he lifts with a fragile hand the snake,
and in molten tears his heart melted away. . . . O the beaming angels
that the wind of purple night dispersed. . . . Woe the stooped forms of
the women. Fruits and implements fell from the rigid hands of a race
in terror. . . . O the voluptuosity of death. O you children of a darkling
generation. . . . O, of the night; o, of the accursed.

# 6

# Eight Labors of Mourning

(All cinders are pollen—their calyx is the sky.)
—Novalis, *Das allgemeine Brouillon*, no. 339

—Can anyone accept working for His Highness Mourning?
—How can one not accept it? That is what mourning is,
the history of its refusal. . . .
—Derrida, *Cinders*

It is not easy to recover from Trakl. The imbrication of voluptuosity and mortality, sensuality and morbidity, ecstasy and melancholy, silvery foot and benighted head, fragile hand and snake, beaming angel and purple night—such an intertwining takes us perhaps as close as we will ever want to get to works of art and mourning, works of a difficult and hard-won affirmation. We will therefore not wish to recover from Trakl, but only to step back for the moment, quietly closing the door. At the same time, we will want to open other doors—eight of them—to sundry labors of mourning in the philosophical work of our time.

Having discussed the haunting presence of something like mourning in two of the classics of deconstruction, *Voice and Phenomenon* and *Of Grammatology*, let us return to more recent works by Derrida—in the present instance his *Feu la cendre*, or *Cinders*.[1] The themes of Derrida's *Feu la cendre* and related texts merit the most careful elaboration, commentary, and questioning. Any one of the themes broached in these books deserves much more space than I can devote to it on the present occasion. Which themes? If I may reduce them to the simple word "themes" and to unadorned titles, the following: (1) cinder and ash, the most ephemeral of traces, the furfuraceous stuff that any wind can disperse—and yet actual stuff nonetheless, material remains, remnants, residue; (2) holocaust, as the disaster of a history—ours, both recent and remote—that exceeds nightmare and outrage, but holocaust also as conflagrations of passion and immolations of sacrifice; and finally, most important for my own inquiry, (3) impossible mourning, mourning as baleful incorporation, rather than successful introjection, of the person (or "object") mourned—that is to say, the cryptic inclusion of the object of prohibited desire in an inaccessible interiority, in an inner sphere that is locked *from* the inside *to* the inside.

None of these themes is easy to invoke, situate, or understand. Taken together, what are they? Moods, modes, motifs? Metaphors, figures, fundamental infrastructures? Whatever they are, I want to argue in what follows that they are not mere exotics that we can take or leave as we like, not mere marginal regions of being. Rather, I believe they are matters already encrypted in the work of many of our contemporaries—current work, but also work that has been going on for decades, if not centuries.

Merleau-Ponty writes of a *phenomenology for us,* in which we feel not that we have encountered yet another new philosophy but that we suddenly recognize what it is we were waiting for. I will for the moment not write *about* cinders, holocaust, and impossible mourning in Derrida's work, but will look for traces of them elsewhere in some areas of contemporary philosophical work. The eight connections I wish to make may seem far-fetched, yet they may be perfectly obvious to those who labor in the respective fields. I offer them as long-distance questions to Derrida, some of which may be worth pursuing, and as local questions to my readers, whom in general I wish to ask: Does one or another of these connections bear any relation at all to the work we have been doing—or *want* to be doing in the most perfect of futures—in contemporary European thought?

## Husserl

In earlier chapters of the present book, Husserlian phenomenology has been portrayed as militant and triumphant, as though mourning and loss were as foreign to it as anything could be. Sometimes the phenomenological movement seems that way, especially in the United States, where rough-and-tumble phenomenologists roll up their sleeves and prepare to tackle any and every human experience, no matter how recalcitrant, no matter how chilling, with gusto and élan. Yet it was not always such cheerful sport for Husserl.

In the third chapter of the third division of *Analysen zur passiven Synthesis,* reproducing the 1925–26 lecture course, "Fundamental Problems of Logic," Husserl inquires into affective awakening through reproductive association in the remote sphere (*die Fernsphäre*), in other words, the initial rousing of memories that are not yet memories as such, the awakening of what has long lain concealed (*die Weckung des Verborgenen*).[2] Here no retention reaches into the past from a vital present; here something like an absolute past resists every phenomenological penetration; here the living present turns its face toward the future alone, as though in amnesia. Husserl is not sanguine about the possibility of a phenomenological account of the awakening of "objectivities that are ceaselessly veiling themselves, and ultimately of those that are already wholly veiled" (173). Rather than the familiar phenomenological mechanisms of primal impression (*Urimpression*), retention, and retrieval (*Wiederholung*), it is here a matter of "the vacant horizon of what has foundered [*Leerhorizont des Versunkenen*]." Rather than the now (*das Jetzt*) serving as the font or source point of evidence, it is here a matter of "the zero [point] of indistinguishability [*das Null der Unterschiedslosigkeit*]." Here the retentional process as a whole, insofar as it is relevant at all, takes on the appearance of "a process of continuous impoverishment," "a progressive diminution of affective force." As the effective affective force of association and potential reproduction dwindles, as the *Urimpression* pales to "vacuous identicality," the line (*Linie*) of retentional synthesis "loses itself in universal nullity" (174), which is very much like a past that has never been present.

What can *Weckung*, whether passive wakening or active waking, mean here? It cannot mean that an alert ego rouses the somnolent object, but only that the object itself "'steps forward' out of the 'fog' [*'hervortritt' aus dem 'Nebel'*]." Whence the dormant object's somnambulistic locomotion? And who would be there to observe its crepuscular peregrinations? How should nullities escape absolute zero, when it is zero that causes them to be nullities? What sort of injection (*Zuschuß*) of affective force from the all-too-distant living present can perform this miracle? For, while Husserl sometimes speaks of the objects as "dormant," he at other times acknowledges them to be quite "dead." Here, in the remote sphere, Husserlian phenomenology must either approximate necromancy or approach mourning.

We cannot in the case of nullity appeal to the chain of temporal constitution, Husserl insists, precisely because we only experience the constitution of time as a chain "thanks to the retroactive awakening [*dank der rückgehenden Weckung*]." The problem is that "the chain" of retroactive awakening "is finally lost on the zero horizon" (176). The dilemma or double bind of retroactive awakening (which ultimately can only be *passive* in an unheard-of sense) is that "the force of intuition, including the weakened forces of derivative intuitions, is limited [*begrenzt*], and in radiating back it ultimately reaches zero [*in der Rückstrahlung wird sie schließlich Null*]—." However, if the retentional process itself ceases (*hört auf*), petering out into "the one zero [*in das eine Null*]" (176), as Husserl repeatedly insists that it does, how can the fog ever lift on any future for a memory that has foundered in the past?

Husserl replies that the zero point itself must be—but what is the status of this *must?*—a kind of persistent, subsistent reservoir or stockpile (*das beständige Reservoir*) that is locked into objects "that have come to living foundation in the living present" (177). Such objects and their encrypted zero reservoir are now admittedly shut off, inaccessible to the ego; yet they remain, inevitably, though inexplicably, at its disposition (*"Für das Ich . . . verschlossen, aber sehr wohl zu seiner Verfügung"*). If the objects are no longer "constitutively alive," they are still there—themselves incorporated or encrypted—as funereal figures ("*in der 'toten' Gestalt*," Husserl writes), as configurations devoid of "streaming life." Their very rigidity—and it is a rigor that is more rigorous than the rigor of all transcendental-phenomenological science—seems to preserve them as potential recipients of an injection of affective force from the sensuous life of the living present. Indeed, Husserl declares that these lifeless objectivities are "enclosed in the null sphere and cannot go astray [*unverlierbar in der Nullsphäre beschlossen*]" (182). In short, what at first seems to be the vanishing horizon and the fog in which all objectivities founder in concealment, what at first is called *zero*, suddenly becomes a *crypt*, a secure *vault*; the nought sphere is ultimately modeled on the "inner sphere" or "sphere of immanence," of which consciousness always keeps the key. What was a bank of fog suddenly becomes a reserve bank, a thesaurus; the vanishing horizon mysteriously becomes a sturdy mausoleum. When the object encrypts the zero as a reservoir in the heart of its being, it secures itself as "that which cannot be lost in the zero sphere." Only through this undiscussed slippage or passage between inside and outside, only through such cryptic haunting—as though phenomenological consciousness were like an animal huddled in the moss near the trapdoor of its burrow, believing itself to be both inside and outside at once—can there be waking and wakening.

And yet the encrypted objects, far from being frozen in a perfection of form, embalmed and rigorously preserved, are in a wretched state. Because they have altogether lost the life they once had lived throughout the entirety of our earlier experience, the objects are themselves in tatters: Husserl describes them as "strips torn from the whole cloth of an earlier experience that is now defunct [*abgerissene Fetzen aus einer verlebendigten früheren Gesamterfahrung*]" (184). If and when they waken and come to the fore in consciousness, they do so discontinuously (*durch diskontinuierliche Weckung*), like flitting specters, by fits and starts (*sprunghaft*). They enrich the lifeworld in the way that Hades and Persephone enrich the upper world: they haunt the land of the living so persistently that we come to believe we can summon them whenever and as often as we like.

One often does Husserl the terrible injustice of taking him to be an evidentiary optimist; one often takes phenomenology to be the Church Militant of apodicticity and adequacy. Those who study Husserl with greater devotion and insight will know that the retentional process—and with it, perhaps, all self-givenness, eidetic essence, and evidence—is, in Derrida's words, "destined, like everything, to disappear from itself, as much in order to lose the way as to rekindle a memory."[3] They will know—whatever confidence and esprit the *movement* that calls itself *phenomenology* often seems to exude—that the *passivity* of genesis and of synthesis invites a sustained meditation on the ashes of evidence and the evidence of ash. Evidence is evidently to be mourned.

## Merleau-Ponty

What is the nameless *adversity* that shakes our confidence, interrupts our itineraries, and frustrates our projects? Although Merleau-Ponty's thought of the living body and the flesh of the world is as generous and generative a thought as we possess, it never fails to acknowledge the shadows. If mourning is always the *other's* experience of mourning, as Merleau-Ponty says, and if the situations of the phenomenologist and the mourner cannot be superimposed, that merely gives the phenomenologist one more thing to mourn (P, 409). If lovers love unequally, and if everyone I know or love possesses "an inexhaustible ground that one day may cause the image of them I've fashioned for myself to explode" (P, 415), if my own life "precedes itself and survives [or lives out beyond] itself," then whether I am alone or with others—especially with my significant others—I am no stranger to mourning. If unobtrusive serenity and equanimity grace every page of Merleau-Ponty's philosophy, and they do, that is only because his philosophy knows that mourning too is unsuccessful: cheer up, mourning doesn't work, either.

A philosophy of ambiguity lives with ashes and accident. Merleau-Ponty evokes "the feeling of my contingency, the anxiety of my being *dépassé*, so that even if I do not think my death I live in an atmosphere of death in general, and there is something like an essence of death that is always on the horizon of my thoughts" (P, 418). If, later on, in the project of a genealogy of truth and an interrogation of the invisible that is *of* the visible, "reversibility" seems to be absolute truth, if the touched touching seems to be the perfect paradigm of a world peopled at last by living bodies in the flesh, reversibility remains, as we heard in Chapter 3, "always imminent [with an *i*, not an *a*, hence either forever futural or absolutely past] and never realized in fact" (VI, 194/147).

It is no coincidence that for Merleau-Ponty's thinking there is no perfect coincidence or coextensivity, not even in our most fervent engagements in the world. "Each political act," for example, "bears in addition to its manifest meaning a contrary and latent meaning" (S, 303). If the philosopher's consent is always halfhearted, as we heard in the Introduction, it is because she or he has learned the lesson of wholehearted sloganeering. "When our initiatives spin their wheels in the sands of the body, of language, or of the recalcitrant world that we are given to complete, it isn't that the will of an evil genie thwarts us: it is simply a matter of a kind of inertia, of a passive resistance, of a failure of meaning—of an anonymous *adversity*" (S, 304). Perhaps it is the inevitable withdrawal, as we saw most clearly in Chapter 2, in the story of Echo and Narcissus, the turning away, the *aversion* and *adversity* we confront in what we most love, that lies at the heart of mourning?

Jean-Paul Sartre felt the sting of this adversity, which can maim friendships—such as his with Merleau-Ponty. I will resist the temptation to quote at length from "Merleau-Ponty vivant," one of the most mournful and magnificent texts of Sartre's oeuvre, and cite only this:

> Merleau, an exile, had very early *felt* what I could only *know.* We can't go backwards, the gesture cannot be reclaimed, the gentle contingency of birth is changed, by its very irreversibility, into destiny. I was not unaware that we proceed along the course of things and never retrace our steps. But for a long time, trapped by the bourgeois myth of progress—Progress, that accumulation of capital and virtues—I cherished the illusion that each day we grow in value. We keep everything. In short, I was approaching excellence. This was the mask of death. Today it is stripped away. But this mask repelled Merleau. Born to die, nothing could restore to him the immortality of his childhood. Such was his original experience of the event.[4]

In Derrida's *Cinders,* one voice asks, "Can one ever accept working for His Highness Mourning?" Another voice replies, "How can one not accept it? That is what mourning is, the history of its refusal, the narrative of your revolution, your rebellion, my angel" (55).

## Benjamin

A certain tension—or a certain *slack* in the tension—with regard to the theme of mourning in Benjamin's "Über den Begriff der Geschichte" ("On the Concept of History," 1940) is telling. For it is truly difficult to see precisely how historicism, historical materialism, and messianism can be rigorously distinguished in the way that Benjamin initially hopes they can be. Perhaps what Benjamin calls the primal ground of mournfulness (*der Urgrund der Traurigkeit*) is constituted by the node or tangle of *all three* relations to history? No doubt a thoughtful reply to this question would require study of Benjamin's *Trauerspiel* thesis and a careful contrasting of mourning-play and tragedy in terms of the dimensions of the "inexpressible" and the "messianic." Such a study lies beyond my competence and the limits of this brief chapter. For the moment, therefore, I will remain within the confines of this uncanny essay, or highly polished fragment, "On the Concept of History."

Historical materialism hopes to break decisively with the empathetic, historicist approach to history—Benjamin alludes to Fustel de Coulanges, but he could have cited Dilthey and many others—which invariably identifies with the victors. For empathetic historicism, time is the stouthearted march of homogeneous now points in contact with an empowering past and moving through a legitimated present toward a perfect future. For the sake of the victims of history, whom he mourns, Benjamin joins forces with those who reassess the concept of time, including thinkers with whom he is only rarely associated—Husserl, Sartre, Merleau-Ponty, and Heidegger among them. Benjamin: "The representation of the progress of the human race in history cannot be disengaged from the representation of its continuous advance [*durchlaufenden Fortgangs*] through a homogeneous and vacuous time. Critique of the representation of this advance must shape the foundation of a critique of progress in general."[5]

It seems as though both Benjamin and Sartre are summoning Marxist and neo-Marxian social-critical theory to a painstaking study of what others call *ecstatic* temporality and to a rigorous deconstruction of the point, line, and circle of time. Could social-critical theory ever accept such a summons? If it were to accept, it would go to encounter the gravest difficulties.

The difficulties in Benjamin's effort mount when Benjamin tries to think messianic cessation or immobilization [*Stillstellung*] as the *monad,* and when he proclaims the day of mourning or remembrance a *monument,* erecting it as a fast-motion or speedup *mechanism (Zeitraffer).* The problem is that the eternal recurrence of such a day of recollection, as an anniversary, is guaranteed precisely by the speedup view of history, which is itself parasitic on the stouthearted march of empathetic historicism. To be sure, in Benjamin's view each instant of future time is given not as a stolid, homogeneous, and empty now point but as what Heidegger calls the *kairotic moment,* Benjamin "the little portal through which the Messiah could step" (261). However, how does one prevent the little portal—or the day that is seized, intensified, and monumentalized as the monad of a historical constellation that is putatively fixed in its import, understood and commemorated once and for all—from gaping as an open door to the worst forms of sentimental empathetic historicism? Is the "school of hatred and readiness for sacrifice" sufficient to prevent the degeneration of historical materialism into vacuous triumphalism— sufficient to prevent its decline into the self-righteous, rancorous discourses of self-proclaimed victims, which today we hear on all sides?.

The school of hatred and sacrifice will be sufficient, Benjamin himself admonishes, only if a *weak* messianic force (*eine schwache messianische Kraft*), emanating from earlier generations of the wretched on this earth, reaches it— not as an injection of affective force from a living present (Husserl), or as the bravado of a generation that has chosen its heroes (Heidegger), but as the faintest cry from the enslaved and defeated defunct, the as yet unmourned dead of the remote past. When Flaubert says that few will ever know how sad it is to resuscitate Carthage, or when Dedalus replies to Mr. Deasey that history is a nightmare from which he is trying to awake, and when Merleau-Ponty speaks of an anonymous adversity that muddies the clarity and force of our engagements, they are perhaps not to be mocked for their inertia of the heart, their *acedia* (torpor, listlessness, melancholy, *Schwermut*). On the contrary, when the historical materialist prides herself or himself on being a "distant observer," cool, ironic, steeled, ready for anything, or perhaps full of wrath, with righteous indignation closing all the gaps on the time line while at the same time secretly opening the door to empathy, historical materialism is at best passionate intensity, at worst the smug and crafty (i.e., thoroughly bourgeois) decision to go with a winner. Without something very much like *mourning* to temper its righteousness, historical materialism plays the vengeful dwarf to historicism—and it will not be able to lose for winning, as the faint cries grow fainter and finally fade away altogether.

However, what of the third—the messianic—grasp of history? In recent works, such as "Force of Law" and *Specters of Marx,* Derrida tries to distinguish what he calls the messianistic from the messianic, and the call for *justice* from the cry for *vengeance.* In *Specters* he notes, however, the unnerving proximity of messianism and vengeance: "If the law [*le droit*] holds to vengeance, as Hamlet seems to complain that it does—Hamlet before Nietzsche, Heidegger, and Benjamin—could one not yearn for a justice that one day, a day that no longer pertains to history, a day that is quasi-messianic, would be withdrawn from the fatality of vengeance? Better than withdrawn—infinitely foreign, heterogeneous in its source, with regard to vengeance? And is such a day ahead of us, still to come, or more ancient even than memory?"[6]

*All* judgments concerning history are tenuous in the extreme when *all* who judge are caught up in a certain kind of progress—and Benjamin, in the "Concept of History," continues to call it *Fortschritt,* even though it is as far from triumphalism as anything could be. *All* are caught up in the storm (*Sturm*) that reduces the past to rubble as it tears us away into an uncertain, imperfect future. The expression of horror on the face of the angel of history, the dismay of the *angelus novus,* is an expression of *impossible* mourning. For everything great or small *falls* in the storm. Whereas the angel would pause to wake the dead (*die Toten wecken*) and mend the shattered victims, or at least attend to their faint cries and erect monuments of memory, the angel too will be blown away. For the firestorm that blasts the angel of history blows from the origin, from paradise (*vom Paradiese her*), as Benjamin himself affirms, and all the messianic and messianistic portals, large and small, burn on their broken hinges.[7]

## Heidegger

As a young phenomenologist Heidegger too insisted that the march of history was ruinance, and he was never certain whether or how ruinance could be resisted.[8] In the early 1930s he devoted himself to the task of awakening (once again the word appears: *Weckung*) the fundamental mood or attunement of philosophizing, which he called *Schwermut,* μελαγχολία.[9] In the late 1950s he described the interplay of joy and mourning in poetizing-thinking as pain, *der Schmerz.*[10] No doubt the theme of mourning accompanied Heidegger's apparently triumphant remembrance of being from the beginning to end.

The final pages of Derrida's *Of Spirit,* immediately before the imagined dialogue between Heidegger and the frustrated theologians, focus on this *Schmerz.* They are perhaps the most difficult pages of that difficult book.[11] For if anything seems to moderate the decisionism and militarism—in a word, the triumphalism—of the *spiritus rector,* and if anything seems to move poetizing-thinking beyond mere flowers of rhetoric—for example, the rhetoric of evil as the rage of malignancy—it is the long discourse on pain in the 1953 Trakl essay, "Die Sprache im Gedicht" (US, 61–64), to which I referred quite briefly in the preceding chapter.

Pain is the only possible link between the sister and spirit: the "sister of stormy melancholy" is the great soul that the poet sings in "Gewitter," "The Storm." Pain is hers—even if her lunar voice recedes from this point on in Heidegger's text. Pain harbors *ein in sich gegenwendiges Wesen,* an unfolding that turns back upon itself; the French translation, as though in recollection of Merleau-Ponty, calls it *adversité.* Pain is the adverse flame of spirit that tears ahead, as a firestorm, and so tears us away (*der Fortriß*); yet it also tears back all concealments and lets us see the past in stark outline (*der zurückreißende Riß*). Such pain embraces all living things: in it all living things are joined— as though by a messianic force so weak that nothing can save them. "Alles, was lebt, ist schmerzlich" (All that lives is pain-ridden). *All* that lives: for the first and last time Heidegger refrains from segregating human beings from plants and animals. Even the stones now seem to live, to see and speak in pain: "Das alte Gestein ist der Schmerz selbst, insofern er erdhaft die Sterblichen anblickt" (The ancient stones are the very body of pain, when pain looks at mortals in an earthly way) (US, 62).

Of spirit and the flame, yes. But also *Of Pain.* We will never really understand the reasons for Heidegger's stony silences. Nor will we ever be able to set aside his corpus, which in some sense—perhaps Trakl's sense—consists of lithographs of mourning. And, finally, no, we will never be able to be rid of Heidegger's metabolic yet unbudgeable corpse.


## Irigaray

*L'oubli de l'air chez Martin Heidegger* is a work of mourning, begun the day Irigaray learned of Heidegger's death.[12] Mourning accompanies its every pace. Even though its theme is "horizontal flowerings," the φύειν of φύσις, the awakening breath of lovers (again, *die Weckung*), the oxygen borne by their blood and the songs bubbling across their lips, each fragment of thought in her work sustains mourning. Not as introjection, not as "successful" mourning, for no lover's investment is ever withdrawn; there is no mockery or rebuke in her text, no pullback, no desire for cheap victories. Not as incorporation, not as encryptment, for Irigaray's voice and her fluid line remain unmistakably her own. Her way *with* Heidegger is not Heidegger's way. With each *efflorescence horizontale*, with each rose blossom and each rose thorn, we come to hear *une autre voix*, we sense a different sort of *bouquet*.

Irigaray's response to Heidegger's readings of Hölderlin and Trakl constitutes one of the most remarkable segments of the book. For Irigaray champions Hölderlin's "all-living nature" against Heidegger's embarrassed recoil. And upon the mouth of the poet she finds the embrace and the brazier of lips: "She, the living one, . . . embrazes all: day and night" (*Elle . . . embras(s)e tout,* 99). Holocaust of the body and of the breath that gives life—yet, again, not as triumphalism or militancy or polemic. Irigaray's is instead a thoughtfully sustained and affirmed *impossible* mourning.

To be sure, it is a mourning that seeks a different place and another venue. To the *il y a là* of cinder and ash, she reiterates a question about an *other* site, an *other* voice. "Is it a matter of the same place? Of the same there? Or will there now be a distance between there and there (*là et là*)? What sort of difference will she make? *Là, quelle?*" (31).

No doubt Irigaray's is the desire for a site—her own—that will not involve the same mindless masters and mastery. "We literally unveil nothing of her, nothing that in the final account does not leave her intact, virginal (that's the only thing he loves), indecipherable, impassively tacit, in a word, sheltered from the cinder that there is and that she is." (That is Derrida, of course, on page 41 of *Cinders,* which is also a polylogue, but it *could* be *une autre voix*.) What persists throughout Irigaray's work on Heidegger, which makes no mention of Derrida, is the thought of mourning and pain—for example, in this one passage, a passage on birth, a kind of ultratranscendental passage but without a hint of triumphalism, an ultratranscendental passage to something like an absolute past, a passage that will have to represent the dozens of passages I would like to have reproduced here:

> The air remains—it is what resuscitates life, yet at first under the form of an absence: nothing is there but what it is, and it does not appear. This provenance of life, this mediation and milieu of life—these give themselves without appearing as such. The first time they give themselves, they are felt as pain. The open air represents the possibility of

life, yet it is also the sign of the loss of that which—or of her who—
gave everything without distance, without hesitation, and without
chagrin. The air, the open, is in the beginning the limitless immensity
of mourning. There all is lost. (43)

## Nietzsche

The very notebook in which Nietzsche writes about cinders—it is the notebook
that immediately precedes the one in which he loses his umbrella—also
contains a large number of notes on two other matters.[13] First, notebook M III
1 (9:441–575) offers us the most striking formulations of the eternal recurrence
of the same (*die ewige Wiederkehr des Gleichen*). The very first of these notes
on eternal return (11 [141]) insists that the thought must be incorporated or
ingested (*einverleibt*). Paraphrasing Heidegger, we may say that Nietzsche never
dreamed of another mode of reception for the thought of eternal recurrence
of the same than our *eating it*, as the *absolute other*.

Yet how are we to incorporate the thought without swallowing it whole,
or allowing it to swallow us, as we are, taking it in as a merely ventriloquized
voice, as the remnant of a cryptic, encrypted forbidden desire? How are we to
incorporate the thought, if not as the work of an impossible mourning? For
does not eternal recurrence express a desire for *the same*, that is to say, the
*metaphysical* desire par excellence?

The second matter broached by notebook M III 1 is this: Nietzsche's most
stringent critique of the word and concept *des Gleichen*, of "the same" (or, as
Heidegger would insist, of the *identical*). There they burn, side by side, *recto
verso* and *en face*, the eternal return *of the same* and the excoriation of *every
appeal* to "the same," the excoriations actually outnumbering the affirmative
presentations of Nietzsche's "thought of thoughts." In the *same* notebook, on
the *identical* site.

Let us be content with one sample, inasmuch as the thought *of* the same
and *against* the same often collude and collide within one and the same note:

11 [202]
The measure of force in the cosmos is *determinate* and is nothing
"infinite"; let us be on guard against such excesses of conceptuality!
Consequently, the number of positions changes combinations and
developments of such force, while monstrously vast and in practice

"*immeasurable*," is in any case also determinate and not infinite. Yet the time in which the universe exercises its force is infinite, which means that force is eternally the same [*ewig gleich*] and eternally active:—up to this moment an infinity has already passed by; that is to say, all possible developments must *already have been. Consequently*, the development occurring at this instant must be a repetition, likewise the one that bore it and the one that arises from it and so on forward and backward! Everything has been, countless times, inasmuch as the collective condition of all forces always recurs. Whether, *apart from that*, anything has ever been the same [*irgend etwas Gleiches*] is altogether undemonstrable. It seems that the collective position forms all *qualities* afresh, down to the tiniest details, so that two different collective positions can have nothing the same [*nichts Gleiches haben können*]. Whether there can be something the same in one collective position, e.g., *two leaves?* I doubt it: it would presuppose that they had an absolutely identical gestation [*eine absolut gleiche Entstehung*], and for that we would have to *presuppose* that the same had subsisted *all the way back through eternity*, in spite of all the mutations in the collective position and the creation of new properties—an impossible supposition! (9:523)

If Nietzsche, six thousand feet above sea level and much higher above all human things (9:494; 11 [141]), thinks the eternal recurrence of the same as the *new* center of gravity, the *new* burden that should give our lives ballast (*Schwergewicht*); and if teaching this doctrine should be the best way to incorporate it, inasmuch as we would have to eat it for *and as* the rest of our lives (*dem Reste unseres Lebens*); what does it mean that incorporation is at least initially, if not always, an interiorization "of the fundamental errors [*Grundirrthümer*]"; and what does it mean that *das Gleiche* is roundly condemned as the primal error—the first fruits of coarse and imprecise representation, faulty memory, excessive fantasy, and sheer laziness? What is left to us on our congealing star but mourning and ashes if the greatest burden turns out to be ingested error? What is left to us clever animals who will never come down to the same (except in mourning, except as ashes) if life itself—the organic as such—feeds on the same error of the same? Finally, apropos of ashes, who will interpret for us this note from M III 1 (9:538; 11 [254]) on pain: "There would be no suffering if there were nothing organic[;] that is to say[,] without belief in **the same**[,] that is[,] without *this error[,] there would be no pain* [keinen Schmerz] *in the world*"?

What would eternal recurrence be *without* the same, *without* anniversary or monument, *without* the fast-motion mechanism, *without* a messiah *ex machina?* How could we think return *without* returns? Who at Nietzsche's wake would be able to incorporate such a thought, think such a double-edged shibboleth, without gnashing the teeth, without going to work for Monsignor Mourning, without "a faint odor of wetted ashes" hovering ever about her or him, without unstillable pain?[14]

## Cixous

For a long time I have observed you when you write, what returns from the breathless race makes its way on a long cinder track.
—Derrida, *Cinders*

In 1972 a young man went to Paris to talk to an expert on James Joyce. She showed him the head of Nefertiti and gave him a book she had just published, entitled *Neutre,* the neuter/neutral.[15] She also jotted down for him a list of books she felt he needed to read. At the top of the list stood "Derrida: *Dissémination* (Seuil)." The young man read *Neutre* immediately, missing most of it, no doubt, except for its account of a desperate race between the subject and the tale told (*le Récit*), a race in which each vainly pursues the other in turn. The outcome of the race? A failed birth, a blind child, a neutering and neutralizing of the writer. "It is in this way that I lost," she wrote, "and there is no one there to weep" (132).

Years later, the man, not so young, took up the books on her reading list. He noticed near the end of "Plato's Pharmacy," and also in the dedication at the very end of *Dissémination* (published in 1972, the same year in which *Neutre* was published), the words *Il y a là cendre,* "There there is cinder." After even more years farther down the line toward the zero horizon, closer to the point of all foundering, he opened *Neutre* once again and reread the first page of the text after the exergues:

Holocaust . . .

   if, without name, without force, without age, and without sight, I am and I follow [*je suis*], lacking air and resources, lacking light and air

and space and also time, not without desire and movement, but with
my extremities cut off from my body, thus
Neuter/neutral
about to engender myself,
who am I, who am I to follow?

. . .

    dense pellicle of smoke oriented from bottom to top, fire masculine,
    smoke feminine, cinder feminine singular or plural,
    no Wind
    and from top to bottom, misunderstood, my mouth.

    The one is not without the other
    "The one is not without the other"
. . . delirium, cinder or ashes, in every direction therefore, : (a mix of
    yellow saffron white gray black and, oddly, carmine ash) descending
    from the top to the bottom of
    Desire

Some say that the time of French feminism and of feminine writing is
absolutely past, that the fire is quenched, that the charred remains of
bitterness and an unrestrainedly masculist political expediency alone survive
as the elements germane to feminism. Yet there are cinders of a more fecund
variety; cinders are what such writing always produced, and I suspect that
these ashes of feminine writing, and feminine mourning, will be with us for
quite a while yet, which would be good for people like me who are so slow
to read even the best of books assigned by the most gracious and talented
and inspiring of teachers. Teachers that trace their lineage all the way back
to

# Empedocles of Acragas

Hölderlin knew that the fire of heaven scorched mortals. Scorched everything—
all the points of time, every discernible epoch and ἐποχή, every source of
(self-)giving—all incinerated to nought. The fiery point is felt always in
searing intensity, always in ardor, always in an excess of intimacy—*zu innig,
zu einzig*—and always in pain. For even if all-living nature and humanity
interact harmoniously, as Hölderlin notes in "Das untergehende Vaterland. . ."

(The nation in decline. . .), so that a new world and a new life germinate Phoenix-like in the cinders of the old, and even if tragic dissolution can be felt only by the heart that senses an inchoate, nascent unification—even so, the modality of possibility remains fixed in mournful remembrance of a past that has gone up in smoke and is lost from top to bottom, forever. Ashen Phoenix is disoriented, displaced, distraught. Only the rare human being—too intense, too singular, trying to rouse the gods and the heroes of thought from the remote past—has such premonitions.[16]

Both Hölderlin and Nietzsche believed that Empedocles of Acragas was such a human being; they wanted to find in the mouth and throat of Empedocles their own poetic, thoughtful voice. Yet neither was blithe about his chances. On September 4, 1795, Hölderlin wrote to Schiller: "I believe it is the property of rare human beings to be able to give without receiving; they can 'warm' themselves even 'on ice.' All too often I feel that I am not at all a rare human being. I freeze and petrify in the winter that surrounds me. As my sky is of iron, so I am of stone."[17]

Irigaray counterposes to Heidegger's Parmenides and to the well-rounded sphere of 'Aλήθεια Empedocles' notion of the asymmetrical alternation of Love and Strife. She also has in mind the Empedocles of Hölderlin or the Empedocles who informs Nietzsche's Zarathustra, at all events the Empedocles who pledges his troth—that is, his life and death—to the earth.[18] For even if Empedocles plays no role at all in Heidegger's reading of the Greeks, and a very minor role in his reading of Hölderlin, there are nevertheless Empedoclean fragments on all sides in contemporary European thought, fiery fragments that continue to burn out of control. If one of the voices of *Cinders* complains that "in Sicily churches are built with the stone of lava" (61), another voice might counter that no known church or messianic portal was ever built on the following affirmation of Empedocles (fragment 17, lines 18–26):

> Fire and water and earth and vast height of air . . .
> And in their midst, Love . . .
> Gaze on her with the mind's eye, do not be astonished.
> You know her, she surges in the limbs of mortals.
> Through her they dwell on loving thoughts and do unifying deeds,
> Calling her by name: Delight! and Aphrodite!
> As she whirls with the other elements there
> No mortal male can make her out. But do trace
> These footsteps of my logos: it will not disappoint you.

## A Polemical Note

Why these eight vignettes? How can the number eight not go horizontal, ∞, and so mark infinity? Who could entertain the Derridian thought of cinders, even for a moment, without invoking Levinas, but also Freud and Lacan, Mallarmé and Blanchot, Genet and Bataille? What about the fate of hermeneutics? What about Socrates and Plato? What about Kant and Hegel? What about Rousseau? Once the door opens to even a few of the names associated quite rightly with Derrida's oeuvre, we are thronged by possible and necessary connections, so that a choice is worse than arbitrary, it is foolish. Did I say a *throng* of names and texts and issues? It is more like a flood, a tidal wave.

This may help us to understand something about the polemic that so often rises to meet—or to flee—Derrida's work. One might have supposed that such polemics could arise only in cultural and academic backwaters. Cambridge, for example (the little one, in England). Or New York (the little one, in the *Review of Books*). Yet the polemic is so widespread and so bitter that it remains truly baffling. It is as mean-spirited as the person it vilifies—the purest of bastards—is gentle and generous. The one saving grace of such polemic is that it is so ill informed, so endearingly stupid.

There are doubtless many reasons for the polemic, but here is one we do not often admit to—it has to do with the breadth and depth of Derrida's work. What happens when scholars who have spent decades working on a particular angle and specialty of philosophy or literature or law or politics or psychoanalysis or feminism or architecture or art history suddenly feel the ground quaking beneath their feet, perhaps after reading only one essay of his, a mere "note on a note," as he likes to say? They look out to sea and do not fail to discern the thirty-foot tidal wave looming out of the distance. From left to right, right to left, the monster is uniformly vast and deep, there is no relief. They look down at their feet and scrutinize the two or three scholarly sandbags they have gathered over the years, with pains, against disaster; they examine the battered life preserver looped over a stooped left shoulder. Once again they look out to sea: the wave is visibly nearer, higher, deeper. Gratitude is not in their hearts.

In their panic, and in the ensuing scramble, they overlook one thing. The wave is not "Jacques Derrida." In fact, this purest of bastards, himself ship-wrecked, is standing on the shore alongside them and all the others who are menaced. (Beckett would exclaim, once again, "What an addition to company that is!") True, the equipment at his feet is more impressive than any we have seen, but his life preserver is in tatters, it will never pass inspection, he'd better come up with Queequeg's pocket-size Tlingit coffin, or he's doomed.

In the end, nothing will withstand the wave. It isn't called "Deconstruction" or "*la machine derridienne*" or "apocalypse." If we shy from calling it grandly "a sending of being" or "an envoy of writing," there is no reason to be shy about saying that it is *die Sache des Denkens,* or, in the plural—if only by way of anagram—a hauntingly familiar command: *zu den Aschen [Sachen] selbst.*

In his "recent" work, say, from the 1980 *Post Card* or even from the 1974 *Glas* onward, Derrida has gone to meet such ashes again and again. In the three final chapters of the present book we shall accompany him there. It will not be a tidal wave that rises to meet us in these final pages, but something far more uncanny. While I acknowledge the need to warn my readers in advance about the strangeness of these last two chapters, I feel powerless to reconstitute the *Asche* into a *Sache,* powerless to make it all clear for thinking. Labors of mourning do not respond well to cries for clarity. The dominant question of these final chapters is Derrida's bastardy *and* purity—his illegitimacy and generosity alike burning in incandescent mourning.

# PART THREE

---

# Mourning Affirmation

# 7

# Knell

MARCELLUS: I tell you, a beautiful woman is something
                 inexplicable. Woman's beauty is an enigma. Our
                 gaze does not penetrate it. One never knows
                 what a beautiful woman can be, what she is
                 compelled to do.
—Georg Trakl, *Maria Magdalena: A Dialogue*

For the most part, the French constitute the nation that most
often speaks of virtue, because among them the individual is
more a matter of his or her peculiarity [*Eigentümlichkeit*] and
natural mode of action. By contrast, the Germans are more
a thinking people, and among them the identical content
achieves the form of universality [*Allgemeinheit*].
—Hegel, *Philosophy of Right*, §150, addendum

*Glas* rarely discusses the theme of mourning and never works through it in a
conceptually rigorous way, never achieves true generality or universality
concerning mourning. Yet the trajectory that the book follows through the
texts of Hegel and Genet, a trajectory without proper beginning or end, is *all
about* mourning, if *about* be taken in a verbal, rather than a prepositional, sense.
*Glas* tolls for the *remains* of so much that we take to be our philosophical and
literary traditions in the West. These remains or remainders, these remnants,
leftovers, and scraps, these traces of mortal dissolution—ashes to ashes—
constitute the waymarkers and indicative signs of Derrida's text. Whether the
topic is Hegel's absolute knowing or Genet's humiliation and glory, dialectic's

stairway to heaven or the fictional scaffold ascended by Genet's flower-laden
lovers, Derrida focuses on the contingency, the accident, the recalcitrant detail,
the pieces of the puzzle that will not fit, the morsels that refuse to be swallowed,
the refuse that refuses to be trashed, the cyst that will not be dissolved and
absorbed without a trace into the system.

In what follows I shall emphasize the scraps of the "Hegel column" in
Derrida's text. However, I will try to read across the entire page of *Glas* and
with as many eyes as I can muster.


## Does Anyone Here Remember Absolute Knowing?

After Darwin, Marx, Kierkegaard, Nietzsche, and Freud, it is distinctly odd to
declare a period of mourning for absolute knowing. After positivism and
neopositivism, pragmatism, and analytic philosophy of virtually every strain
and variety, it would be absurd actually to mourn what Hegel's *Phenomenology
of Spirit* calls *das absolute Wissen*. If Derrida devotes so much labor to this
reading of Hegel, and to a reading of the writer whom Hegel would have
abhorred most, arguably even more than Friedrich Schlegel, it must be because
he suspects that the *remains* of absolute knowing—if only in the form of the
absolute phantasm—still inhabit or haunt all our brave pronouncements and
even our modest claims, all our professionalism and even our cynicism. If Hegel
is the last great fling of speculative philosophy, Derrida suspects that we who
sail or sink in Hegel's wake are still being flung by the dream of absolute
knowing and absolute self-possession: we ourselves are remnants of Hegel, as
the professing Hegelians today constantly remind us, taking their sole joy in
the rigor and rancor of the system and the sting of universal history. We are
the bolt ends of the whole cloth of German Idealism and Romanticism, scraps
on the table of the beggars' banquet, the spilled milk of a dying spiritual galaxy,
one big unhappy holy family.

If *reste(s)* is (are) one of the guiding threads of Derrida's *Glas*, a second such
thread is *the family*. In the parade of industrious fathers and sons, productive
husbands and wives, pious and pure brothers and sisters, and invisible but
efficient mothers, in the procession of all the loves and execrations of the family
romance, Genet limps along like Kaiser Sóse behind a Hegel on the march.
Whether it is Genet wanting to bathe his mother's head in spit or Hegel wanting
to join Mary Magdalene at the feet of Christ, the grasp or concept of *love* and
the grip or drive of *desire*—the stuff of which families are made and undone—

are also the objects of Derrida's tireless investigation. The third thread, therefore, the one that somehow manages to twist the other two (remnants, the family) into a common cord, is *love*, love in the *family*, or in whatever is *left* of families. For the principal insight into the Hegelian system of philosophy in Derrida's *Glas* is that consciousness, reason, and spirit alike are always *family affairs*, that familial love is both a passing moment and a perpetual threshold of spirit, so that Hegelian spirit is anything but self-possessed and singular, anything but a solitary *Bei-sich-sein*.

Derrida's *Glas* also remains sensitive to certain accidents and remnants of *writing*. If absolute knowing, *das absolute Wissen*, becomes the French *savoir absolu*, signified by the paraph or acronym *sa*, then it is also, by homophony, *Ça*, the *id* of French psychoanalysis. Further, absolute knowing is always said of the feminine, it is *sa*, "hers," even when, as we shall see in the following chapter, it is Saint Augustine's, SA's. Finally, *savoir absolu* can be heard in French as *s'avoir absolu*, absolute self-having or self-possession, so that the goal of absolute knowing and the fantasy of perfect presence to self appear to be indistinguishable. These accidents of homophony help to create the wayward constellations of religion, politics, feminism, psychoanalysis, fiction, and metaphysics that populate Derrida's written text or palimpsest. And these vagrant constellations of writing appear as mournful remnants of love in the night sky, traces of the love of men and women in sundry positions and combinations. For love is what makes the familial spirit tick, what makes the rabbit run, what makes the owl of Athens take flight at dusk.

Remnants, families, and loves: odd subjects for a book on Hegel, and every bit as odd, albeit it in an asymmetrical way, for a book on Jean Genet. Let me begin with some general remarks about remains, the family scene, and the coils of love. For each of these is anomalous, though each pertains, as we shall see, to mourning.

What is odd about remains, remainders, or remnants is that they appear both to undergird and to undermine the system. What endures and lasts, what *remains* after everything else has come and gone, after all accident and caprice are done, is the very essence of things, that which *always was* and *always* (as we have heard Heidegger insist) *has been* the case. There is a certain stability, a fundamental solidity and stolidity, about what *remains* the case. When Faulkner wants his readers to know the essence of the South, he only needs to write of Dilsey, "She endured." The classic formulation of *remaining* (or one such formulation, inasmuch as a dozen passages from the dialogues of Plato would serve our purpose every bit as well) is Aristotle's *Metaphysics Z*, whose doctrine of being we may recapitulate in six steps.

1. Aristotle asks whether being as such, essential being, οὐσία, is matter, ὕλη. What induces him to ask such a thing? The fact—noted by Antiphon of Athens—that matter is what seems to *remain* after every form has vanished: essential being at first seems to be safeguarded in what is left over after all accidents, contingencies, and composite elements have been stripped away or have themselves dissolved. What remains is the ὑπομένον (1029a 12). It is this word—not yet the ὑποκείμενον, but the elliptical and even cryptic ὑπομένον, the under-maining—that Derrida's *Glas* solicits. It is the prepositional prefix ὑπο- that will serve as the fundamental clue that leads Aristotle and all later Aristotelians to conclude that οὐσία is ὑποκείμενον, the underlying, the sub-sistent sub-stance, sub-strate, and sub-ject. Whatever underlies, undergirds, underpins, or under-stands *remains.* And what properly remains is what we call essence, that which *was* or always *has been* in being (*das Ge-Wesene*), τὸ τί ἦν εἶναι (1030b 5; cf. 1031a 12). For Aristotle, however, and for all metaphysics after him, essence is not matter but . . .

2. The soul. "Primary substance," οὐσία ἡ πρώτη, which is what endures and remains, is ψυχή. Soul or spirit is the under-maining of matter. Yet soul or spirit can be what it is only when it dwells within matter, only as indwelling, which is to say, only as . . .

3. Form, τὸ εἶδος. Substance is indwelling form, οὐσία ἐστὶ τὸ εἶδος τὸ ἐνόν (1037a 29). Such indwelling form serves as . . .

4. The general or universal, τὸ καθόλου (1038b 3), which in turn is always . . .

5. The definition, account, formula, proportion, ratio, or reason in its full generality, ὁ λόγος ἁπλῶς (1039b 20–21), which in the end is and remains . . .

6. The primary, and thus final, cause of being, αἴτιον πρῶτον τοῦ εἶναι (1041b 28).

In a word, being is what remains. Remains remain (in) being.

By contrast, or precisely by the same token, unsalvageable leftovers and dross, *caput mortuum,* and whatever else is sloughed off, are also called *remains.* The French word *reste,* as defined in *Robert,* is instructive here, first of all because its definition is compelled to refer to itself: *le reste* is defined as *ce qui reste (!) d'un tout,* for example, *un somme d'argent, du lait, de sa vie.* Used in an absolute sense, that is, without any obvious reference back to anything else, *le reste* is "everything that in any given case is not the thing previously mentioned: *pour le reste, quant au reste.*" With the indefinite article, *un reste* is defined in the same self-referential manner, but this time with more trenchancy: a remnant or remainder is an *élément restant (!) d'un tout,* a whole "whose integrity has not been preserved." Remains entail a loss of integrity. To that extent, *un reste* joins all the other favorite words of Derrida's vocabulary: *trace, supplément, parergon, vestige, débris.*

The dictionary examples of such remains or remnants do not vary, whether on the French or English and American scenes: the leftovers of a meal; mortal remains, whether interred, exhumed, or incinerated; the result of subtraction in arithmetic. If one turns to the verb *rester,* which is employed in both definitions in order to say what remnants *are,* or *remain,* the connection to Aristotle becomes compelling: *rester* means *continuer d'être dans un lieu, demeurer, s'éterniser, se maintenir, séjourner, habiter, persister, durer, subsister,* all the classical translations of ὑποκείμενον as ὑπομένον, the substance as under-maining and remaining.

However, tucked in among all those words for staying put is the word *mourir,* to die. For mortals, what remains is the place where, or the event in which, one is interred, even if the remains turn out to be exhumed and incinerated, and room thus made for other remains. The under-maining is also the under-mining of mortals—and perhaps of all indwelling forms.

What remains is the very essence of things. Yet remains are the scraps that fall from the table, precisely what does not enter into the system of essential nourishment. A corpse lying naked on the slab—Descartes's fresh cadaver, with its springs and levers still flexible, its knees unimpaired, its volatile pineal gland still intact, but with all of these things on the very verge of dissolution—that is the very essence of remains. What remains is precisely what passes, decomposes, and in the stench of its corruption—the green spots of decay on its exquisite hands—elaborates the very definition of what is *inessential* for philosophy. The question "What (of the) remains of absolute knowing?" therefore asks about both what *endures* at the end of metaphysics and what *disperses* into scattered, unassimilable, and essentially corrupt remnants.

Mourning, for its part, has to do with a certain lasting impression, and a dogged depression, concerning our situation at the end(s) of metaphysics: we remain trapped within it, or in the remnants of it, suspended in its systems and vocabularies, precisely as those who are destined to *be* remains and remainders. Mourning has to do with what remains: a certain transience, a raveling of the thread, an irremediable loss.

The *family,* too—moving on now to our second raveling thread—both lasts and breaks up, perdures and dissolves. Whether the house is that of Atreus or Addie Bundren, the family is always a matter of survival and demise, as one lay dying, and as the others prepared the remains for the funeral. For Hegel's spirit, the family is both a passing moment—for the demise of the family is the very birth of the nation-state and civil society—and a perdurant condition: spirit will come to know itself only in the family way, and only in a nation and civil society that continue to be constituted by families and family functions, whether that communal form is expressed as a divine trinity, a holy family, the conjugal bond, the establishment of a natural species, the rearing of offspring, the passing of generations, the endurance of corporations, or the survival of a moribund monarchy.

Yet can the family as such ever be stripped of its natural, material, mortal dross, so that its essential structure, both canceled and preserved, both sublated and relieved (for *restance* and *remnance* are merely the last remaining words for *Aufhebung*), will come to know itself as spiritual? If the family remains, does it not do so precisely as the *family crypt* of spirit?

Finally, *love* too comes on the scene, or has always already done so, as the ultimate reconciler, the final expression of a wholly holy spirit. Spirit—at least at the level of religion—is love. Yet love is and remains a (mere) sensation (*Empfindung*), an emotion, which is why it never lasts. Or, if it does last, conquering even death, love burns brightly and smolders in turns, raging then retiring, continuing to surprise us with its jealousies and infantile remnants, its dirty linen, its obsessions and betrayals and ressentiments. A spirit that knows itself absolutely and has itself absolutely in hand is perpetually undone— that is all that lasts—by whatever it is that love loves to love. Writers of fiction seem to make a career out of depicting this undoing, this humiliation, as though love were a death sentence: Genet gives the homophobic male or female continuous grounds for something more than discomfiture, while in our own language James Joyce teases us mercilessly with Bloomian infantilism, as in the following passage from "Cyclops":

> Love loves to love love. Nurse loves the new chemist. Constable 14A loves Mary Kelly. Gerty MacDowell loves the boy that has the bicycle. M. B. loves a fair gentleman. Li Chi Han lovey up kissy Cha Pu Chow. Jumbo, the elephant, loves Alice, the elephant. Old Mr Verschoyle with the ear trumpet loves old Mrs Verschoyle with the turnedin eye. The man in the brown macintosh loves a lady who is dead. His Majesty the King loves Her Majesty the Queen. Mrs Norman W. Tupper loves officer Taylor. You love a certain person. And this person loves that other person because everybody loves somebody but God loves everybody.[1]

Derrida discovers that the hand and mouth of love open and close upon what is irreducibly *other* in Hegel's system, even after all the foldings and refoldings, doublings and redoublings of phenomenological consciousness, even after all the fiery purges of desire, the dismantling of sexual differences, the flight from every possible site of Pandemian Aphrodite or *Venus vaga,* the rarefaction of sensibility into the wispy vapors of spirituality and ethicality, intellectualism and voluntarism. Even after all these purgations, something of love remains, overflows, dribbles onto spirit's patent-leather shoes, obscures the reflection, confounds the self-knowing that thought it knew it all.

When one surveys the vast circuit of Derrida's *Glas,* one feels defeated and undone by its scope and complexity. Even when (out of ignorance) one focuses on the "Hegel column," one is astonished at the itinerary, which I shall here reduce to five stages:

1. An introduction to the remnants and remnance, the residues, remains, and remainders (*le reste, les restes, la restance*), of a "Hegel," of a "Rembrandt," of a "Genet": the religion of flowers, the religion of animals, the religion of the phallus; morality, ethicality, genealogy, the family, and love; signature, *Klang* (sound, resonance), *langue* (tongue, language), *tombe* (tomb, fall), and *glas* (death knell). Here (*Glas,* 7–26/1–19) Derrida pays special attention to Hegel's *Philosophy of Right,* §§141–59, and the *Phenomenology of Spirit,* "Natural Religion."

2. Derrida now (*Glas,* 26–95/19–82) shifts his attention to Hegel's early texts, the works prior to the *Phenomenology of Spirit,* focusing on the meaning of the family—for example, in the Jewish and Christian religious traditions. In a painstaking reading of Hegel's 1798–1800 *Spirit of Judaism* and *Spirit of Christianity,* Derrida analyzes the πλήρωμα, or fulfillment of the Law by Love, that the life of Jesus—Hegel's Jesus—elaborates. Of particular importance in this regard are the "Last Supper scenes" involving Mary Magdalene (to whom we shall soon turn) and, at the last of the last suppers, the apostle John.

3. The scene now shifts to the question of *life,* and eventually to Hegel's analysis of the organic realm of nature in the 1805–6 Jena lectures on *Realphilosophie.* Here (*Glas,* 95–135/82–117) Derrida offers a careful reading of what one might have the temerity to call Hegel's "dialectic of genitality."

4. Derrida now (*Glas,* 135–225/118–201) focuses on Hegel's theory of the human family as a theory of developmental consciousness. Among the themes of this section of *Glas* are desire, marriage, brother and sister, incest, struggle, and death. Among the texts discussed are Kant's *Anthropology from a Pragmatic Standpoint* and Hegel's *Phenomenology of Spirit, Philosophy of Right,* and correspondence.

5. The final stage of Derrida's reflection on remains, family, and love in Hegel's system (*Glas*, 225–91/201–62) focuses on the mechanism of *Aufhebung* in speculative dialectics. In doing so, it raises questions concerning fetishism, imperialism and colonialism, the figure of the mother and the virgin, the phantasms of immaculate conception, autoinsemination, absolute self-having and self-knowing, and, at the end as in the beginning, the solar-sounding statues of Memnon—which are finite in their memory and resonance.

Nothing can prevent the five-stage itinerary above, however, from reducing *Glas* to something considerably less than it is. And nothing can prevent such a reduction from being an act of exclusion that invariably leaves an unassimilable remainder. When one reduces the five-stage itinerary to particular constellations—such as remains, family, and love—one may wind up with the following three star groups:

1. Love, sexual difference and sexual opposition, desire, and the family, as they appear in nature (flowers, animal species, etc.), religion (Jewish "hard-heartedness" and Christian "sacrifice," etc.), politics and society (Athens at the time of Sophocles, Germany at the time of the Hohenzollern, etc.), through the mirrors of Genet's fiction and Hegel's speculative system.

2. Logic, the concept, speculative dialectic, and absolute knowing, as opposed to the discourses of psychoanalysis and fiction, the fetish, contingency and accident, dispersion and disintegration; the absolute phantasm of absolute self-having.

3. The philosophical as opposed to the literary text; and, common to both, the spoken tongue as opposed to written language; issues of phonology, glossematics and graphematics, signature and trace.

But enough of these attempts to swallow and disgorge *Glas*. In the context of works of mourning, art, and affirmation, I will simply choose three moments of *Glas* for close reading, three tintinnabulations of the knell, without any claim or hope that they are typical of the whole or in any way representative or encompassing. My three moments will be:

1. Mary Magdalene's anointing the feet of Jesus: Hegel's *Spirit of Judaism* and *Spirit of Christianity* (a discussion of *Glas*, 38–74/33–63);

2. Teaching the children, washing the corpse: family functions in Hegel's *Phenomenology of Spirit* and *Philosophy of Right* (a discussion of *Glas*, 149–64/131–45);

3. Foam in the cup: absolute knowing in Hegel's *Phenomenology* and absolute phantasm in Derrida's *Glas* (a comparison of the two final pages of *Glas* and the *Phänomenologie des Geistes*).

Fig. 9.   H. L. [Hans Loi?], "The Coronation of the Virgin," altarpiece, central panel,
Stefansmünster, Breisach, Germany

My three moments are taken from the second, fourth, and fifth stages of
the five-stage itinerary through *Glas*. Discussion of the third stage—that of
organic life in general and the dialectic of genitality in particular—waits upon
a separate investigation.[2]

## Mary Magdalene at the Feet of God

One of the main features of the Stefansmünster at Breisach on the Rhine is the
wooden altarpiece, "The Coronation of the Virgin," a triptych executed by the
master H. L. (presumably Hans Loi) during the years 1523–26. At the center
of the central panel the Virgin is being crowned by God the Father and God
the Son. The Virgin's feet, if she has any, are covered by the folds of her robe.

Fig. 10.   Detail of Figure 9

Fig. 11.   Detail of Figure 9

In contrast, the feet of the Father and Son obtrude, the big toes of each figuring prominently, protruding to the outermost surface of the high relief. Moreover, the big toes of these thrusting feet—the left foot of the Son, the right of the Father—are themselves flexed upward and outward, erect and impressive, even if they are mere reflections of a divine reflex: the left arm of the Son and the right arm of the Father are stretching out into the central panel in order to place the crown on the head of the Virgin, and the corresponding feet and toes are flexing in tandem with the divine arms and hands.

There are subtle differences between Father and Son: the careful observer will note that the left foot and toe of the Son are viewed in profile, even though the naked upper torso, including the gash low on the rib cage, is viewed almost full front; the observer sees the raised foot of the Father from below and frontally, even though the upper body turns as sharply toward the Virgin as the Son's. There is something particularly ungainly about the Father's gesture, something perhaps of unresolved tension at the moment of this coronation. The upper body and head of the Father appear to be slouching, while the Son's gaze seems to be riveted on the Father, as though some unspoken question or confusion is about to disrupt the solemnity of the occasion. The Virgin Mother, demure, inclining slightly toward the Father (but is it her Father or her Spouse?), seems to be reaching with her crossed arms to the figures on either side of her, as though to reconcile Father and Son (but is it her Son or her Spouse?). The Son and the Virgin appear to be about the same age, whereas the Father is much older than they. Whatever the differences between them, however, Father and Son share the Virgin Mother—and the big toe.

Georges Bataille, who figures less prominently in *Glas* than one might have expected, has a remarkable text, "The Big Toe," an early text for the "Critical Dictionary" of *Documents* (in 1929). There Bataille writes:

> The big toe is the most *human* part of the human body, in the sense that no other element of this body is as differentiated from the corresponding element of the anthropoid ape (chimpanzee, gorilla, orangutan, or gibbon). This is due to the fact that the ape is tree dwelling, whereas man moves on the earth without clinging to branches, having himself become a tree, in other words raising himself straight up in the air like a tree. . . . But whatever the role played in the erection by his foot, man, who has a light head, in other words a head raised to the heavens and heavenly things, sees this foot as spit, on the pretext that he has it in the mud.[3]

Bataille takes the mud in which the foot and the big toe try to gain purchase to be the principal figure of evil in traditional moralities. "Human life entails, in fact, the rage of seeing oneself as a back-and-forth movement from refuse to the ideal, and from the ideal to refuse—a rage that is easily directed against an organ as *base* as the foot" (20–21). The word *refuse* here reminds us of the *remains* that preoccupied us earlier. It is as though the big toe and the foot from which it projects are inexorably bound up with the lowly, the rejected and dejected, the fallen and corrupt, detritus, debris, and leftovers. To the foot we attribute "the most nauseating filthiness," a filthiness otherwise associated only with the nether parts—except that, of course, the feet are as nether as one can go. The Greek and Latin root for things of the foot, *pod-*, is also the root of the posterior, or anal, region of the body, what contemporary German, for example, calls the *Po*. Bataille pursues the sexual nature of the shamefulness and squalor of the foot, finding it reflected in many cultures; he focuses in particular on the *hilarity* that often explodes when one even imagines the toes. The toes thus become fetishes of the flesh in all its protuberances and folds:

> The play of fantasies and fears, of human necessities and aberrations, is in fact such that fingers have come to signify useful action and firm character, the toes stupor and base idiocy. The vicissitudes of organs, the profusion of stomachs, larynxes, and brains traversing innumerable animal species and individuals, carries the imagination along in an ebb and flow it does not willingly follow, due to a hatred of the still painfully perceptible frenzy of the bloody palpitations of the body. . . . Blind but tranquil, and strangely despising his obscure baseness, a given person, ready to call to mind the grandeurs of human history . . . , is stopped in mid-flight by an atrocious pain in his big toe because, though the most noble of animals, he nevertheless has corns on his feet; in other words, he has feet, and these feet independently lead an ignoble life. (22)

What does it mean, then, that God the Father and God the Son can be represented as having feet, indeed, feet with distended toes, seeking purchase? What will it mean that the one who is fit to wash and embalm the corpse of God is the Magdalene, who goes to the feet? Bataille reminds us that the toe is "psychologically analogous to the brutal fall of a man—in other words, to death" (22). Furthermore, the possibilities of seduction in this base realm are far more powerful than they are in the exalted realm of the head. Mary Magdalene—whom Bataille does not mention—is the right woman in the right place at the right time.

Naturally, Hegel could have known nothing of Bataille's podiodigital meditation, and it is not known whether the Swabian philosopher ever made it to Colmar and Hans Loi's Marian masterpiece. Yet the Hegel of *The Spirit of Judaism* and *The Spirit of Christianity*, texts composed during the years 1798–1800,[4] is fascinated by that Mary who is presumably other than the Virgin—Mary Magdalene, at the feet of the Son. Hegel describes with loving care and in considerable detail her anointing the Christ with chrism—this all-important pleonasm by which the Magdalene's chrism christens the Christ—as though naming him and defining his sacrificial essence for all Christendom. For his part, Derrida shares Hegel's fascination with and absorption in those details.

The context is a Jewish nation whose supreme legal and religious representatives repudiate the Son of Man. So "hard of heart" are they, so sclerotic (σκληροῖς καρδίᾳ, 1:329), and so "harsh" are their "expressions" (σκληροὶ λόγοι, 1:377), that only the embodiment of their lowlife, their *canaille*, that is to say, only a whore, can respond to the love for which the elevated ones are never pliant enough. To be sure, it is a reformed whore, an Augustinian whore, as it were, a Monica in the making, that is represented by Mary Magdalene the penitent. Yet there is a remarkable irony in the Magdalene's repentance, and Derrida does not neglect to emphasize it: according to Hegel, the only sin or infraction of the Law that Jesus refuses to absolve in the otherwise universal amnesty granted by the πλήρωμα of Love is that of a woman (that is, a wife) who betrays her husband—an adulteress. The Magdalene's virtue lies in her having been a mere fornicatrix. For had she been married, not even the God of Love or the Love of God could have forgiven her her sin of Love, no matter how lovely her hair upon His feet. In short, Mary Magdalene hovers in the greatest possible proximity to the unforgiven; hers could readily be the sole sin that Jesus will not or cannot expiate. And yet precisely she is taken to be the exemplary penitent and, beyond that, the exemplary Jew, the only Jew who is capable of love and beauty. Ever since Abraham, writes Hegel, the wretched Jewish people and their jealous God alike are unreconciled to "the perdurant need of Love" (1:277, 292). As we shall see, Hegel revels in the well-nigh Hellenic beauty of her deed at the feet of Christ.

The Magdalene's beauty and love are first introduced into Hegel's initial sketch of *The Spirit of Christianity*, the so-called "basic conception," precisely at the point where love itself is acknowledged as a *problem* rather than a panacea for everything that is wrong with Judaism. For, as Abraham also knew, love is a need, *ein Bedürfnis*. Without it, life is gone; with it, tranquillity. Love is actually intuited as "the wound," *die Wunde*, so that the need or craving for love is always bound up with a certain melancholy, *mit einer Wehmut*, that presumably has to do with mourning. It is in the context of craving, unrest, laceration (perhaps as Freud too envisages it in his essay on narcissism: 3:49–50), and melancholy that the name *Maria Magdalena* now flows from Hegel's pen (1:306).

Faith and love suffice for the forgiveness of sins, inasmuch as total love (the essence of religion) encourages and even demands forgiveness of others. Only one who has faith in human beings, only one who "has felt the entire depths of human nature" (1:306–7), can be relieved of sin, if not of guilt and punishment. Yet the vulnerability of the wound—unhappy redundancy—is felt over and over again in Hegel's own text: love is not only a spur to meditation or reflection on marriage and the family but also a sensibility or sensation, and no sensibility or sensation is wholly amenable to reflection (1:308). Perhaps for this reason the stolid apostles themselves are insensitive to the beauty of Mary Magdalene's deed. For the beauty of the deed consists in "an unconstrained and beautiful outpouring [*Ergießung*] of a loving soul" (1:311). Hers is, as Matthew 26:10 calls it, a καλὸν ἔργον, "a beautiful deed." Hegel remarks that it is "the sole deed in the history of the Jews that merits the modifier καλόν" (1:311).

As noted earlier, the principal theme of *The Spirit of Christianity* is the fulfillment of the Law through Love, which as inclination and sensibility complements the objective possibilities of legality. Hence the discussion soon turns to love between man and wife, marriage, and divorce. According to Hegel (1:328–29), Jesus contrasts both the duty of fidelity and a husband's right to divorce his wife with the higher claims of love. Such love excludes desire or craving, *Begierde*, an exclusion that will be a constant in Hegel's later works, such as the *Philosophy of Right*. Only in one case, to repeat, does Mosaic Law preserve its absolute sway: if a wife has given her love to another, her husband retains the right to divorce her: "the husband cannot remain her bondsman [*ihr Knecht*]." Neither Hegel nor, apparently, Jesus invokes the possibility of a case in which the adulterer is the *husband*. Presumably, if a husband is unfaithful, the bondage of the wife remains intact. Adultery is of woman.

Jesus can forgive Mary Magdalene because she knows the depths of human nature without having become a wife. That is the advantage of her profession. Hegel writes: "A beautiful example of a recurrent sinner also comes up in the story of Jesus: the famous beautiful sinner, Mary Magdalene" (1:357). The Magdalene is a beautiful example, a πάρεργον of the most perfect sort, and she herself, like her deed or ἔργον, is a beauty, precisely for a people who are generally too hard-hearted for beauty. Hegel offers the following syncretic account of her beautiful story:

Mary, conscious of her guilt, hears that Jesus is eating in the house of
a Pharisee, at a large gathering of upstanding and righteous persons
(*honnêtes gens,* the most bitter recusants of a beautiful soul's mistakes).
Her inner being drives her through the company straight to Jesus. She
steps behind him, drops to his feet, weeps, bathing his feet with her
tears and drying them with her head of hair; she kisses his feet and
anoints them with unguents and with undiluted, precious spikenard.
Timid, proud, self-sufficient virginity cannot utter aloud the needs of
love; even less can it in its soulful outpouring (her sins consist in her
having isolated herself from the righteous folk) make bold reply to the
legalizing stares of the Pharisees and the apostles; but a deeply wounded
soul, on the verge of despair, must cry out louder than its own awkward-
ness permits, and in spite of its own feelings of propriety must both
give and enjoy the entire plenitude of love, allowing its consciousness
to founder in this intense enjoyment. (1:357–58)

It may seem odd that virginity, *Jungfräulichkeit,* is attributed to the
Magdalene. Yet it is certainly meant to underscore the fact that she is not a
wife, inasmuch as marriage would exclude her from the πλήρωμα of which
she is the sole beautiful example. She is not a mere πάρεργον but a paragon,
herself at the heart's core of the beautiful ἔργον. No wonder she has been so
often painted, so often sculpted! Hegel feels no need to expatiate on her
consciousness of guilt, *Schuldbewußtsein.* He notes that she is more a pariah
than a sinner, inasmuch as her sin "consists" in separating herself from the
righteous folk who are so happy to mount her, then accuse her; their abuse
makes it seem as though there were no inherent guilt in that profession by
which she learns the dark secrets of human nature. Indeed, in the beautiful
scene to which we are now privy, the Magdalene regresses to the age of
awkward, though proud, innocence. Her profession has not hardened her heart
to love—if anything, the reverse: she is overcome by her amorous feelings.
Because she cannot murmur mere words of love, she weeps, kisses, laves with
her tears, and anoints. Her deeply wounded soul—for it is her childlike, though
knowledgeable, soul that is beautiful, and not her body, which seems to
incarnate the vulnerability of love in all its restlessness and craving—swoons
in the overwhelming enjoyment of love. Hegel writes of her pleasure or
enjoyment, her *Genuß,* which rhymes with her *Erguß,* the ecstatic pleasure of
her first truly divine orgasm, the jouissance of God.

Simon Peter finds all this liquidity abhorrent. How can Jesus have gotten
mixed up with such a creature? If he were a genuine seer, a masterful messiah,

thinks Peter, would he not know a whore when he saw one? Neither Peter nor the casuistic Pharisees grasp the beauty of the situation; worse, they insult "the holy ejaculation of a loving heart" (1:359) by mixing it up with baser matters. "Why do you trouble her, says Jesus: she has performed a *beautiful* work for me—and [Hegel adds] this is the only item in the story of Jesus that bears the name *beautiful*. . . . Only a woman who is filled with love—so frank, so free from any purpose having to do with any advantage in either deed or doctrine— can express herself in such wise" (1:359).

What has any of this to do with the work of *mourning*, which *Glas* presumably is *about?* Hegel's Jesus himself gives reply: "She has anointed me for my burial ahead of time." The "fine fragrance" of her spirit, according to Hegel, is redolent of the floral arrangements at a wake or a grave site. Whether because of her consciousness of sin (but in precisely what does her consciousness of sin consist? what isolates her from her hypocritical folk other than their hypocrisy and sclerosis?) or because of the nature of that sin itself (but what precisely is that sin? does it have to do with her being at the very worst an accomplice in men's adultery?), Mary's beautiful deed betrays a faint odor of wetted ashes. It is almost as though her mortal sin itself, which is a certain hyperbolic interpretation of the πλήρωμα of Love, makes her own mourning possible. It is almost as though the deadly sin could never be pried loose from the beauty of her deed. Hegel writes: "Might one say that it would have been better if Mary had adapted herself to the destiny of Jewish life, if she had become an automaton of her times, normal and proper, and if her life had run its course without sin and without love? Without sin, for that period in her people's history was one in which the beautiful in heart did not live without sin; but during this period, as at every other, the beautiful in heart could be brought back to the most beautiful consciousness by means of love" (1:359).

Mary Magdalene expresses the mystery of a love that—at least for a certain period of history—cannot be severed from sin. In *all* periods, however, her sin can be elevated to consciousness, that is, to a level that by definition cannot be base, through the power of love. Nothing that Hegel writes here, not even his most adventurous effusions on the Magdalene's necessary sin, her essential wound, her stammering virginity, her helpless outpourings, her beautiful deed, dissolves the mystery that has surrounded her since ancient times.

One might interrupt Hegel's (and Derrida's) account of Mary Magdalene by asking how Hegel would respond to a somewhat different account of this figure, one that sees her power less in a guilty conscience than in a glorious— indeed, divine—genealogy. For certain Gnostic (noncanonical, apocryphal) gospels assert that Jesus loved Mary Magdalene more than any of the apostles, that he often kissed her and called her (without irony) "the woman who knew the universe." For certain medieval traditions she is Mary the Light-Bearer, Mary Lucifer. For the *Pistis Sophia* she is Christ's "questioner," addressed always as "Dearly Beloved." Certain fathers of the Church identify her as the Mother of All, the Great Goddess, now of course in the form of *Ecclesia*. In short, Mary the Whore is but a mask of Mary the Virgin—or vice versa—so that it is she, the Magdalene, the one who would quite readily show her feet, who is being crowned in that triptych in Breisach on the Rhine. Mary Magdalene is the Triple Goddess of the tower, Mari-Anna-Ishtar. In that capacity she tends the tomb of one of her many consorts, Jesus of Nazareth. "Mari Ishtar the Great Whore anointed—or *christ*-ened—her doomed god when he went into the underworld, whence he would rise again at her bidding. That is, she made him a Christ. . . . In the *Epic of Gilgamesh,* victims were told: 'The harlot who anointed you with fragrant oil laments for you now.'"[5]

Hegel's attribution of *Jungfräulichkeit* to the Magdalene is not at all strange if we remember the sacred prostitutes that were sponsored by Popes Julius II, Leo X, and Clement VII. Even Innocent III, who had a testy vocabulary when it came to concupiscence, called them *virgines*. That appellation survives in many tongues, as in German, where prostitutes are occasionally still called by their old-fashioned name, *Freudenmädchen*, "maids of joy." Mary Magdalene, the beautiful woman who, at least in the fantasies of the Father and the Son, remains a mere slip of a girl, a professional maiden, haunts Hegel's text each time the "pathology" of love is mentioned—the fact that love is an inclination and sensation as well as a meditation (1:362), an undefinable feeling that resists words and the concept (1:363); each time a supper or common meal is mentioned (1:364–69); each time religion is cited as the πλήρωμα of Love, the fulfillment of the Law (1:370); each time the inadequacy of the Jewish reception of Christ is averred (1:381–82); each time the beautiful soul is set in opposition to the Jewish essence, inasmuch as Jesus turns out to be related to Mary Magdalene as a soul sibling (1:385); each time marriage, man and wife, and the union and divorce of couples is cited (1:387); each time the liquidity of love—for example, in the total immersion that a catechumen experiences in baptism—is described (1:391); and, at last, toward the end, when Jesus' failure to marry a woman and have children by her is cited, when the beautiful soul's isolation from both nature and the community, its passivity and flight, are mourned (1:400–405).

Derrida is intrigued by the role of Mary Magdalene in Hegel's *Spirit of Christianity* precisely because she interrupts the man-to-man discourse of what may be called "the speculative family," that is, the mystical union of Father and

Son that so bedazzles onto-theology. As a sinner of the flesh, in the flesh, she represents the flood that instills in the postdeluvial Jewish essence a fear and distrust of nature; as the beautiful Jewess, an anomaly to her own people because she is capable of a καλὸν ἔργον, she represents Greek harmony rather than Jewish discord. Yet she can respond to Jesus—and he to her—only as a harbinger of death: her ejaculations and outpourings of the little death are inevitably subservient to the greater death, which Hegel identifies as absolute life, the life of spirit. Which means either that she remains Jewish or that Christianity's fulfillment of the Law is only another enactment of death, ultimately in service to death. Christianity's cut about the phallus is, as Derrida notes, if anything, "higher up" than the Mosaic cut: the Magdalene is the Medusa of Christendom.

Why then does Hegel tarry near her? Perhaps, Derrida surmises, because Hegel's own mother's name—Maria Magdalena Louisa Fromm—encourages him to associate the mother with the maid, *Magdalena* being an offshoot of the *Magd.* Maria Magdalena, rather than Mary or Martha or Monica, is the name of Hegel's (m)other. Yet it is the dramatic, energetic beauty of her desperate deed that dazzles Hegel. Derrida's account of that deed—spinning off from Hegel's own account—is as follows:

> To what beauty was Jesus sensitive? To that of the overflowing of love, certainly, to the kisses, the tears of tenderness, but above all, let us believe Hegel on this, to that perfumed oil, to that chrism with which she coats his foot. It is as if in advance she took care of his corpse: she adored it, pressed it gently with her hands, soothed it with a holy pomade, wrapped it in cinctures the moment it began to stiffen. This whore who behaves like a virgin "'. . . has embalmed me in advance,' Jesus says, 'for my burial.'" The oily balm makes the body of Christ glisten; a kind of funereal glory caresses it. A shiny yellow and waxy stain in a very somber picture. Destined for virginity, the prostitute stays beside the Son of God. The weeping woman also melts over him like a candle. (*Glas*, 73–74/62–63)

Mary Magdalene instigates the death of the natural. She is the life of nature dying in order to give birth to spiritual life. Christ is the object of her love because he is the one who is destined for the passion of death. Mary Magdalene is thus the crowning irony of life: herself immured against her earlier sins of the body, yet in some way opened by those very sins to love, she prepares the body of God—with special attention to the feet—for entombment. She is perhaps one of those partial or component erotic drives that Freud calls the pallbearers or avatars of death, *Trabanten des Todes* (3:249). She herself will die without children, never a wife, in this way too proving herself the sister and bride of Christ. His Echo, perhaps?

## Teaching the Children, Burying the Corpses

Insofar as she embalms the Christ for burial, however, Mary Magdalene does everything a wife can do for a husband, a sister for a brother, or even a daughter for a mother or a father. As a herald or minister of death, Mary marks several kinds of death in and for the family—on the way to spiritual life or religion. As a penitent, she marks the death of sex—the end of pleasure, desire, and the sexual opposition as such. Presumably, the enjoyment in which she founders over Christ's feet, the swoon into which she falls, the outpourings she undergoes, have nothing to do with sexual opposition and union. Although she is not married, and cannot be if she is to be forgiven, she is the perfect wife, inasmuch as she does not let herself be enjoyed. In her, sexual pleasure is demoted (*herabgesetzt*) and suppressed (*zurückgedrängt*), as Hegel says of the married woman in general (*Philosophy of Right*, § 163). She *is* woman, not so much by virtue of her natural capacity to bear children, as through her spiritual capacity: she is the one who will arrange her husband's interment. She is a family unto herself.

The family is for Hegel the site of the multiple deaths that transpire on spirit's way to the larger life of the state and civil society. The family *is* what it is, is all it can be, at the sounding of the knell. The first tolling of the funeral bell occurs at school. For upbringing and education constitute the single most important moment in the transition from mere natural life to conscious life. In fact, Hegel is so anxious to subject children to pedagogy that he cannot wait for them to be born: in the "general remarks" on ethicality in his *Philosophy of Right*, before the family is even introduced, much less children produced, Hegel stresses the importance of pedagogy for the life of spirit. Beyond natural and even moral law, and presumably even beyond Mosaic Law, ethicality can be identified with spirit as such. If ἦθος is a becoming-accustomed, a habituation (*Gewohnheit*), pedagogy is the art of such habituation or "customization":

> Pedagogy is the art of making human beings ethical: it observes the human being as natural and shows the way upon which such a being

can be regenerated [*ihn wiederzugebären*], transforming his first nature into a second, spiritual nature, so that the spiritual in it becomes a *habit*. In this second nature, the opposition of natural will and the subjective will disappears; the subject's struggle is *broken*. Thus habit pertains to the ethical, just as it pertains to philosophical thinking, inasmuch as the latter requires that spirit be molded in such a way that it resist arbitrary notions, which are to be broken and overcome in order that rational thinking achieve an open path. (§151, addendum; 7:302)

Education of the children and the eventual dissolution of the family constitute the final moment of the family as the *immediate* ethical substance of spirit. If the first moment consists in the subordination of natural, sexual love to the ethical love between husband and wife, parents and children, the last consists in the subordination of the family as such to civil society and the state. Children represent the objectification of the love husband and wife have for each other, love no longer as mere sensibility (*Empfindung*) but as spirituality and religion. Spirituality, religion, ethicality—these break the back of the *naturalness* of love.

Yet love *remains* a sensation and a sensibility: Hegel repeats this lesson over and over again, as though he himself has learned it in the school of hard knocks, in the university of life. For his part, Derrida is impressed by the atavism of the amorous sensibility, the adamantine persistence of love as a feeling, in the Hegelian system. Hegel may not be able to depict the dialectical sublation or relieving of love step-by-step, handbook style, but he is an expert at formulating its recalcitrant mystery. He writes: "Love is therefore the most monstrous contradiction, one the intellect cannot dissolve. For there is nothing harder than this punctuality of self-consciousness, which is negated, yet which I ought to possess affirmatively. Love produces and resolves the contradiction at one and the same time: as its resolution, love is ethical unity" (§158, addendum; 7:308). Education or upbringing breaks the back of this monster, first for the parents, by suppressing their pleasure, and then for the children, by suppressing theirs, which was so fragile in the first place—for children are driven to abandon their own state in order to be just like the grown-ups. Pleasure is the very touchstone of naturalness, and if rearing is the least natural but most necessary thing in the world of nature, it is only because, as Flannery O'Connor's "misfit" maintains, "It's no real pleasure in life."[6]

Hegel does not elaborate in the *Philosophy of Right* on the mortuarial character of the family. There it is more a matter of the death of the father as the occasion upon which the family's *property* passes on to the widow and the children, eventually dispersing into the wider family circle and the social fabric as *commonweal*. Yet this mortuarial character is stressed in the much earlier *Phenomenology of Spirit,* and I want to return to this text for an instant (as Derrida does) in order to look briefly at "The ethical world; the human and the divine law; man and woman."[7] Hegel is here concerned with the way in which the dead individual is gathered up, removed "from the long sequence of his dispersed existence," rescued "from the restlessness of his contingent life," and erected as a complete and singular configuration, elevated to "the tranquillity of simple universality" (PG, 321). As a family member, the dead one is merely a bloodless, marrowless shade; as a citizen, however, the dead one is still actual and substantial. The remaining family members must see to it that the transition is properly made; hence the crucial role they (especially the women) play in the funereal life of spirit.

Death cannot be allowed to remain something that *happens* to a family member, to say nothing of the family *head* or *chief,* and least of all to a *burgher.* Death too must be something that is done, effected, or achieved (*ein* getanes). The blood relatives must transform and accomplish what is otherwise a merely natural, not to say ghoulish, movement. They must append a conscious act to nature's bunged-up kidney or clotted heart. Wife and children must snatch the family head from his natural destruction; or, rather, since the dead one needs that destruction for his own effective transit to a higher order of spirit, they need to take such destruction on themselves. They must deflect the community's attention from the utterly passive being-for-others that the once powerful one has now become to his perdurant accomplishments and deeds. They must rescue the family head from the shame to which every cadaver is exposed, must prevent the dishonor that "cravings without consciousness" have in store for the corpse—whether those "cravings" are of maggots and foul gases or, as Derrida prefers, of the bereaved and tormented blood relations themselves, who may have read Freud's *Totem and Taboo* and who may therefore have some deeper unconscious cravings in mind. Whatever the case, the family members prepare the corpse for burial and "betroth their relative to the womb of the Earth" (PG, 323).

If wedding bells are breaking up that old gang of mine, the gang I knew since the days when school bells chimed, those bells too are fundamentally funereal, and they need not detain us here. In the end, it will be the responsibility of the women of the family, all the pious Magdalenas, to see to it that their loved ones—but especially the men, and among the men, especially the chief—are erected into stone.

## Foam in the Cup

Both Hegel's *Phenomenology of Spirit* and Derrida's *Glas* refuse to terminate. Yet the ways in which these two books arch back to their beginnings differ. The experience or itinerary (*Er-fahrung*) of phenomenology is "the circle that bends back into itself, presupposing its beginning and reaching it only at the end" (PG, 559). Sometimes that itinerary seems to be sheer regression, as in the final two pages, where Hegel appears to move proleptically *from* the as yet unwritten science of logic *back to* the presentation of the science of consciousness—which is and *remains* phenomenology. Yet when phenomenology arches back, it does so with ever greater suppleness: even though it appears to begin at the beginning again, without bias or advantage, *unbefangen . . . anzufangen*, as though it had forgotten everything that earlier configurations of spirit had inculcated in it, bracketing out everything that earlier adventures on that same itinerary had taught it, phenomenology always begins (again) "at a higher stage," saved by the internalizing remembrance (*Er-Innerung*) that propels spirit. Its arching back and beginning again constitutes, in effect, an upward spiral. Nothing is lost to spirit: all is archived in the kingdom of spirits (*Geisterreich*), and each configuration of spirit inherits the wealth of its predecessors as spiritual commonweal. Absolute knowing completes (*vollbringt*) that spiritual kingdom's organization, contingently as history, but conceptually as science. Science and history *together* culminate in the powerful images with which the *Phenomenology of Spirit* closes: the science and the history of the knowing that appears (*des erscheinenden Wissens*) "together form the internalizing remembrance and the Golgotha of absolute spirit, the actuality, truth, and certainty of its throne, without which it would be the lifeless solitary; only—

> From the chalice of this kingdom of spirits
> Does his infinity overflow with foam.
>                                 (PG, 564)

Derrida is intrigued above all by this *déferlement* of foam, the froth of infinity, the spume in the wake of all transcendental passage, the trace of all *Er-fahrung*. He is also intrigued by the place where that foamy chalice resides, the Place of the Skull, as the site of an internalizing remembrance that has come to its absolute: Golgotha as the site on which only the lifeless *solitary* is undone, but presumably never the *familial* spirit.

Derrida's *Glas* also ends doubly, with memories not only of Golgotha but also of Lydia, with Christ and Dionysos as the fragmented gods, the divine remnants. It ends, one can also say, with the petering out of its two erected columns. Because neither column terminates in a full stop, the question of the text's arching back, whether in order to go full circle or to spiral or to go into a tailspin, becomes a decisive question—or at least a decisive (if undecidable) moment in our reading of Derrida's text. The two columns terminate as follows—although where one *begins* to cite such an impossible end already frustrates the decisiveness I have been flaunting here:

A time to perfect the resemblance
between Dionysos and Christ.
Between the two (already) is elabor-
ated in sum the origin of literature.                   What I had dreaded, naturally,
But it runs to its ruin, for it counted          already, republishes itself. Today,
without                                                          here, now, the debris of

The two concluding prepositions, "without" and "of," beg for an object to complete the thought. The object under discussion in the Hegel column is literature, the spiritual work of art, whether as tragedy or comedy. In a sense, column A is already inclining toward column B, Hegel bowing (stiffly, unforgivingly) to Genet, absolute knowing to the language of flowers. Between Dionysos and the Christ hovers the Magdalene, which *could* be the name of a character in any of Genet's novels or plays or journals.

Even though the word *what* that opens each column at the outset of the book begins with a lowercase letter, suggesting that columns A and B could revert to either or both commencements, there is some sense in saying that only column B is open to such reversion:

                                                              *"what remained of a Rembrandt*
                                                              *torn into small, very regular*
what, after all, of the remain(s), today,    *squares and rammed down the*
for us, here, now, of a Hegel?                    *shithole"* is divided in two.

No doubt, the "today," "here," and "now" at the end of column B recall the same words at the outset of column A. However, the phrase "Today, here, now, the debris of" also seems to flow quite naturally back to *"what remained of a Rembrandt . . ."* Thus one could just as easily argue that the terminations of both A and B revert to the outset of B, that philosophy (to say it far too crudely) reverts to literature.

To be sure, Derrida is not merely double finneganing us. What *remains* of any such reversion of terminations "is divided in two," remaining as indeterminable as all remnants and remainders remain, at least in matters of the family and love. Yet both columns of *Glas* flow into literature—if it is literature that falls to the tomb, loves and mourns without the saving grace of absolutes, ruins from within all its sundry logics, and yet steadfastly refuses to neutralize or absorb into its system its own (m)other.

Genet: "Our-Lady was given the death penalty" (16/10 B).

Derrida: "The work of mourning as work of the tongue, teeth, and of saliva" (40/31 B). And: "Milk of mourning sealed up (congealed, pressed, squeezed, hidden, coagulated, curdled).

"I begin to be jealous of his mother" (290/261 B).

## 8

# Mourning Monica, Our (M)Other

... so that whoever reads this will—at your altar—remain mindful of Monica [*ut quotquot hoc legerint, meminerint ad altare tuum Monnicae*].
—Augustine, *Confessions* IX, 13

*I confess my mother, one always confesses the other.*
—Derrida, *Circumfession*

How quickly mourning overtakes us, and how long it lasts! It seizes us in that proverbial moment for which we are "never prepared" and spans our lifetimes, each new death adding an epicycle, a loop of time *perdu*—time *tellement perdu.* Sudden *and* perdurant? A seizure or rapture *and* the rhythm of a lifetime? How can that be? When does mourning commence? Does it slice into an already constituted time, or does it in some way serve as time's instauration?

Such questions take us back to matters that occupied us in Chapter 5, matters having to do with Heidegger's analysis of ecstatic temporality. In the present chapter I return to that analysis with an eye to what Augustine calls seizure and suddenness—*rapere, raptus, raptim.* I then offer a genealogical critique of the mourning that pervades Augustine's *Confessions,* a critique inspired principally by Nietzsche and Freud. I follow this with an attempt to read one of Derrida's purest of bastardly texts, namely, his circumfessional response to Augustine and Monica, the mother of Augustine, in *Circumfession.*

Finally, I close by returning to the question of ecstatic temporality and mourning—what one might call the raptures of mourning.


## Entrückung, μεταβολή, Raptus

Three words, still quite foreign to our ears. According to Heidegger they mean the same thing, namely, the metabolism of time in our lives, time *as* our lives. As I mentioned in Chapter 5, I have tried over the years to uncover the sources of Heidegger's analysis of temporality in *Being and Time* and in the lecture courses surrounding it. Suffice it to say that these sources are well hidden. Whereas we may be certain that Aristotle's "treatise on time" (*Physics* IV, 10–14) is a crucial source, Heidegger's own extensive analysis of the *Physics* does not discuss the *existential, ecstatic* moments of that treatise at all—it neglects the ἐξαίφνης, the "suddenness" that is at the existential core of the Aristotelian analysis, a core that, admittedly, comes at the very end of the treatise. Likewise, when Heidegger writes of Augustine's *Confessions* in his 1924 lecture, *The Concept of Time,* he cites the passage from chapter 27 of book XI in which Augustine speaks of "the times that I measure in my mind," yet says nothing of *rapere, raptus,* and *raptim* throughout the *Confessions.* Yet in what other Latin text he may have been reading at the time would he have found the word *raptus,* later employing it as a translation of *Entrückung,* the mechanism, as it were, of ecstatic temporality itself?

For Heidegger, time *is* ecstatic: each νῦν, each "now," is outside itself. In *Being and Time* he does not shy from saying that time is utterly centrifugal, and he says it with a glance—as we saw—to Hegel: "*Temporality is the original 'outside itself' in and for itself*" (SZ, 329). When the time comes to explain how the temporal ecstases of having-been, present, and future temporalize, how they release or give birth to one another, he chooses the word *Entrückung:* "transport," "seizure," or "rapture" (SZ, 338–39; 350). This time it is a nod to Plotinus and Tertullian, for whom, however, rapture is the union of the soul with God by grace of transport *beyond* the secular, *beyond* time. For Heidegger, the *beyond* is derived time, *inappropriate* time. In a 1927 lecture course he insists, "Time in itself, as future, having-been, and present, is *enraptured* [entrückt]" (24:377).[1] Even when, in a later lecture course, he searches for the unifying *horizon* of ecstatic temporality, *horizon* being the word that for phenomenology always means a *meaning-bestowing,* Heidegger remains adamant: as we earlier heard him say, the "totality of the *Entrückungen,*" and that means the *unity* of the ecstases and their horizon, "is itself ecstatic" (26:268).

We know that for Heidegger such an ecstatic or, as he once calls it, "ecstematic" horizon has to do with death, or with an experience of the nothing. That experience must somehow be related to mourning, if only as a vicarious mourning of one's stretched and self-stretching self, or as time's mourning of its own ecstatic passage into the absolute past. We may also be certain that Augustine's *Confessions* contributes to the ecstatic analysis of time. Yet Heidegger himself gives us very few clues about that contribution. To be sure, when Heidegger calls human existence by the name *care*, we can be certain that Augustine is as crucial a source as Seneca, Hyginus, and Goethe's *Faust*, all of which, along with the Vulgate and the Stoic μέριμνα, he explicitly cites (SZ, 199n.; cf. 20:418–20). Indeed, in Heidegger's own education, Augustine plays a key role: in a 1925 lecture course he explains that seven years earlier, that is, in 1918, he "stumbled across" the notion of *Sorge* in Augustine (20:418). Yet I know of no such attribution, no such "stumbling across," in the case of *rapere* and *raptus* or the adverb *raptim*, which is particularly important because of its connection with the Aristotelian ἐξαίφνης.[2]

While *rapio* itself derives from ἐρέπτομαι ("to feed on") or, by inversion, from ἁρπάζω ("to seize or snatch," which implies the Harpies or Raptors of time), the adverb *raptim* in Augustine's *Confessions* surely does have something to do with ecstases or raptures. In chapter 15 of book XI Augustine, in search of the fleeting present of time, notes that whatever can be called "present," no matter how minute, "flies suddenly out of the future into the past": *raptim a futuro in praeteritum transvolat*.[3] This sudden flight can scarcely have escaped the notice of the young phenomenologist—for whom, it is true, the care and concern of existence itself had not yet been expressly understood in terms of temporality. When, after those seven years are gone, he begins to sketch out *Being and Time*, and when, three years later, he refers explicitly to *raptus* as a word for the metabolic movement of time, I cannot doubt that both Aristotle and Augustine have been remembered. In a moment we will examine several more uses of *rapere* in Augustine's text, but not before noting that Augustine's principal word for the "timing" of time, *distentio*, can be discovered in Heidegger's account of the "stretch" of temporalizing time, *Erstreckung*, itself crucial for Heidegger's thinking of self and history.

We recall that Augustine's explicit role in *Being and Time* has less to do with temporality than with "falling," that is, with that lapsing into everyday dispersion that Heidegger characterizes as the bane of an existence that would be appropriate to itself. So it seems. Yet "falling" occurs in and as the ecstasy of the present, according to Heidegger, and it seems to describe—especially to those of us who are always so busy—the way in which our future flies *so suddenly* into a past. I have reported elsewhere (in the second chapter of *Daimon Life*) on Heidegger's account of dispersion and benumbment and their relation to Augustinian hebetude, the *vanus hebesco* of book X, chapter 35, and so will say little about these matters here. Yet the suddenness of *raptim* and *rapio* will bring us back to hebetude, dullness, and bedazzlement, which, like mourning, strike us abruptly but last a long while.

If the key reference to the temporality of the sudden is *raptim . . . transvolat* (XI, 15), other uses of *rapere* in the *Confessions* are nonetheless instructive. Our senses snatch up images quite suddenly, in order to lock them away in our memory, whereby both the suddenness of the action of our senses and the perdurance of the vestiges in our memory never cease to amaze us: images *quibus sensibus raptae sint,* "seized by our senses," have a staying power that only the most potent typography, the most efficacious iconography, and the most subtle engrammatology can seek to explain.[4] The sudden seizures by which we *learn* and spiritually grow are therefore also ambivalent in the extreme. Such ambivalence, which is appropriate to the mystery of time as such, comes to the fore in two apparently opposed instances of rapture. First, Augustine confesses himself "ravished away by lust," seized, *rapiebat,* by the very raptures of Eros; during one period of his life, even theater plays sent him into ecstasy, *rapiebant* (II, 2; III, 2). And we know what staying power such seizures had, especially those tenacious raptures Augustine suffered at the hands of the women in his life. Second, Augustine records his long conversation with Monica at Ostia, in which the two of them, mother and son, review the supreme pleasures of carnality and spirituality, flying ever higher, soaring ever more swiftly, until they are seized by a singular exultation that ravishes them, *rapida cogitatione attingimus . . . haec una rapiat* (XI, 10). Whether one learns from one's mother or from a ravishing woman, in either case the learning involves rapture. Indeed, rapture comes into play even when one learns from the father.

Earlier in book IX Augustine had marveled at how suddenly, *subito,* it was made easy for him to accept the embraces of his heavenly father, embraces that released a flood of tears; at the end of book IX, the son is suddenly seized by a fit of weeping for his dead mother. Whether the torrents of joy and sorrow, the overflow of tears, *confluebat in praecordia mea . . . transfluebat in lacrimas,* can be tied to the ecstatic flight of time, *transvolat,* I cannot say; that the violence of mourning in particular, *violento animi imperio,* is a violence in and of time, I do suspect, and for the most excellent Augustinian reasons (IX, 12).

Whether the lamentations of his natural son, *puer Adeodatus exclamavit,* can be described as a kind of seizure, whether Augustine's own pain, as though from a recent flesh wound, *vulnus recens,* can have been caused by thrusts of time, I am uncertain; whether the bloody wounds inflicted on his soul, *sauciabatur anima,* that is, wounds as troubles or cares, and the bloody fragmentation of his life, *dilaniabatur vita,* that is, fragmentation as a life utterly lost to itself—whether these can be subjected to a temporal analysis, an *ecstatic* temporal analysis, is a question that surely would have occurred to Heidegger, if only when he presented a copy of *Sein und Zeit* to his mother on her deathbed (*Basic Writings,* 23). Whether in Augustine's account the temporality of an everydayness that fails to assuage the pain of mourning—through neither redoubled sorrow over his sorrowfulness nor the cult of the dead nor steam baths is his mourning of Monica alleviated—can be counterposed to an appropriate temporality of soothing sleep, *noctem sopora gratia,* a sleep that alone ameliorates the suddenness of the deprivation, *qua subito destitutus sum,* I do not know; yet it seems certain that Augustine's tears, released from the shackles of shame to flow when they will, *et dimisi lacrimas . . . ut effluerunt quantum vellent,* themselves constitute something like a *temporal flux.* Finally, whether or not confessions laid out in written ciphers to be read and interpreted by the eyes of any and all, including Heidegger, *can weep temporally, can weep as time,* if only for the smallest part of an hour, *exigua parte horae,* let no one mock the confessor, let no one laugh in the face of what may be the origins of time—the liquid spacing of time. That, at least, would be Heidegger's fundamental mood and Derrida's plea. We will return to the constellation of mourning, tears, and time at the end of the chapter.

## The Ultimate Inhibition

Friedrich Nietzsche writing in Nice—the city in which Derrida's mother, Georgette, lives after 1962 and in which she dies on December 5, 1991—a letter dated March 31, 1885, to Franz Overbeck in Basel:

> I recently read for rest and recuperation the *Confessions* of Saint Augustine, full of regrets that you were not here with me. Oh, this old rhetorician! How false and squint-eyed [*augenverdreherisch*] he is! How I laughed! (For example, over that youthful "theft," at bottom a mere schoolboy prank.) What psychological falsehood! (For example, when

he says concerning the death of his best friend, the friend with whom he shared *a single soul,* that he "determined to live on, so that in this way his friend would *not altogether* die": such talk is a nauseating deception.) Philosophical value = zero. *Platonism for the masses,* that is, a mode of thought that was invented for the highest aristocracy of souls cut down to size for servile natures. In addition, with this book one is looking into the belly of Christianity: I stand alongside with the curiosity of a radical physician and physiologist.—[5]

Doubtless Freud and Derrida alike—albeit for very different reasons— would argue against Nietzsche that Augustine is perfectly right to live on after his friend, to survive him, to accept the ultimate irony—survival as the conso-lation prize—and precisely through his own labors of mourning to preserve the memory of the dead one. Doubtless a practiced thief, a Jean Genet, for example, would take real joy in Augustine's description (II, 4) of the pleasure of the stolen pears—pears fit for pigs, but the stealing fit for an outlaw prince. Doubtless the genealogist himself must remain grateful to Augustine for opening his own belly and his own bellyaching to the radical physician and physiologist, whose best vivisection, after all, is on his bellyaching self.

Yet anyone interested in prayer and confession might do well to pause over some of Nietzsche's more detailed notes on Augustine, especially the following note, from the spring of 1885:

> The *unmanning* and perhaps even *emasculating* impact of excessive *prayer* is also a part of the damage wrought by the Reformation on the very being of the Germans. In any case, it is a matter of bad taste to beg a great deal instead of giving a lot: the mixture of obsequious servility with an often quite haughty and boorish obtrusiveness, with which for example Saint Augustine in his *Confessions* grovels before God, reminds us that human beings are perhaps not alone among the animals that possess religious feeling—the dog has a similar "religious feeling" toward the human being.—Trafficking in prayer with God breeds moods of humiliation and posturing, attitudes that still assert their rights in times that are no longer pious: Germans nowadays are known to wither in the face of princes or party leaders, or when they hear the phrase, "Your most humble servant." We should put all that behind us.[6]

Derrida never cites in his *Circumfession* the scornful report on Augustine that Nietzsche addresses to Overbeck from Nice. Nor does he refer to any of the many references to Augustine in Nietzsche's oeuvre. Derrida's somewhat abashed reference to the weeping Nietzsche in *Memoirs of the Blind*, to which I alluded at the end of Chapter 2, suggests that Nietzsche is increasingly becoming a goad to him, a necessary but painful corrective—even if in *Circumfession* he calls the lachrymose Nietzsche and Rousseau "my two positive heroes" (26).[7] In that spirit, the spirit of painful correctives and a heroism of tears, we will soon begin to read Derrida's *Circumfession*, but not before undertaking two preliminary genealogical diversions. First, we will take a glimpse at what Freud considered the ultimate inhibition, the inhibition expressed by Hamlet's ghost when he warns young Hamlet,

> Taint not thy mind, nor let thy soul contrive
> Against thy mother aught. . . .
>
> (act I, scene V)

Second, we will undertake a far less sympathetic examination of Augustine than Derrida's. We will consider the Augustine Derrida is perhaps too generous to read, in a word, the *genealogist's* Augustine—Stendhal's, Baudelaire's, and Nietzsche's Augustine, as it were.

At the outset of *Inhibition, Symptom, and Anxiety* (6:235–36, a work to which I referred in the Introduction because of its concluding reflections on mourning), Freud defines inhibition (*Hemmung*) as "the expression of a *limitation in the functioning of the ego,* a limitation that itself can have quite various causes." In cases of highly specialized functions—involving, for example, that of a pianist at the piano, a writer at the desk, a city dweller walking—the limitation of function in the fingers or toes is normally due to "an excessively strong erotization" of those organs or parts of the body. Erogeneity or sexual significance reduces the ego function of an organ. Freud's confessedly bizarre (*skurril*) example is that of a cook who will not work at her stove because the lord of the house has become her lover. Her household function, by which she earns her living (thus surviving as an ego), diminishes as she hears the slippered feet of the lord outside the galley door. Freud's less scurrilous examples are as follows—and both of them will have cut Derrida to the quick:

> Writing consists of causing liquid to flow from a tube onto a piece of white paper. If writing has taken on the symbolic significance of coitus, or if walking has become a symbolic substitute for tramping upon the body of Mother Earth [*des Stampfens auf dem Leib der Mutter Erde*],

then both writing and walking will be abandoned, for it is as though one were performing the forbidden sexual act. The ego renounces the functions that pertain to it, in order not to have to undertake yet another repression, *in order to avoid a conflict with the id.* (6:236)

On Derrida's testimony in *Circumfession,* one might suppose that his mother had never been in the kitchen, but only at the poker table, playing until dawn, up to the last minute refusing to surrender a good hand in order to give birth to him; now, once again, and for years, seemingly forever, she is bedridden and amnesiac with Alzheimer's disease. He recalls that she was as beautiful as a picture, as beautiful as the Winter Garden Photograph that Roland Barthes never reveals in *Camera Lucida,* as beautiful as those mothers who, when they die, leave too little for sons like Maurice Merleau-Ponty or Roland Barthes to live for.[8] The writer's anxiety is that his mother's death, the closing of those eyes, will mean his own death, or, rather, that the two deaths cannot be kept apart. It is as though the mother-son relation were the only relation that breaks the mortal rule—the rule that one person will have to die after the other, hence that the survivor will have to mourn her or him, the rule that we will not see one another die any more than we will see ourselves die. *Nous nous verrons mourir* is an impossible saying—except for a boy and his (m)other, a Narcissus and his original, anaclitic Echo. Our inability to keep the two deaths apart is not a perfection, however, but an inhibition. What the writer writes is this crack, fissure, abyss, wound, or bedsore that will not close upon an identity or a proper name: "Step on a crack, you break your mother's back," as the children say. The writer can neither tramp nor stamp, neither inscribe nor tread the lines of his—or her—text: ". . . *fear of absolute inhibition*" (21).[9]

Freud notes that when psychic energy must be devoted to a strenuous task—his example is that of *mourning*—the quelling of sexual fantasies will demand so much force that the ego can scarcely function at all. The mourner might be lame for days at a time; or, if the mourning should become depression or melancholy, ultimately leading to self-destruction, the mourner may find himself or herself in the paralyzing position of *Allgemeinhemmung,* universal inhibition, which is the absolute shadow of absolute spirit, spirit as absolute past.

However, what if the scurrilous writer were to elaborate lines of writing that evoke a sexual fantasy about the (m)other, involving titillation, invitation, *jouissance,* and implacable self-recrimination? And what if that sexual fantasy were simultaneously a fantasy of mourning, involving sedation, withdrawal, quiescence, and impossible pardon? Would such lines be possible? Would they not frustrate every attempt to systematize, whether that systematizing effort were psychoanalytic or philosophical? In his *Circumfession*, Derrida is about this apparently impossible task, on the scent of universal inhibition, hard on the heels of systemic disaster.

Before examining that impossible task, however, let us undertake our second, more protracted genealogical effort, reading Augustine's *Confessions* without piety or pity. From the outset, Augustine worries about the tainting that must have occurred in and through his mother's womb, a tainting concerning which neither his mother nor his father can inform him, but which can only be inferred from the (probable) experience of his infancy. Fortunately, that tainted gestation in the mother's womb and tainted infancy at her breast are swathed in an oblivion so profound that the primal tainting seems never to have occurred:

> Therefore, O Lord, this age which I do not remember to have lived, which I have taken on trust from others, which I conclude myself to have passed through from observing other infants, although such testimonies are most probable, this age it irks me to join to this life of mine [*piget me adnumerare huic vitae meae*], the life I have lived in this world. In so far as it belongs to the dark regions of forgetfulness it is like that which I lived in my mother's womb. But "if I was conceived in iniquity," and if my mother nourished me within her womb in sins [*et in peccatis mater mea me in utero aluit*], where, I beseech you, O Lord my God, where or when was your servant innocent? But, see, I now set aside that period [*sed ecce omitto illud tempus*]: and what does that matter to me of which I recall no trace [*cuius nulla vestigia recolo*]? (I, 7)

Much later in his *Confessions* (X, 22), Augustine pursues the parallel mystery of his recollection of past *happiness:* whence the joy, the febrile memory of which he pursues when he pursues the father? He, the perfervid fornicator, does not dream or imagine or even write that the source of all joy may have been that dark intrauterine period, *illud tempus,* which he says does not matter because it apparently has left no trace in him, the period spent in the sinfully celestial realm of his mother's womb. Yet who is this (m)other? Some initial words about Monica, her mettle, her misery, her mystery, and her miasma.

Monica's mettle lies in her connivance to replace Augustine's father, Patricius, with the Lord, to overcome the man to whom she is politically and institutionally subject but intellectually and spiritually superior (I, 11). It lies also in the deference, the surreptitious manner, by which she deflects and avoids her husband's wrath. For all her deference, and despite her costume, however, she is virile in her faith (IX, 4: *muliebri habitu, virile fide*). While the foolish Patricius looks forward to the grandchildren that will flow from Augustine's loins, Monica relentlessly warns her son against fornication and adultery (II, 3).

Monica's misery lies in her inheritance from Eve of the very things that seduce her son to "carnal corruptions of the soul": inexplicably but inevitably, hers is the source of the slime (II, 2: *limosa concupiscentia*, bound up in some undisclosed way with the *ex limo terrae* of the traditional Christian creation story) that Augustine struggles to escape in order to prepare a dry spot for the Lord. Why the Lord has these slimy agents as his most menacing competitors— in other words, in what way the ostensibly lowest level of beastly embodiment can displace the putatively highest level of divine spirituality—is a question Augustine is reluctant to ask, even though the whole of his *Confessions* circum- scribes it, circumfesses it, and circumvents it like a cat circling hot porridge while a larger carnivore circles them both. Paul at least is clear about it: whoever touches a woman will not be receptive to the embraces of the Lord. Augustine: "I should have listened more heedfully to these words, and having thus been made a eunuch for the sake of the kingdom of heaven [*abscisus propter regnum caelorum*], I would have looked with greater joy to your embraces."[10]

Monica's mystery lies in the temple of her breast, from which Augustine sucks the milk (III, 4: *lacte matris*) of Christ's name. Indeed, Augustine soon attributes that creamy breast to the Lord and Father: "What am I, when all is well with me, except one sucking your milk [*sugens lac tuum*] and feeding on you [*fruens te*]" (IV, 1; cf. VII, 18). Monica's virile milk is mirrored in the flood of tears that flow from her eyes on account of her lubricious son, a flood that waters the earth (and produces slime?) wherever she prays (III, 11). That "chaste, devout, and sober widow," who in spite of her virile faith and manly hope is "no less assiduous in weeping and mourning," so prods a bishop with her concern for her son that the holy man assures her, "It is impossible that the son of all those tears should perish [*fieri non potest, ut filius istarum lacrimarum pereat*]" (III, 12). Her saline tears are sweet to her and to the Father, as are all the tears of bitterness and mourning (IV, 5). Whether or not such sweetness is concupiscent Augustine is reluctant to ask—inasmuch as the time is ripe not for questioning but for confessing (IV, 6). Indeed, the altar of Augustine's *Confessions* serves as a memorial to Monica's life and death, a monument to her heart's blood and her tears for her son (V, 7, and IX, 13).

Monica's miasma lies in the swamp her tears create, a bog that well-nigh entraps Augustine and prevents him from making his way to Rome. For the son knows what Monica does not see clearly enough: that only a sea voyage

from Africa to Rome, only a bath in the waters of Roman grace, will dry up
"those rivers flowing down from my mother's eyes, by which, before you and
in my behalf, she daily watered the ground beneath her face" (V, 8). Scene:
mother and son are at the harbor; she pleads with him, begs him to stay. She
desires his presence. He, thinking solely of another heading, pretends to relent,
gives her assurances. Augustine convinces Monica to overnight in a nearby
convent—then secretly sets sail in the night. Even if he is halfway across the
Mediterranean, he can, like a novelist or rhetorician, paint the scene of Monica's
subsequent hysteria, the scene of the carnality that ties pious mother to profligate son, or, as the worm turns, pious son to a mother profligate in her tears:

> The wind blew and filled our sails, and the shore receded from our sight.
> On that shore in the morning she stood, wild with grief, and with
> complaints and groans she filled your ears. But you rejected such things,
> since you carried me away on my own desires so as to put an end to
> those desires, and thus the carnal longing that was in her was beaten by
> the just scourge of sorrow [*et illius carnale desiderium iusto dolorum*
> *flagello vapularet*]. For she loved me to be present with her, after the
> custom of mothers, but much more than many mothers [*sed multis*
> *multo amplius*]. She did not know how great a joy you would fashion
> for her out of my absence. She knew nothing of this, and therefore she
> wept and lamented. By such torments the remnant of Eve within her
> was made manifest [*atque illis cruciatibus arguebatur in ea reliquiarium*
> *Evae*], and with groans she sought the one to whom with groans she
> had given birth [*cum gemitu quaerens quod cum gemitu pepererat*]. Yet
> after her denunciation of my falsity and cruelty, she turned again to
> beseech you in prayer for me. She went back home, and I went on to
> Rome. (V, 8)

As a relic of Eve, tormented by the impending loss of her little one, Monica
for once in her life obstructs the Lord's plan. For all her piety and virility, for
all her paternal (m)ilk, Monica is a reliquary of evil, the evil ensconced in that
by which she gave birth. Yet the mother, strong in maternal piety, *mater pietate*
*fortis*, and even stronger in her man's faith, soon pursues Augustine to Rome
(VI, 1). By now it is clear to him that baptism alone will liberate him from the
manacles of Monica's fanatical mother love, from Monica's monocular vision
of his future. Augustine still doubts whether he can do without a woman's
embraces (VI, 11: *si feminae privarer amplexibus*): "Caught fast in a disease of
the flesh with its deadly tenderness [*deligatus morbo carnis mortifer suavitate*],

I dragged along my chains and was fearful of being loosed from them" (VI, 12). Ambrose is astonished that Augustine is "stuck so fast in the birdlime of that pleasure [*ita haerere visco illius voluptatis*]," birdlime betraying the color of mother's milk and the viscosity of the semen that is the seed of woman in every man, the color and viscosity of pallid slime, the very stuff of naturalness, the spawn of death.

Principally through the urgings of his mother, Augustine puts away the woman with whom he has lived for thirteen years, the nameless woman out of Africa who has given him a son, Adeodatus, "gift from God." Or, rather than put her away himself, Augustine submits to her being torn from his side, *avulsa a latere meo*, thus hiding in the utterly passive voice behind which the lordly (m)other works her will. Even after the enthrallment of his marriage to another woman, and on the very verge of his baptism, Augustine is "still tightly bound by the love of women [*tenaciter alligabar ex femina*]" (VIII, 1), entangled in the chains of "a harsh bondage" (VIII, 5). Only the fear of death, the very death into which his unquenchable lust is ostensibly causing him to waste away, curbs his concupiscence: as was undoubtedly the case for Mary Magdalene, the wretchedness of Augustine's carnality announces itself in the very paroxysms of his pleasure. In the bower and bowel of desire, the storm clouds of death gather head.

Louder than the cries of Augustine's self-laceration rises the initially "feeble voice" of Continence, "virtuously alluring," serene and joyous, attractive yet not wanton. She, *continentia,* stretches forth her arms to lift Augustine out of the slime: she is not barren, however, but unlike the Magdalene is the fruitful mother of many sons, *fecunda mater filiorum,* sired by the Lord (VIII, 11). She smiles and murmurs to him, encouraging him to surrender his hesitation: "Turn deaf ears to those unclean members of yours, so that they may be mortified [*inmunda illa membra tua, ut mortificentur*]." Under a fig tree, of all places, a mortified Augustine weeps, his conversion complete. He rises and goes to his (m)other. Her desires to marry her son off—vestigial Patrician desires, the desires of a man "weaker than woman," as Creon says—are now quelled. The (m)other rejoices. "You turned her mourning into a joy far richer than that she had desired, far dearer and purer than that she had sought in grandchildren born of my flesh." No longer must Augustine scratch the itchy sore of lust (IX, 1: *scalpendi scabiem libidinum*) in order to fulfill the parental desire. He pores over the scriptures, his lungs deteriorate, his teeth go bad, he is compelled to resign his professorship of rhetoric: all goes well with him.

Finally, as an afterthought, he remembers what his mother has confessed to him: a sin of her youth, her weakness for wine. The (m)other was a bibbler.

The nascent saint therefore confesses the liquidity that has so tormented those two souls, (m)other and son alike, who so furiously wanted to be dry (IX, 8). Yet by now the (m)other can sense that her son despises aqueous life even more than she does: her prayers have been amply answered, and she has gotten even more than she asked for. For if she is about to die, so is her son, who has outdone the (m)other in mortification. By the time she goes on to glory, he will be as moribund as she. One secret bout of tears in memory of her, along with one somewhat more protracted bout of commemorative writing, and he will have put her away forever. Or she him—it is difficult to say.

## Confessing the M(O)ther

Let our genealogy of Augustine end here, for it is at this point, with the scene of the (m)other's imminent death, that Derrida's *Circumfession* begins and ends. Derrida seeks a certain "rawness" of language for his task, not the cooked concept, but the unrefined language that will defeat any conceptual or "theological" presentation of his ideas. He admits to "having never loved anything but the impossible" (1), and avers that "one writes only at the moment of giving the contemporary the slip" (12). It is to the impossible scene of his (m)other's deathbed that his *Circumfession* transports or abandons us readers. It will be a scene of bedsores and blood, the blood of the (m)other's wounds and of the son's circumcision: "I always dream of a pen that would be a syringe, a suction point rather than that very hard weapon with which one must inscribe, incise, choose, calculate" (2). Derrida seeks not the truth of these scenes, inasmuch as confessions, even circuitous circumnavigatory ones, can only *make* truth, not perceive it or comprehend it as already there. Not a verity, but a severity, a severity of avowal, is his aim, an avowal that has to do with "the deaths of our respective mothers" (3).

To be sure, at the time of the writing (January 1989 to April 1990), Derrida's mother has not yet died. She is bedridden in Nice, where eventually she will die and be buried—like Augustine's mother, Monica, she will have to accept a grave on the far side of the Mediterranean, far from the Africa that was her home. A number of contingencies rise to influence Derrida's text, from the Santa Monica near which he is writing in California to the rue Saint-Augustin where he spent his first four years in colonial Algeria. Yet the most terrible contingency is the way in which this labor of mourning imposes itself on the writer *before* his mother's death, as though the writing here and the dying over there were somehow in alliance with one another, the writing "in alliance with death, with the living death of the mother" (27), or as though they were caught up in a race with one another, a terrifying race the son can only (hope to) lose.

Sultana Esther Georgette Safar Derrida no longer recognizes her son by the time of the writing, at least as far as he can tell. There is no intimate, edifying conversation between them in Nice as there was between Augustine and Monica in Ostia. The writer cannot garner the mother's blessing or celebrate her courageous acquiescence in a foreign burial. Deaf to the warnings of psycho-analysis, the writer records with a verisimilitude that is painful and shocking to the reader his mother's wandering words. For example, these: "'I have a pain in my mother,' as though she were speaking *for* me, both in my direction and in my place, although in the apparently amnesiac confusion in which she is ending her days the memory of *her* mother is very present to her" (4). The reader, especially if his or her mother is still alive, worried by illness perhaps but still alive, is scarcely reassured by the writer's insistence that he is "writing *for*" his mother. Each disclosure or exposure of her ("'Because I'm attractive'") cuts like a stiletto. The reader will want to cry out ("The bastard!") against a narcissism that writes of the anaclitic (m)other so uninhibitedly, so mercilessly, simply because *she* can no longer recognize *his* face in *her* pool.

Derrida is aware of the reader's outcry; he provokes it, counts on it. For this scene will be about cruelty, a cruelty without inhibition, beyond genealogy. The death scene will involve a writer who now "posthumes" as he breathes—like Nietzsche, born posthumously—while over his head a conceptual system is being built from the debris of "deconstruction." Writing beneath and against Geoff Bennington's exposition of "Jacques Derrida," Derrida is driven to write "*unpredictable things*" and to seek "the salvation of a backfire" (5). Once again the reader will inveigh against a narcissism that so values its philosophical corpus that it will raise the amulet of a mother's moribund body against the system: "it is as if I were trying to oblige him [i.e., Geoff Bennington] to recognize me and come out of this amnesia of me which resembles my mother while I say to myself when I read this matrix there's the survivress signing in my place and if it is right, and it is, faultless, not only will I no longer sign but I will never have signed, is this not basically what I have always meant to say." The writer takes momentary comfort in the guilt that is always poised to assault him, whatever she or he does or does not do with respect to the (m)other: "me who, among other remorse with respect to my mother, feels really guilty for publishing her end, in exhibiting her last breaths and, still worse, for purposes that some might judge to be literary, at risk of adding a dubious exercise to the 'writer and his mother' series, subseries 'the mother's death,' and what is there to be done, would I not feel as guilty, and would I not in truth *be* as guilty if I wrote here about myself without retaining the least trace of her, letting her die in the depth of another time" (7). "In the depth of another time." At the heart of this forbidden discourse on the mother, which is in some sense a discourse *of* the mother, lies concealed the question with which we began— time. Ecstatic, existential time, which is (as Heidegger says) in each case *mine*, is also shared with the (m)other, is perhaps even *granted by her*.

Yet what a bizarre, bathetic treatise on time! The reader's fear of bathos will dissipate only if the pathos of the text overwhelms him or her, and nothing here can help the reader any more than it helped the writer. Derrida's will have to be a text that answers the demand made by Nietzsche's daimon with respect to eternal recurrence of the same: its thought must be incorporated or ingested, *einverleibt,* more than introjected, and must either maim or make us. In the notebooks on circumcision, notebooks "dreamt of" after his father's death in 1970 (shades of Freud's *Interpretation of Dreams*), begun after *Glas* and continued into the 1980s, Derrida writes: "*if this book does not transform me through and through, if it does not give me a divine smile in the face of death, my own and that of loved ones, if it does not help me to love life even more, it will have failed*" (15). That the stakes are high—as high as in Nietzsche's thought of eternal return and *amor fati*—and that the pathos is genuine are realizations that grow on the reader as the reading progresses, even if the writer insists that "a circumfession is always simulated" (24), so that no mere avowal, such as mine, here, can help.

The realization commences perhaps when the mother's words, "I want to kill myself," terrifyingly clear among her confused mutterings, are recognized by the son as forming a sentence of his own: her words are "me all over," he says. The writer sees in that sentence the secret of the child "about whom people used to say 'he cries for nothing,'" and the continuing secret of the adult who is driven by "a sort of compulsion to overtake each second," each second of ecstatic time as it flees forever into the past. This is the childish secret that no systematic account of Derrida's thought can express, even though those who program or scan the perfect deconstructive system will, like sons burying their father, have to believe that they comprehend everything: "and already I catch them out seeing me lying on my back, in the depth of my earth, I mean, they understand everything . . . except that I have lived in prayer, tears, and imminence at every moment of their survival, terminable survival from which 'I see myself live' translates 'I see myself die,' I see myself dead cut off from you in your memories that I love and I weep like my own children at the edge of my grave, I weep not only for my children but for all my children, why only you, my children?" (7).

Thus the son occupies the position of the (m)other, stretches out in the very bed, the deathbed, of the (m)other, and the reader is only more troubled. "'I'm losing,'" the mother says, as though still at poker, poker being "the passion of her life, they say, her passion of life" (8). The son is not about to accept the consolation prize of survival, however, and in the poker game in which the stakes are highest, there are no winners, none who gain the other side:

> wondering at every moment if she will still be alive, having nonetheless stopped recognizing me, when I arrive at the end of this sentence which seems to bear the death that bears her, if she will live long enough to leave me time for all these confessions, and to multiply the scenes in which I see myself alone die, pray, weep, at the end of a circumnavigation trying to reach its bank in a story of blood, at the point where I am finally this cauterized name, the ultimate, the unique, right up against what, from an improbable circumcision, I have lost by gaining. (8)

If the mother is "the eternal survivress," and if absolute knowing (once again, *Savoir Absolu,* SA, this time as Saint Augustine) is a maternal figure, one that traditional philosophers of spirit cannot do without, even if they must rigorously sterilize, cauterize, mutilate, and defeminize it, then the *mother's* agony and dying (*pace* Freud) are the ultimate crisis of the philosopher's living, writing, and thinking. The surviving son must beg forgiveness "for the crime, blasphemy, or perjury in which consists presently the act of writing," even as he knows that "writing is only interesting in proportion and in the experience of evil" (9).

Whether such an experience runs in tandem with or counter to Augustine is difficult to say: it runs *against* Augustine when the saint's *Confessions* are content to grovel in self-recrimination, but *with* Augustine when the writer says of the origin of evil, "I know not what or whence [*nescio quid aliud*]" (25; *Confessions* V, 10), and when he rebukes his Lord, "You enjoin continence: give what you command, and command what you will [*da quod iubes et iube quod vis*]" (X, 29, 31, and 37, a rebuke not cited by Derrida). Derrida's experience differs from Augustine's in that he (Derrida) is more sanguine, or at least more candid, about "the supplement of pleasure" granted by tears (19). Yet Derrida accompanies Augustine when the latter "tracks the origin of evil" to "that monstrous mother, the infinite sea containing an immense but finite sponge" (20; cf. *Confessions* VII, 5).[11] Derrida's guilt is double and contradictory, and we will have occasion to return to it near the end: he fears both that he will survive his mother and that his mother will survive him, both that the survivress about which he has written so intensely and so often will fail in her role and that her life will swallow his. When a viral infection—the same infection that we saw ruining the Cyclopic eye of the self-portrait in Chapter 2—causes the left side of his face to freeze in paralysis, the (m)other's uninterrupted stare gazes back at him from his mirror as though from her deathbed. The eye that will not close "is looking at me from my mother" (12, 18, 20). That paralyzed eye will also be the volcanic and bloody bedsore (*escarre*) that remains a wretched sign of indefatigable life in the (m)other, and the ritual scar or cut on the infant son that will not heal (16–17, 43). The same water or saliva that dribbles from the mouth of the bedridden woman dribbles from the son's face when it is struck by paralysis (19). And, like Monica's tears on the slimy earth, that saliva will turn up elsewhere as well.

Two contingencies haunt the situation of mother and son: two siblings, two brothers, die on either side of the birth of "Jackie," as her mother calls him. Paul Moïse Derrida dies in 1929, a year before Jacques's birth, and Norbert Pinhas dies in 1940, when the writer is ten. "Jackie" therefore substitutes for Paul and survives Norbert, whom he watches his mother mourn. One can likewise imagine Nietzsche mourning his little brother, Josephchen, who dies not long after their father's death and who haunts Nietzsche all his life; one can imagine a life of mourning in which the very figures of father, brother, and survivor are fused and confused in the figure of the mourning mother. One can imagine that even God, the sole witness, may be transformed into this preeminently maternal figure of mourning, a *schechina* of the Jewish tradition (11, 30), and one can further imagine that such a God must be a *Doppelgänger,* both breast and knife blade. Indeed, the (m)other, who has two or more sides and is as *doppelgängerisch* as any father could be, is held to be the circumciser: "The cruelty basically being hers" (13), she is the one whose blade the writer will escape only vicariously, only by sparing his own sons. He will escape the knife by not circumcising his sons, by breaking the pact, by being for his own family "the last Jew" and "*the end of Judaism*" (24, 57).

As the figure of Zipporah, to whom I alluded while discussing the Echoes of Chapter 2—"the one who repaired the failing of a Moses incapable of circumcising his own son, before telling him, 'You are a husband of blood to me,' she had to eat the bloody foreskin, I imagine first by sucking it" (13)— the (m)other becomes both the wielder of the stone knife and the source of all nurturing tenderness.[12] She becomes in Derrida's wayward fantasy the faithful Catherine of Siena, embracing her nuptial ring, but also the concubine, "my first beloved cannibal, initiator at the sublime gate of fellatio."[13] Thus the peritomy that is circumcision, the conversion by which the penis is cut back to size, becomes the example—albeit in a "region that is no longer that of an example" (14)—of an impossible position with regard to both love and religion, both the family and the community. Derrida's confession, or circumfession, will be "restrained," inasmuch as it "will not have been my fault but hers, as though the daughter of Zipporah had not only committed the crime of my circumcision but one more still, later, the first playing the kick-off, the original sin against me, but to reproduce itself and hound me, call me into question, me, a whole life long, to make her avow, her, in me" (14). Further, such a confession or indictment will have to be sucked and eaten rather than merely read—*manduco bibo*, Augustine says; "*like the foreskin,*" Derrida says (15; cf. 29). It will be the circuitous eucharistic and accusatory confession of a (m)other's son who is caught between the names Jackie and Élie, between the public "Christian" name, as it were, and the secret Hebrew prophetic name that is bestowed upon him at circumcision.

His uncle, Eugène Eliahou, holds the seven-day-old baby on his lap. It is his mother's birthday, but she is barred from the ritual. Circumcision produces in this case a hybrid creature: the object of the sacrifice is neither Jew nor Gentile, but a kind of *Jackelie* (20), doubtless related to the jackal. The name of God would nevertheless be heard as a name in *her* mouth, no doubt "when she was praying, each time she saw me ill, no doubt dying like her son before me, like her son after me."

> and I'm mingling the name of God here with the origin of tears, the always puerile, weepy, and pusillanimous son that I was, the adolescent who basically only liked reading writers quick to tears, Rousseau, Nietzsche, Ponge, SA, and a few others, that child with whom the grown-ups amused themselves by making him cry for nothing, who was always to weep over himself with the tears of his mother. . . . I weep from my mother over the child whose substitute I am, whence the other, nongrammatical syntax that remains to be invented to speak of the name of God, which is here neither that of the father nor that of the mother, nor of the son nor of the brother nor of the sister. (23)

Derrida's *Circumfession* is not meant to be a literary confession or a form of "theology as autobiography," however much it may borrow from Augustine and however much it may harp on divinity. The writer is interested instead in "memory and heart" and, as though it meant the same, "the depth of the bedsore" (17). To be sure, it is not a matter of the history of the present as present, or of knowledge and truth (26: "a confession . . . no longer has anything to do with truth"), or a matter of any simulacrum of "deconstruction" (17, 58). Here it is to be a matter of the family escutcheon, the ἔσχατον, and the *escarre:* the family (as in *Glas*), the outermost point, and the scar.

Jackelie is both the favorite and the excluded son of the family, the valued ersatz for one brother who dies before him and another who dies after him, but an ersatz nonetheless. The sacred name of Élie or Elijah, the prophet who presides over circumcision but who also represents a certain vacancy, an empty chair at the dinner table, will be one of the secrets of this confession: Élie, Elijah, Eliahou—*il y a là: cendre*, a name whose personal and historical destiny will be traced in ash, "the name of God in the ash of Elijah [*la cendre d'Élie*]" (19, 35, 51).[14]

One of the strangest parallels between Augustine's *Confessions* and Derrida's *Circumfession* is the relative absence of the father from the text—at least if one discounts the rhetoric of the divine Lord and Father in Augustine. Patricius has lost his virility to Monica, and Derrida's father is mentioned only a few times in the text. In Derrida's case, however, the whole project is "dreamt of" only after the father's death, and the father is invoked at the side of Uncle Eugène Eliahou and in the context of writing, a writing his mother never will have read. The father will insist that the son write only "on the most irrepressible of drives," precisely in the way that the father himself meticulously composes his own death notice (19, 25, 27). Yet it remains the mother who, after a stroke, poses the question "Who am I?" The son finds even the syntax of the question difficult to follow, if only because the *suis* may derive from *suivre*, in which case the mother would be posing the question of "obsequence," as the question proper to the survivress and to the "logic of the living woman," namely, the question "Whom do I follow?"[15] He imagines her "protesting in silence, impotent, impatient, faced with the incorrigible narcissism of a son who seems to be interested only in his own identification, but no, that of his double, alas, the dead brother" (27). The absent brothers, the all-but-absent father, never more absent than when the name of God is uttered, and the absent daughter, whom the writer will never have (28, 40, 56), are all represented by the (m)other. *Circumfession* thus revolves about the mother as other, the m(other) who speaks as the mouth of God, the (m)other as the immortal one who is nonetheless dying, the surviving (m)other of the writer who is driven to confess—circuitously.

> Quick, memories, before the thing arrives. . . . I confess my mother, one always confesses the other, I confess (myself) means I confess my

mother means I own up to making my mother own up, I make her speak in me, before me, whence all the questions at her bedside as though I were hoping to hear from her mouth the revelation of the sin at last, without believing that everything here comes down to turning around a fault of the mother carried in me, about which one might expect me to say however little, as SA did about the "surreptitious" taste of Monica, never, you hear, never, the fault will remain as mythical as my circumcision, do I have to draw you a picture. (29)[16]

If Monica's surreptitious taste is for wine—wine, family pride, obeisance before the Father, and insatiable ambition for her son—Georgette's surreptitious taste (apart from her passion for poker) is swallowed in silence or else writ large as myth. Derrida's taste is not the misogyny that sees in every (m)other the victim *and* the perpetrator of castration. Nor is it the enthusiasm (as misogynist as misogyny) that sees in every (m)other a repentant Maria Magdalena or a militant Monica. Can we say anything at all about Derrida's surreptitious taste, his secret sin, the sin of his (m)other? Derrida's taste is "*this incredible supper of the wine and blood, let people see it how I see it on my sex each time blood is mixed with sperm or the saliva of fellatio . . . make all the readers drool, wet lips, high and low, stretched out in their turn on the cushions, right on the knees of 'godfather' Élie*" (30). Derrida's taste thus involves an expansion of Augustine's own metaphors of milk and birdlime, of tears, lime, and slime, the quickening blood, the paternal breast, the steamy waters, and the viscous concupiscence that are so intertwined in Augustine's experience that his memorial for Monica always leaks, always exudes more liquids than can be contained in memory of her.

Derrida's guilt—the guilt of the purest of bastards, bastards such as Ishmael or Adeodatus—would therefore have to do with many things, and we might as well list them. His guilt arises from the happpenstance that God comes to "circulate among the unavowables" in his writing and is invariably brought down to earth—in "the violence of the void through which God goes to earth to death in me" (30, 51); that there is "*too much* love" in the writer's life (30); that the Narcissus at the heart of this mama's boy practices nothing so much as "*autofellocircumcision*"; that the petty thefts—of grapes or pears or ribbons—are essential to his own *Circumfession,* inasmuch as "confessions of theft [are] at the heart of autobiographies" (31); that his mourning, rather than withdraw its investments, as Freud advises, "capitalizes" on and consumes the other, eating the anaclitic (m)other, himself acting out the role of the (m)o(u)ther; that his mourning betrays or slanders or salivates over both the mother and the son (32); that the writer is at best "a half-mourning satyr," deriving more public pleasure from tears than even Augustine or his imploring mother, always the little boy crying to the mummy who is always crying over him when he is ill or in danger or about to set off on a journey, and that the satyr deceives both her and his readers, whom he loves to "'zap'" in writing (33–34; 40); that he wishes on his own mother the euthanasia she wishes for herself, or would continue to wish if the lethargy and oblivion due to her disease were not so total (34); that the writer in the depths of himself is heartless, ultimately "'without-interest,'" the perfect Kantian, before his own circumcision and the death of his own mother (36); that he prides himself on his adolescent rejection of every "nonproteiform identity," after the manner of Gide (37); that he is like a virus that attacks the immune system, homing in on the "destinerrancy of desire" with a certain ruthlessness (38); that the one who has had too much love in his life has "*no doubt never known how to love*" (40); that he fakes a circuitous confession through "the ruse of avowal" in order never to have to own up to all his very real failings as a writer and as a man, his failure to be sufficiently lucid, his failure to love enough, his failure to aid the Jews of Europe during World War II, when, admittedly, he was a fourteen- or fifteen-year-old boy in Algeria (41, 58–59); that he confuses the most sacred rite of his people with other so-called profane and obscene matters—"*imagine the loved woman herself circumcising (me), as the mother did in the biblical narrative, slowly provoking ejaculation in her mouth just as she swallows the crown of bleeding skin with the sperm as a sign of exultant alliance, her legs open, her breasts between my legs, laughing, both of us laughing, passing skins from mouth to mouth like a ring, the pendant on the necklace round her neck*" (41); that he, the purest of lubricious bastards, is thus also "the truest of false prophets" (42); that he is more destructive of Augustine's text than any genealogist can be, when, for example, he transforms the sublimity of Augustine's "book of the heavens," "spread out like a skin" (*Confessions* XIII, 15), into his own insistent fellative fantasies, which simply have to be quoted in full here each time they occur, as in the present instance: "I do not have the other under my skin, that would be too simple, the other holds, pulls, stretches, separates the skin from my sex in her mouth, opposite or above me, she makes me sperm in this strange condition" (43); that he will also be made to pay the penalty for such offenses, joining "the adorers of the goddess" who one day will run through the streets (for how long? one must wonder) "with their severed penises in their hands before throwing them deep into the houses" (44), except that this writer throws his onto the page; that the writer fears the fact that he *resembles* his mother more and more, and that his mother is daily becoming "a more and more dead desire" (46–47); that the thinker writes in order to subvert both Descartes and Freud ("I am, I think . . . without narcissistic counterpart"), yet continually collapses back into an eternal recurrence of self-preoccupation ("I am sighing to know until when I will be going round myself in this way") (48); that the little boy who weeps for his mum is guilty in fact of mummification, "as though I were proceeding with the interminable embalming of Mother alive," even though he promises to denounce what he is doing at some later, more vigilant moment, "letting my mother go or letting her down, already burying her under the word and weeping her in literature" (49); that the one thing he is willing to "sign" for is the fact that in the history of humanity he is *both* the happiest, luckiest, and most euphoric of persons, "drunk with uninterrupted enjoyment," *and* simultaneously "constantly sad, deprived, destitute, disappointed, impatient, jealous, desperate, negative and neurotic," along with the fact, mentioned above, that his family *both* singled him out as its favorite *and* excluded him, hence that he was "an excluded favorite" (50, 52); that he toys with suicide in the terrifying ambiguity of giving and taking a life ("*I don't take my life, mais je me donne la mort*") (53); and, finally, that he toys with his by now thoroughly zapped, benumbed, insensate, and livid readers in such a variety of ways that "nobody will ever know what is happening between us" (54).

Such guilt, so richly and multifariously deserved, culminates in the most culpable and vulnerable (*coupable*) of all deeds or omissions, namely, the writer's admission that the need to be "charged," to be accused, is the greatest indulgence of all. Derrida notes "the extent to which avowal, even for a crime not committed, simply secretes meaning and order, an intelligibility that arrests"; the subject is thus "constituted by the category [κατἀγορεῖν, public accusation], the hiatus finally circumscribed, edged, the subject configured by the knife of this economy"—*je suis . . . coupable,* I am both culpable and "cuttable" (56). Accuse me, make me your cutout, even if, as the Joker says, it's so hard to stay in the lines. To convert, to circumcise, one needs self-recrimination and groveling above all, or beneath all, as Nietzsche will have said: "*to begin with scenes of guilt in some sense faultless . . . , you have to let yourself be 'charged,' as they say in English . . .* this fault which nonetheless is all Hebrew to me," although circumcision is "older than Abraham" (57–58). A guilt that announces itself as an indulgence, however, is either feigned guilt or feigned indulgence: it is not so much *true* as a *making* true, a made-up true, a circumfabulation, avowed with all the force of faith, with the full conviction of the faithful witness. Faithful witness? Perhaps more like a perjured witness, a Marrano, a "pig."[17]

*Marrano,* "pig," too slippery and too catholic to be either Jew or Christian; Echo, too protean and too polymorphous to be Narcissus as either man or woman in either thigh or jaw or throat. If Derrida is merely one of the many who claim to be the last Jew, he is doubtless the first man to exhibit penis envy while gazing on his sex. "It only happens to me," he mutters at the end, precisely in this "*Everybody's Autobiography*" of *Circumfession.*

Yet for all the shiftiness, for all the confessing without apology, for all the (dis)simulation, there will have been *something like* witness. It is the distracted, traumatized, yet wily witness of a bloody remnant—the remains and remainders of a (m)other and of a (m)other's son or daughter. If both the narcissism and the anythingarianism are so excessive that their echoes are endless, this distracted, traumatized, but ever wily witness, this *distrait* who taints his mind and contrives with all his might, *will nevertheless never cease to mourn,* even if his mourning will disperse and disseminate in the contingencies and happenstances, the leakages and seepages that make our life the perilous sea voyage that it is—a life headed on the (m)other heading, but forever without destination. A life in that sense doubled over, bereaved, and ultimately abandoned by the phantom (m)other, who in the end does fail to survive, who goes *zu den Aschen selbst.* A mourning thus utterly bereft of witness: "this secret truth i.e. severed from truth i.e. that you will never have had any witness, *ergo es* [therefore you are], in this very place, you alone whose life will have been so short, the voyage short, scarcely organized by you, with no lighthouse and no book, you the floating toy at high tide and under the moon, you the crossing between these two phantoms of witnesses who will never come down to the same" (59).

## Raptures of Mourning

In the suddenness and the long while of mourning, in the *Angst* and the *tiefe Lange-weile* that Heidegger thought might serve as the grounding attunement of human existence as such, may we find the ties that bind time and mourning? Can there be a temporal interpretation of mourning *and* a mourning of temporal interpretations? One of the ways of understanding Heidegger's thought after *Being and Time* is the way of mourning, in which the death that is in each case mine pales before the abandonment of beings by being. Ironically, such abandonment introduces into Heidegger's thought an element of ἔρως, so that one may begin to dream of a history or sending of being in terms of the erotic—something we never dreamed Heidegger could have considered. Yet if I am right, in the *Beiträge zur Philosophie* of 1936–38 he does conjure up such an erotic or daimonic history, although quite cryptically and anxiously. There is a Heidegger who thinks the erotic, and precisely in the context of abandonment and withdrawal. There is a Heidegger who dreams of becoming a Derrida, just as there is a Derrida who marvels at the staying power of Heidegger's analysis of existence and temporal ecstasy. Perhaps they meet in raptures of mourning.

It would be foolish, however, to wish to conflate Heidegger's and Derrida's Augustine, or Freud's and Nietzsche's Augustine, into one figure. Why should Augustine be *one* figure for anyone? And why should one wish to collapse Derrida back into Heidegger, or project the spirit of Heidegger forward as a Heidegger *revenant* in Derrida, even if Derrida does insist that only a matter of *style* separates them? If Heidegger turns to Augustine because of *cura, concupiscentia oculorum,* and (as I am insisting, without the evidence to prove it) the *raptim transvolat,* Derrida is himself not untroubled by care, concupiscence, and the suddenness of blood. If Heidegger places his incomplete magnum opus upon his mother's deathbed nine days before her final breath, Derrida writes his opusculum in Santa Monica eighteen months before his mother's final demise, already brooding on the loss of destination in the writing and the dying. Perhaps there never was anyone to write for, but the philosophers now know this better than ever.

When does mourning commence? Without the *possibility* of mourning, Heidegger and Derrida and Augustine would agree, whether it be a proleptic mourning of one's own death in readiness for anxiety or an equally proleptic mourning of one's own (m)other, there would be no commencement, no *transibo.* Mourning does not slice into an already constituted time; rather, in some unthought and undiscerned way, mourning opens time, whether in the desire to have a conscience, if memory is conscience, or the desire to confess—and confess in writing—the (m)other.

One of the motivations for thinking about ecstatic temporality and mourning is the possibility that such thought will enhance our reading of the *Confessions* themselves. Augustine's text would not be a life story that, having raveled to its end, cursorily mourns the mother and then philosophizes interminably about memory, time, and eternity. It would instead be a text that at each ecstatic instant of mourning—mourning its own past life, its mother and both its fathers, its own bastard child, its lovers in and out of Africa—is transported by sudden suffering, swept away by its peculiar ecstasy of tears. The book itself would take and give time to recount the things that happened so suddenly, as the future fled to past; it would take and give all the time in the world to work through each precipitate loss. Taking and giving the time to confess, it would confess time even as it professes eternity. For both time and eternity, that is, both appropriate and inappropriate time, are instants of seizure or rapture. What relevance would a perdurant "now" have for an ecstasy that is always flying by, dashing ahead, or crossing on another heading, an ecstasy in which no excess of piety delivers us to the farther shore? What relevance would an altar and a monument have unless they contained a reliquary, a crypt for that slippery relic of Eve that is Augustine's (m)other in himself—the self of his self, the wash of the sea, secretion of milky tears, ecstasies of spending?

# Conclusion

## Affirmation Without Issue

This chance (affirmation without issue) can come to us only
from you, do you hear me? Do you understand me? (. . .)
And I, the purest of bastards, leaving all sorts of bastards
just about everywhere . . .
—Derrida, *The Post Card from Socrates to Freud and Beyond*

. . . the *hybris* of the prophet sent off for having had himself
assigned a mission whose indecipherable letter arrives only
at himself who understands it no better than anyone else . . .
—Derrida, *Circumfession*

I stand, so to speak, with an unposted letter bearing the
extra regulation fee before the too late box of the general
postoffice of human life.
—James Joyce, *Ulysses,* "Circe"

Shifty and traumatized at once, the purest of bastards zaps his readers and loses
his contemporaries, but always for the sake of the promise of memory.
Trenchant, merciless, relentless in his pursuit of undecidability, he is always at
work on mourning, always with considerable art, and always affirmatively. In
the end, we have a right to ask about this odd mix of purity and bastardy; we
doubtless are obliged to ask about the possibilities of affirmation. For what can
affirmation mean to a thought that is dedicated to undecidability? What can
affirmation mean to a thought that dismantles, deconstructs, "destructs,"
disquiets, and disconcerts? Even if one quells one's own hysteria in the face of

the tidal wave, what about that unshakable, decisive, apparently always already decided undecidability? Would not undecidability breed halfhearted affirmation? Would not deconstruction find itself always on the verge of affirmation, yet never quite making it? And *can* one remain on the very verge of affirmation? Can one hesitate on the hither side of affirmation? Or must one alter the question in the following way: Can one today do anything else than hesitate on this side of affirmation? Must one today mourn affirmation?

What remains today, here, now, of absolute affirmation? As Hegelian absolute knowing fades away beneath the sound of the *glas,* does Nietzschean unstinting affirmation whir through the air like a leaping arrow? Does affirmation in the grand style, launched as the Nietzschean cry *da capo! da capo! take it from the top!* shatter the spell of mourning? Or does such a cry remain stuck in our throats, as though we were the last human beings, the scarred and flummoxed human beings who are members of a decomposing race, creatures who know nothing of the bow's tension and the arrow's flight?

Even if we should muster the strength for a double affirmation, for a *yes* to our every *yes,* how should we prevent the Zarathustran cry *ja! ja!* from dwindling to the asses' braying *I-A! I-A!?* How should we prevent affirmation from becoming a consolation—yet another hee-haw from our domesticated beasts of burden? Can one escape the decadence of redemptive *willing?* Can one who is caught up in the work of mourning, tracing withdrawals and losses in works of art and philosophy, affirm and reaffirm affirmation *without issue?*

If one can no longer affirm the innocence of becoming without recoiling like a new angel before the terrors of a history haunted by guilt, what becomes of Nietzschean golden laughter? Or if, by contrast, one can never affirm the innocence of becoming one time only, once and for all, does not reaffirmation itself inevitably involve strains of mourning? Finally, does not such mourning remain eminently unsuccessful, nonrecuperative, perhaps altogether impossible and even in default?

Are not our works of art and thought distraught, are they not works of ressentiment? Is not our laughter a kind of shadow play, a snigger at worst, at best a weary and jaded chortle, a kind of secondhand laughter by hearsay, a *ouï-dire,* a *oui-rire?* Does not affirmation today become an engendering of little bastards *oui oui* just about everywhere? Once they are engendered, do we not abandon them, so that they are absolutely vulnerable to the most insidious kinds of contamination? Do we not expose them without mercy or remorse to the worst sorts of violence, as though the little bastards, crying *oui oui oui oui* all the way home, were no issue at all for us, as though we ourselves were absolutely sterile and without issue?

Does affirmation have any chances today, here, now? Is *aujourd'hui* an *aujourd'oui?*

—Yes! yes! say some.

—No, not at all! others demur.

—Yes and no! say the majority, in this age of pusillanimous compromise and cagey correctness.


## Mourning and Affirmation Revisited

The oeuvre of Jacques Derrida, from the beginning up to the present moment, and let us hope well beyond the here and now of today, elaborates affirmation as such with every breath of its body, albeit always with a sense of the sacrifices that affirmation elicits from those who affirm. The labors of deconstruction proceed always and everywhere as potlatches of dissemination: nowhere do they yoke the beast of burden to its traditional toil; never do they seek to console. And yet the beast of sacrifice is never far off: there there is always the forfeit, the gage to language, hostages to history, and promises made to the world. Always there there is ash.

In a number of books, especially since *Memoirs for Paul de Man,* Derrida has linked the question of affirmation with mourning and with a very vulnerable sort of memory. As noted at the outset of the present book, it is the *promise* of memory that structures the double or even numberless *oui oui* in the dire situation of a frustrated mourning, an always unsuccessful mourning, a mourning in default:


. . . dem
Gleich fehlet die Trauer.[1]


If the stratagems of successful mourning are foiled, if introjection and incorporation of the bereaved friend or family member are well-nigh indistinguishable, and if I am left bereft, in memory of the mourned other, left *alone* in order to bear his or her name, then the very promise of memory appears as a kind of slipping away, a kind of *lapsus*. In the words of Heidegger, as modified by Paul de Man, *Die Sprache (ver)spricht (sich):* language promises itself, but in so doing misspeaks. Successful mourning, according to Freud, must withdraw one by one all its once fond but now excruciating memories of the beloved. It must surrender the departed friend or parent or child to oblivion, clutching at the consolation prize Freud laconically calls *Amlebenbleiben*, "staying alive." Such success—Derrida counters—would jeopardize our fidelity to the memory of the other. However, the stratagems of both the limited interiorization of introjection and the infinite interiorization of encryptment miscarry, and they do so in such a way, as I shall suggest by way of conclusion, that the very default of mourning opens a space for the double yes, the *oui* to the *oui*.

No doubt the tonality of such double affirmation differs from the halcyon tone of Zarathustran yes-saying, the golden laughter of "the convalescent." Yet Nietzsche too struggles to avoid asinine affirmation; he too insists on saying *no* and doing *no* in the face of the history and horrors of the world. Likewise, Pierre Klossowski affirms the amnesia that lies at the heart of a recurrent, intermittent affirmation, the anamnesic amnesia that expels every stable self— every Narcissus, though not the anaclitic Echoes—from the circuit of affirmative return.[2] To will eternal recurrence of the same one more time, to remember the thought and to welcome it once again with exhilaration, is to suffer periodic oblivion and recurrent fragmentation: as we saw in Chapter 6, thinking eternal recurrence of the same demands the *surrender of the same* once and for all, but always once again, one more time, the same old thing forever. Both Nietzsche and Klossowski understand affirmation as impossible mourning and as the yes to laughter. Derridian affirmation shares the tonality of this *amor fati* that can be neither sheer enthusiasm nor paltry consent, neither gregarious good cheer nor pious acquiescence. It is the tonality of an affirmation that is always on the verge.

Nevertheless, the tonality of Derridian affirmation, affirmation without issue, is not simply somber, and never truly lugubrious, even if mourning always sets the tone. Everywhere in Derrida's texts on memory and mourning we find an irrepressible *mirth*, the periodic *éclat de rire*, the recurrent undertone of hilarity, the generous spray of chuckles. Always in these texts (such as *Memoirs for Paul de Man* and *Two Words for Joyce*)[3] there is storytelling, tales that recount travels and travails, from the man who says he has never known how to tell a story. Tales of a yogurt in Ohio called *Yes* (which advertises: "Bet you can't say No to Yes!"), or of a typical American tourist in a souterrain newspaper kiosk in Tokyo (who confronts Derrida: "So many books! Which is the definitive one? Is there any?"), or of the puissant international society of Joyce scholars, the most terrifying bastards in the world of literary criticism (who, when Derrida, over the phone, refers to the French word *lui*, reply to him: "The Louis have not yet been detected in Joyce as far as I know"). Always and everywhere a kind of errant storytelling, a protracted archeology of the frivolous. Not merely as comic relief—which, however, is where the work of modern tragedy often gets done—but as a recurrent interruption of the earnest rhetoric. The storytelling seeks to avoid all down-in-the-mouth discourse by means of an ephemeral euphoria. (It seems to me that this is often the function of at least one of the voices in Derrida's recent polylogues: to shatter the spirit of gravity even when the matters under discussion are grave.) It is not cheerfulness or a will to good humor or equanimity or sanctity. It is, rather, an illicit love of chance, a dalliance with droll coincidence. Not black humor or even Jewish humor, not *Galgenhumor* or sardonic humor, but an affirmative laughter light on its feet and easy on its reader, as though unwilling to sacrifice anything to Zarathustra's dwarf, especially when it comes to the most serious matters, such as works of mourning, art, and affirmation. In short, there is in Derrida a kind of *gratia* that enables a theory of mourning to go hand in hand with a joyous, joyceous praxis, letting mockery go, turning a deaf ear to the scornful laughter of the all-powerful and responding with "laughters low."

Granted all this affirmed and affirmative generosity, however, why the talk here and throughout the present book of bastardy? For in the English and American idioms in which I am writing, in the language of the streets, bastards are made, not born: a bastard, a *true* or *real* bastard, as we say, is one who consistently maltreats others, deceiving, cutting, and undercutting them. Zapping them.

I once asked Giorgio Agamben at the Collegium Phaenomenologicum in Perugia (the year was 1987) whether the bastard reasoning of Plato's *Timaeus* (52b 2: λογισμῷ τινι νόθῳ), which he was addressing in his seminar, might be more accessible to "a real bastard" than to a poet or thinker of *Gelassenheit*. Derrida turned to me and interjected: "But that is the problem, isn't it? What is a *real* or *true* bastard?"

Herewith my response, somewhat delayed, but well considered.

## The Purest Bastard of the West

It is, I confess, still difficult for me to identify the purest bastard of the West, certainly more difficult than it was for Heidegger to identify the purest *thinker* of the West (Nietzsche's Socrates) or the *last* thinker of the West (Socrates' Nietzsche). For there is competition for the nomination. Whoever in the end will walk off with the laurels, one thing is certain: the purest of bastards

throughout Occident and Accident alike will be the one who allies himself or
herself most intimately with *writing*. Yet the bastardisms of writing and of
being—of what Heidegger calls *Seinsverlassenheit*, the abandonment of beings
by being, and of what Derrida calls *destinerrancy*, the radical insecurity to which
all destining, sending, and writing are exposed—still call on us to *think*, so that
a confusion of all the old grandfathers is probably inevitable. Allow me in the
final pages of the present book, however, to turn exclusively to the bastardism
of *writing*.

Derrida's genealogy of writing in "Plato's Pharmacy" is by now classic. If
the *logos-père* is that-which-is, then the *logos-fils*, mimicking that-which-is,
writes itself in two forms or moments of familial repetition. The traditional
domesticity of being and *logos* depends on our being able to distinguish, between
two repetitions of writing: the one sort of writing is putatively originary,
memorious, ἔνδοθεν, *für sich, ganz-bei-sich, chez soi;* the other sort is derived
and deprived, hypomnesic, ἔξοθεν, extrinsic, estranged, and errant. As
Derrida's *Glas* demonstrates in some detail, the genealogy of writing in the
West has always been an affair of speculative fathers and sons, the (m)other (as
the prohibited-desired) having been abandoned on the shore or at the grave
site and bypassed in a conspiracy of silence. Writing is forever an affair that
secretes itself again and again as (impossible) legitimation, (inevitable)
contamination of all domesticities, (invariable) confusion and interweaving of
lines and alignments, and (unstoppable) proliferation of genealogies. Writing
is the orphan-bastard in distress, without public assistance, without ever having
had a proper apprenticeship; writing is both a wandering phantom abandoned
by the father and a subversive parricide living off the fruits of his deferred crime:
"It [i.e., the orphan-bastard of *writing*] rolls (275e 1: κυλινδεῖται) this way
and that like someone who has lost his way, who doesn't know where he is
going, having strayed from the correct path, the right direction, the rule of
rectitude, the norm; but also like someone who has lost his rights, an outlaw,
a pervert, a bad seed, a vagrant, an adventurer, a bum. Wandering in the streets,
he doesn't even know who he is, what his identity—if he has one—might be,
what his name is, what his father's name is."[4]

How does such duplicitous writing contrast with or conform to the double
writing of yeses, of affirmation without issue? Who is this *logos-fils*, this son
of the *logos?* It is both a he and a she in the dative, a *lui*, and it is also a yes,
a *l'oui*. Hence a Louis—who has not yet been thoroughly researched by the
Joyce scholars. For Louis is one of the purest of bastards. That is to say, Louis
Hegel, the firstborn son of Georg Wilhelm Friedrich Hegel, the bastard son
of spirit.

# A Gift of the French

Hegel could have named him Adeodatus, "Gift of God," but he did not. He named him *Ludwig*, or *Louis*, after his brother. Louis Hegel was born in 1807, the year of spirit's own birth in the *Phenomenology of Spirit*. He died at the age of twenty-four in 1831, some ten weeks before his own illustrious father's death. Ludwig Hegel, called *Louis* as a young boy, as though he were a gift of the French, was the illegitimate eldest son of Hegel and the third illegitimate child of Christiana Burckhardt-Fischer, Hegel's landlady in Jena. Louis, the bastard son of spirit, was removed from his wayward mother's influence (the two other children to whom she had already given birth were by two different fathers) when he was four, and sent to spirit's bookseller, Friedrich Frommann. He was sent thence to Frommann's sisters-in-law, who ran a boarding school for boys. In 1817, at the age of ten, he was taken back into the bosom of his father, joining his stepmother, Marie von Tucher, and the couple's two legitimate sons, Karl and Immanuel, born in 1813 and 1814, respectively. Young Louis was always treated well in his paternal home—of that the editors and biographers of spirit are quite certain. Louis received the best of care, both as a lad in the schoolmistresses' household and as an adolescent in the house of his father and stepmother. Marie was always kind to him, we are assured of that. No doubt she assumed too great a burden when she received her husband's bastard into her own home; yet she was always decent to the boy, always treated him fairly, although things were particularly difficult for her at the gift-giving time of Christmas and on birthdays.

Despite all the generosity and largesse of spirit, son of spirit waxed listless, grew moody and morose as he entered puberty. While attending the French *Gymnasium* in Berlin (once again, a gift of the French), Louis determined to become a doctor of medicine. He was clever enough to become a physician, and he was also quite capable in languages, especially Greek, Latin, and French. However, Louis's father demurred. Hegel insisted on a mercantile career for the boy. Louis, whatever his patrimony, was not to the professions born. Farmed out once again to the same family, that is, to spirit's bookseller's in-laws, who were now living in Stuttgart, and pursuing an apprenticeship with a merchant, a jobber by the name of Jobst, son of spirit was still listless, moody, and morose. However, he now grew increasingly cunning, spiteful, and rebellious. He fought with one of the schoolmistresses' sons. Frau Frommann took the view that the bastard was hard-hearted. For no apparent reason, Louis pilfered the paltry sum of eight groschen from his adoptive family—or so the accusation ran. There were scenes of recrimination; he was expelled from his apprenticeship and from both his bastard families. His father denounced and disowned him, having already deprived him of the world-historical name *Hegel*. For Louis now bore the name Fischer, the maiden name of his defunct mother.

Louis's half sister, Auguste Theresia, six years his elder, was the only person in the world before whom Louis's brittle heart softened. *And this is the sole being, this sister of mine, the only one in the world with whom I have not had the slightest hint of a quarrel, not an inkling of strife.* From the scanty documentation we have, it seems clear that she too loved him. Not that a bastard sister's love avails. It avails not. Louis was doomed.

Spirit apparently arranged an enlistment for Ludwig Fischer (no longer a *Hegel*, now a mere tattered remnant of the son of spirit) in the Dutch Foreign Legion. Before Ludwig set sail for Djakarta in 1825, at age eighteen, he saw to it that his old guitar and his autograph album found their way to his beloved half sister. His autograph album is not without distinction: into it, in the year 1817, on the occasion of the ten-year-old boy's departure from Jena for the house of his father, the prescient Goethe, who knew what it takes to make true bastards, wrote the following verse:

> Als kleinen Knaben hab' ich Dich gesehn
> Mit höchstem Selbstvertraun der Welt entgegen gehn;
> Und wie sie Dir im Künftigen begegnet,
> So sei getrost von Freundes Blick gesegnet.

> I saw you when you were a little boy,
> Striding confidently into the world's employ;
> No matter how that world may treat you in the end,
> Take solace from the gaze of your friend,

Jena, March 30, 1817                                    Goethe

Another acquaintance of Ludwig's cited Goethe's line "Edel sei der Mensch" (Let the human being be noble), jotting it into the boy's book, then adding: "As I pass on to you this fecund saying, my dear Ludwig, to accompany you on your way, I think of your excellent father, who will show you in life what the poet here promises."

Two months after his six-year term of military duty expired, on August 28, 1831, Ludwig Fischer died of "*febris inflammatoria*," which could have been due to anything from malaria to cholera to a sexually transmitted disease, in a military hospital in Djakarta. Ten weeks later his illustrious, estranged father died in Berlin of a mysterious fever that may have been caused by a cholera epidemic, said to have "come out of the East." To the bitter end the son of spirit remained one of the purest of bastards—for he himself wrote very little, and almost nothing has been written about him.[5]

## Redoubled Affirmation

The purest of bastards, devoted to his sister, or half sister, would surely have applied himself to the thought of the χώρα, the receptacle, (m)other and nurse of all becoming. For the χώρα is the proper subject of a bastard discourse. "She" is ungenerated yet not quite eternal, a form invisible yet seen as through a glass darkly, a thought accessible only to a bastard logistics. Ficino translates λογισμῷ τινι νόθῳ as *adulterina ratione,* while Schelling tries desperately to separate it from "true, in-forming imagination," *wahre Ein-bildung,* condemning the bastard logistics as *die falsche Imagination.* No matter how we may translate it, however, bastard logistics is the site of (the thought of) writing, the site of the purest bastardy.

And yet, to pose the question once again: Why the hint of malfeasance in the *true* or *real* bastard? It is as though the contamination of "good" writing by the "bad" produced something far more monstrous than mere textuality—or as though textuality were more malicious than we supposed. It is as though contamination of the generous *yes* by the complaisant *yes,* contamination of unstinting affirmation—affirmation with no ax to grind, affirmation without mastery or mockery, without outcome or end, affirmation without issue—by the rancorous or burdensome *yes,* were more insidious than we believed.

It is undeniably true that Derrida himself plays constantly with such malice and perfidy, for example, in the *Circumfession* discussed in the last chapter and also in the "Envois" of *The Post Card,* which we shall now—by way of conclusion—peruse.[6] For here too the purest of bastards loses his contemporaries, gives them the slip, and it is a slip covered with writing. Each time the presumed addressee, the beleaguered reader, begs to know who is writing to whom about what, the presumptuous bastard that is writing rises off the page to meet him or her with joker in hand. It is as though "he" were the seducer whom Hegel so mightily fears in his *Philosophy of Right.* The writer declares "his" passionate love to "her," is all commitment—and yet *no contract, no debt, no sealed security, no memory will hold us—not even a child.* "He" proclaims "himself" devoted to memory, *me, the obsessive "passivist," the great fetishist of remembrance,* vows he is all ears, all hers, *I am but a memory, I love memory alone, and I love to remember you,* and yet calls upon "her" to prepare a conflagration *in order that affirmation is reborn at each instant, without memory.* "He" insists *that the absence of memory and the faith that is unsworn would be our chance, our condition,* and that *everything began with the joyous decision to write no more, the sole affirmation, our sole chance,* at which point "he," ever the faithful writer, writes *somewhat without believing a thing,* so that *from the first sending, there is no gift without absolute oblivion.* Thus "he" shares "his" intimacy with "us": *it is a loveletter, you have no doubt, and I am telling you, "Come," come back quickly,* and he solicits our clandestine participation in a *secret rendez-vous, Nôtre Dame Sunday afternoons in the crowd, during the organ concerts, or at a Grand Synagogue in the brouhaha at the end of Yom Kippur. Everything would be possible there.*

Yet the perfidy, the postal pestilence, and the scrivener's cruelty go farther. What scholar does not tremble with rage before the bastard? For "he" confuses Father Plato with other matters. *I want to reread the entire* corpus platonicum *and reside there permanently, as in a high-class bordello.* The venerable sires of an entire tradition *the old couple of bearded grandfathers* he attacks from behind, *I aposteriorize,* the bastard! Deftly evading every grasp *Oh, but yes, my overbidding, almost all my lapses are calculated—you will not catch me* writing and erasing simultaneously with the vengeance of a posterior Plato *unseen unsnatched, I am founding an entire institution on counterfeit money by demonstrating that there is no other kind,* he proves himself the bastard son of a menacing Socrates, a writing Socrates, *son of Hermes and Aphrodite,* and wends his wicked way. *Whence this infinitely subtle text . . . with a soulful candor that does not preclude the possibility of immense resources of bad faith.*

And so it goes, from *Socartes* [sic] to *Des Cartes* and beyond all possible postal *Pancartes.* Sparing no one *holocaust of children* the cruelest of memories, sparing not even "himself" *I'm destroying my own life* (in English in the original), the purest of bastards spares not even religion, confuses the faith of his fathers and mothers with chance *because the feast of Esther (Purim) is a feast of luck:* the purest of pure bastards *"Pur, that is the lot"* (in English in the original). Thoroughly irresponsible "himself," and cunningly so *Therefore, never a response or a responsibility . . . and, yes, that is our tragic lot, my sweet love, the terrifying lottery, but I begin to love you from the moment of what is impossible,* "he" elsewhere challenges "us" to read Heidegger and Levinas precisely in terms of responsibility. The selfsame bastard plays at being both Nietzsche's Empedocles *it is without end, I will never get there, the contamination is everywhere and the fire would never enkindle us* and Oedipus or Hamlet Senior *there are only poisoned legacies, and I myself have been terribly poisoned.* Yet it is all Kleistian puppet theater *I am more like the marionette, I am trying to follow the movement* from beginning to end. And does anyone in either France or the Midwest seriously believe for a single moment that there is a yogurt in Ohio called *Yes?*

Advocate of a bastard writing and an engorged philosophy, "he" titillates us with "his" scripted voice, yet in the end withholds the message and refuses to deliver *guess what she says.* The unregenerate bastard—as insolent as being itself when it abandons its beings—transgresses and betrays the very tradition he transmits transcribes translates *the vengeful conspiracy called* Platonism. He refuses to the bitter end to accept full or even partial responsibility for what "he" has written. *Obviously, when they read these words beneath my public signature, they will be right to (. . . to do what, exactly?) but they will be right: it isn't at all like that that that comes to pass, as you well know, my intonation at this moment is altogether different          I can always say 'This isn't me.'"*

In short, a bastard monstrosity *the only chance was monstrosity* and a monstrous bastardy are Derrida's dog tags. *I am monstrously faithful. You too. Fido, Fido, that's us.* The purest bastardism: affirmation of the absolute indistinguishability and undecidability of family lines and familiar identities *the nonfamily is still the family, the same network, the same destiny of filiation,* the flight from responsible family planning *my son's skateboard,* regression to the primal narcissistic phase *this miracle before which I shall always remain a child,* the ambivalence of all behaviors *I love my sadness like a child born of you,* and the polyversity of all languages, with the resulting false attributions, misquotations, and not by chance *Ich kenne* Dein *Los* instead of *mein Los* (from Nietzsche's *Echo Homey*), the creation of bastard phantasms by mental marital side steps, or *Seitensprünge, "to make one more leap on the side,"* projected by way of opposition *I have the impression that I am writing to my most alien homonym* and unleashed in order to perform lascivious solipsistic acts single-handedly *to give the other time, to allow them to cream all alone . . . , the purest gift of love,* until the inevitable crushing guilt, the groveling, the desire to be accused (we saw it most outrageously in the last chapter), the mourning, and the melancholy *le deuil—of me, of us in me.* Thus the confusion of generations *I shall speak of you, they will not know it[,] and of the I/us of my only daughter* culminates in incestuous thalassic fantasies *I shall drown myself in you, in your tears, in memory without end* and dreams of absolute reconciliation *This would be a sending of me that would not come from me,* etc.

The bastard, for all his hilarity, inevitably turns morose, moody, jealous, listless, chagrined, and ready for deception *you are right, I love you cannot be published, I shouldn't go crying it from the housetops* and yet infinitely cunning, *rusé,* spawning a narrative *full of secret dedications, full of collective murders, full of abortions right there in the confessional, . . . and the virgin who traverses it all with a lovesong. . . . They will believe that we are two. . . . We are the good-in-itself and they shall never find us* disseminating texts like little bastards on all sides, little bastards everywhere whispering little nothings, inventing dialogues that come to nothing "*—Hey, Socrates!—What?—Nothing.*" Laughing up his sleeve, as Alcibiades says of Socrates, who is the purest thinker of the West but the perfect bastard of irony, and laughing at whom? At his readers. Derrida's "dear readers," as John Llewelyn calls them. *The naive ones will believe that all the while I've known who I'm talking to, that the banks are shored up, one only need analyze. You don't say? . . . I am still laughing . . . I am always laughing . . . and as far as readers are concerned, at bottom I do not love them, not yet.* His struggling, bemused, abused, lost, unloved, utterly zapped, and virtually impossible addressees *will believe that we are two, that it is really you and I, that we are legally and sexually identifiable.*

You and I? Who is "you"? Here is one passage from *Circumfession* (section 49) that I neglected to cite in the foregoing chapter:

> and for 59 years I have not known who is weeping my mother or me— i.e. you "*when he says 'you' in the singular and they all wonder, who is he invoking thus, who is he talking to, he replies, but you, who are not known by this or that name, it's you this god hidden in more than one, capable each time of receiving my prayer, you are my prayer's destiny, you know everything before me, you are the god (of my) unconscious, we all but never miss each other, you are the measure they don't know how to take and that's why they wonder whom, from the depth of my solitude, I still address, you are a mortal god, that's why I write, I write you my god*" (9-4-81), to save you from your own immortality.

The purest of bastards believes that he is the Son of God, that God is his mummy. And she is.

Yes, yes, this delectable bittersweet malice, he is eminently capable of it; it is made for him, *lui,* yes, *l'oui,* the bastard. His bow, as Nietzsche would say, is unbearably tense, shooting its barbed arrows of love farthest, though never in a straight line. Yes, yes, affirmation without issue: affirmation without delimitable *Sachen,* always with *Aschen,* affirmation without exit, affirmation without progeny. Mourning itself is affirmation without issue, unless it is an abandoned litter of *oui oui*'s as a forfeit to language, to history, to the play of the world, and to the vicissitudes of friendship and love.

What is left to say? Or to write? The most appropriate response to the otherwise entirely understandable cries of "Bastard!" would be careful study of Derrida's recent eulogies for Emmanuel Levinas, Louis Marin, Louis Althusser, Gilles Deleuze, Sarah Kofman, and others. These texts are being edited and translated into English at the moment by Pascale-Anne Brault and Michael Naas, who have also commented on them more insightfully that I ever could here.[7] Allow me therefore to say only that the remarkable *tenderness* and *trenchancy* of these eulogies in each case let the work of the deceased come to word in the most telling way. In them the friendship of mourner and mourned is confirmed—and the promise of memory affirmed—in ways no reader is likely to forget. Of bastards real and true, it seems to me, Derrida is the *purest*.

What is left to say? Or to write? Only the need and desire to embrace today, here and now—through this my signature, signed by the flesh of my own hands—the malicious orphan who prowls among the legitimated thoughts of the legitimate thinkers, all of them validated by the academy, all of them blessed by their fathers and by their fathers' fathers' fathers' fathers (as Stan/Loretta says), under the shadows of hoary great-great-grandfathers—*Logos, Vernunft, Geist, Sein, das Unbewußte*—and who makes the acolytes of these legitimated thoughts quake and howl.

What is left to say? Or to write? Only the need and desire to affirm— without apology to those who cannot bear the strain of the bow or the barbs of the love or the curvature of the line—the great privilege and pleasure that has befallen me by a singular stroke of luck, which is to say, my having encountered numberless times now, as a half brother or half sister but always an integral friend, the purest of bastards.

# Notes

## Preface

1. See Catherine Malabou and Yvon Brès, eds., *Revue philosophique de la France et de l'étranger*, numéro spécial "Derrida," Presses Universitaires de France, no. 2 (April–June 1990). See 229–38 for an earlier version of my Conclusion, "Le plus pur des bâtards (Affirmation sans issue)."

## Introduction: *Memoria in Memoriam*

1. Friedrich de la Motte-Fouqué, "Undine: Eine Erzählung," in *Rittergeschichten und Gespenstersagen* (Munich: Verlag Lothar Borowsky, n.d.), 76; translation by the author, as are all other translations unless otherwise noted.

2. See Thomas Aquinas, *Summa theologiae*, prima secundae, q. 35–40, on the concupiscible appetites of *tristitia* and *dolor* and the irascible appetite of *desperatio*. I consider Descartes and Spinoza briefly later in this introduction. My thanks to the philosophers at Creighton University, especially Richard White, who invited me to be the Henri Renard Lecturer in 1994 and who on that occasion discussed an earlier version of the Introduction with me.

3. Friedrich Nietzsche, *Frühe Schriften*, ed. Hans Joachim Mette et al., 5 vols. (Munich: Deutscher Taschenbuch Verlag, 1994; a reprint of the historical-critical edition of the 1930s published by C. H. Beck, Munich), 1:21.

4. F. W. J. Schelling, *Abhandlung über das Wesen der menschlichen Freiheit und die damit zusammenhängenden Gegenstände*, vol. 7 of *Sämmtliche Werke* (Stuttgart: J. G. Cotta, 1860), 399.

5. I take the liberty of repeating these Homeric lines, which form the basis of a chapter (the third) in my *Daimon Life: Heidegger and Life-Philosophy* (Bloomington: Indiana University Press, 1992); the lines in question, from book XVII of *The Iliad*, are 426–47.

6. *The Epic of Gilgamesh*, ed. and trans. N. K. Sandars (Baltimore: Penguin Books, 1960), 91; cf. the German edition by Albert Schott and Wolfram von Soden (Stuttgart: P. Reclam, 1988), eighth tablet, p. 71, lines 3–8.

7. James Joyce, *Ulysses* (London: Bodley Head, 1960), 541.

8. Benedict de Spinoza, *Ethica*, pars III, definitiones no. 32; ed. and trans. Jakob Stern (Stuttgart: P. Reclam, 1977), 418–19. On the theme of mourning, see also propositio 67 of pars IV, 580–81: "The free human being thinks less of death than anything else."

9. René Descartes, *Œuvres et lettres*, ed. André Bridoux (Paris: Pléiade, 1953), 793; trans. John Cottingham, Robert Stoothoff, and Dugald Murdoch, *The Philosophical Writings of Descartes*, 2 vols. (Cambridge: Cambridge University Press, 1985), 1:402.

10. My analysis here owes much to that of Geoff Bennington in *Jacques Derrida* (Paris: Seuil, 1991); English translation published by the University of Chicago Press, 1993. See 140–56 in the French, 148–66 in the English. I shall cite this work as JD, with French/English pagination.

11. Jacques Derrida, *La voix et le phénomène* (Paris: Presses Universitaires de France, 1967), 106–7; trans. David B. Allison as *Speech and Phenomenon and Other Essays on Husserl's Theory of Signs* (Evanston, Ill.: Northwestern University Press, 1973), 95–96. Cited henceforth in the body of my text as VP, with French/English pagination.

12. Jacques Derrida, *Signéponge/Signsponge*, trans. Richard Rand, with French text *en face* (New York: Columbia University Press, 1984), 24–26; henceforth cited as SP, with page numbers.

13. See Jacques Derrida, *Glas* (Paris: Galilée, 1974), trans. John P. Leavey Jr. and Richard Rand (Lincoln: University of Nebraska Press, 1986), 8B of the French, 2B of the English. I shall cite the French/English pagination throughout my own text. For a reading of *Glas* that focuses on the theme of mourning, see Chapter 7. On the theme of remains and residues, see also Derrida, "Cartouches," in *La vérité en peinture* (Paris: Flammarion, 1978), 211–90; trans. Geoff Bennington and Ian McCleod as *The Truth in Painting* (Chicago: University of Chicago Press, 1987), 183–253.

14. Throughout my text I cite Freud according to the *Studienausgabe*, 10 vols. (Frankfurt am Main: Fischer, 1982), by volume and page.

15. See Nicolas Abraham and Marie Torok, *Le verbier de l'Homme aux loups*, with a preface by Jacques Derrida entitled "Fors" (Paris: Aubier-Flammarion, 1976).

16. Sigmund Freud, *Aus den Anfängen der Psychoanalyse*, ed. Ernst Kris (New York: Imago, 1950), 221.

17. Jacques Derrida, *Mémoires pour Paul de Man* (Paris: Galilée, 1988), 43; trans. Cecile Lindsay, Jonathan Culler, and Eduardo Cadava as *Mémoires for Paul de Man* (New York: Columbia University Press, 1986), 21; cited henceforth as MEM, with page numbers.

18. John Llewelyn, *Derrida on the Threshold of Sense* (London: Macmillan, 1986), 123.

19. Jacques Derrida, *Adieu à Emmanuel Lévinas* (Paris: Galilée, 1997), 12.

## Chapter 1: Broken Frames

1. Jacques Derrida, *La vérité en peinture*, 44–94/37–82. (I cite the French edition first, then the English, by page number.) My thanks to Ashraf Noor and Sabine Mödersheim— my friends for so many years now—for encouraging me to engage in these reflections. My thanks also to Professor Iris Därmann of the University of Lüneburg for sending me her recent book *Tod und Bild: Eine phänomenologische Mediengeschichte* (Munich: Fink Verlag, 1995). See esp. "Rahmenauffassung" (247–53), which focuses on the question of the frame. Professor Därmann's remarkable study takes its departure from both Plato and Husserl,

though its principal inspiration may be from Derrida and Barthes. It views the photographic image as an attempt to confront—but also, equally, to evade—the death of the other. The book's sustained meditation on portraiture and photography concludes with a consideration of "Trauer und Tod," mourning and the mortality of the other. Professor Därmann's book arrived too late for me to give it the attention it merits—I hope it will be a part of my readers' future, as it must be of mine.

2. I am thinking here as much of Moses Mendelssohn's, Christoph Martin Wieland's, and Johann Georg Hamann's responses to the question "Was ist Aufklärung?" as I am of Max Horkheimer and Theodor Adorno's "Dialektik der Aufklärung," the former in *Was ist Aufklärung?* ed. Ehrhard Bahr (Stuttgart: P. Reclam, 1974), 3–8, 17–28, the latter in *Dialektik der Aufklärung: Philosophische Fragmente* (Frankfurt am Main: Fischer, 1969 [1944]), esp. 151–86, "Elements of Anti-Semitism: The Limits of Enlightenment."

3. In what follows, I cite Immanuel Kant, *Kritik der Urteilskraft*, ed. Gerhard Lehmann (Stuttgart: P. Reclam, 1966), as KU, with page number, in the body of my text; Kant's *Kritik der praktischen Vernunft*, ed. Joachim Kopper (Stuttgart: P. Reclam, 1966), I refer to as KpV. In order easily to distinguish "Parergon" the chapter from "Parergon" the section, I place the former in italics rather than quotation marks.

4. G. W. F. Hegel plays on the word *Bei-spiel* in *Phänomenologie des Geistes*, 6th ed., ed. Johannes Hoffmeister (Hamburg: F. Meiner, 1952), 80 and 484. See also Derrida's *Glas*, 266A/238A.

5. An aside: in the English word *color* the glutinous or viscous nature of *Farbe* is altogether suppressed; in the English-speaking world, the world of Newtonian optics, color is translucent and well-nigh colorless, like a veil of gauze; it does not smell, does not stain the clothing; German *Farben* are essentially more complicated, more *material*, more *pitchlike*. *Pigment* is therefore much the better translation.

6. Charles Baudelaire, *Œuvres complètes* (Paris: Seuil "l'Intégrale," 1986), 546–65, esp. sec. 11, "Éloge du maquillage," 561–63.

7. In *Marges de la philosophie* (Paris: Minuit, 1972), 31–78; trans. Alan Bass as *Margins of Philosophy* (Chicago: University of Chicago Press, 1982), 29–67.

8. "Economimesis" is especially relevant to my discussion of Kant's third *Critique*. See Sylviane Agacinski et al., *Mimésis des articulations* (Paris: Aubier-Flammarion, 1975), 55–93.

9. Martin Heidegger, *Nietzsche*, 2 vols. (Pfullingen: G. Neske, 1961), 1:126–35; in the English translation, 4 vols. (San Francisco: HarperCollins, 1991), 1:107–14; henceforth cited as N, with German/English pagination.

10. Nietzsche may have come across Stendhal's remark (in his *Naples, Rome, and Florence,* 1854) in Baudelaire—in the very essay cited earlier, "The Painter of Modern Life." There, in the first section, "The Beautiful, Fashion, and Happiness," Baudelaire cites Stendhal, that "impertinent spirit," whose impertinences nevertheless lead us closer to the truth than anyone else's wisdoms, "en disant que *le Beau n'est que la promesse du bonheur.*" Baudelaire faults Stendhal for attaching beauty to something as variable as "happiness," yet affirms that this formulation at least puts the usual error "of the academicians" to rout. Baudelaire doubtless would have had less difficulty with the definition if Stendhal had chosen the rather more suggestive word *jouissance*. See Baudelaire, *Œuvres complètes,* 550.

11. Friedrich Nietzsche, *Kritische Studienausgabe*, ed. Giorgio Colli and Mazzino Montinari, 15 vols. (Berlin and Munich: Walter de Gruyter and Deutscher Taschenbuch Verlag, 1980), 5:347. (I shall henceforth cite Nietzsche's works from this edition by volume

and page in the body of my text.) The fact that the statues are undraped, *gewandlos*, makes one imagine that Nietzsche is in some way anticipating the entire problem of parerga here.

12. James Joyce, *Ulysses*, 225, 257, and 334.

13. See Jacques Derrida, *Éperons: Les styles de Nietzsche* (Paris: Flammarion, 1978), and David Farrell Krell, *Postponements: Woman, Sensuality, and Death in Nietzsche* (Bloomington: Indiana University Press, 1986), esp. the introduction.

14. Immanuel Kant, *Die Religion innerhalb der Grenzen der bloßen Vernunft*, ed. Rudolf Malter (Stuttgart: P. Reclam, 1974), 67n and 198–270, passim.

15. One wonders what the relation might be between Kant's elevated *pulchritudo vaga* and the figure of woman that Hegel most fears, namely, that of *Venus vaga:* in his *Philosophy of Right* Hegel clearly wants to banish the wandering goddess of love, to subjugate Venus Kallipyge, or at least to domesticate her by chaining her to the hearth of civil society. Does Kant too want to tether *pulchritudo vaga*—to morality? See G. W. F. Hegel, *Grundlinien der Philosophie des Rechts*, Theorie-Werkausgabe in 20 vols. (Frankfurt am Main: Suhrkamp, 1970), § 161, 7:310. See also David Farrell Krell, "Lucinde's Shame: Hegel, Sensuous Woman, and the Law," in *Hegel and Legal Theory*, ed. Drucilla Cornell, Michel Rosenfeld, and David Gray Carlson (New York: Routledge, 1991), 287–300; revised and reprinted under the same title in *Feminist Readings of Hegel*, ed. Patricia Jagentowicz Mills (University Park: Pennsylvania State University Press, 1995), 89–107.

## Chapter 2: Echo, Narcissus, Echo

1. The myth is recounted by Robert Graves, *The Greek Myths* (Baltimore: Pelican Books, 1955), sec. 85. Echo does resurface in a recent text by Derrida entitled *Prégnances: Quatre lavis de Colette Deblé* (Paris: Brandes, 1993). Here Derrida celebrates Echo's ruses, her "echography": Echo is docile but ingenious, latching onto the final phonemes in a signifying chain and altering them to her own purposes. Thus, always in proximity to the elemental, and especially to the element of water, Echo both exposes herself to the painters' narcissism and exposes the inevitable *rupture* of such narcissism. She teaches a love of self that is in effect a love of an other, an other from whom we are separated, although conjoined in the same elementary solvent.

My thanks to Pascale-Anne Brault and Michael Naas for the invitation to write this chapter, first delivered as a lecture at their conference "Drawing from Philosophy: Derrida's *Memoirs of the Blind*," February 5, 1994.

2. Jacques Derrida, *Mémoires d'aveugle: L'autoportrait et autres ruines* (Paris: Réunion des musées nationaux, 1990); trans. Pascale-Anne Brault and Michael Naas as *Memoirs of the Blind: The Self-Portrait and Other Ruins* (Chicago: University of Chicago Press, 1993); cited henceforth in the body of my text, with French/English pagination.

3. Jean-Jacques Rousseau, *Essai sur l'origine des langues*, ed. Charles Porset (Paris: A. G. Nizet, 1970), 29. This announcement, on the second page of the very first chapter, which acclaims writing or drawing as a "livelier" expression of love, stands in sharp contrast with the later celebration of the *speech* of lovers who gather at the well—in chap. IX, "Formation des langues méridionales," esp. 123. This lively movement of the stick, *ce mouvement de baguette*, is precisely what spurs Derrida to one of his earliest formulations of the arche-writing

within speech: see *De la grammatologie* (Paris: Minuit, 1967), 327–44; trans. Gayatri Chakravorty Spivak as *Of Grammatology* (Baltimore: Johns Hopkins University Press, 1974), 229–42. Hereinafter cited as G, with page references.

4. My position in this chapter partly coincides with that of the "painter-beholder" described by Michael Fried in *Absorption and Theatricality: Painting and Beholder in the Age of Diderot* (Chicago: University of Chicago Press, 1980) and in *Courbet's Realism* (Chicago: University of Chicago Press, 1990). In the former work (at p. 92), Fried indicates that Diderot's desideratum for a work of art was that it "reach the beholder's soul by way of his eyes," and this by means of a three-stage process: (1) the work must call the beholder and draw her or him into the work (*attirer, appeller*); (2) the work must arrest the beholder, retaining him or her in intense absorption (*arrêter*); and (3) the work must enthrall the beholder (*attacher*). My position coincides insofar as I am a beholder of these works, appearing to fulfill "the one primitive condition" exacted by works of art, to wit, that they work on a beholder (p. 4). However, the discrepancy arises from the fact that I know nothing about the makers of the drawings I am beholden to in this chapter; in my ignorance and clumsiness, therefore, I shatter the hyphen of Fried's "painter-beholder."

5. Whether "Cigoli" (i.e., Lodovico Cardi, 1559–1613) is late enough to be a part of the seventeenth-century tradition of absorption, a tradition that declined before its resuscitation during the age of Diderot (Fried, *Absorption*, 43), I do not know. Yet Cigoli's *Narcissus* does absorb the eye of the beholder into the self-absorption of the hero himself. It may be that the mirror surface of the pond that separates the viewer from the hero, the pond that reflects yet also decapitates and desexualizes the hero, is the principal device by which both the beholder and the principal subject of the drawing are thoroughly absorbed.

6. Jacques Derrida, "Circonfession," in JD (cited in the Introduction).

7. It was an obsession that absorbed me, annulled me, utterly. Perhaps Félicien Rops, like Gustave Courbet, desired to *annul* the identity of the beholder—and even the "painter-beholder"—outside the work, desired to draw her or him wholly into the work, without anything left for the distractions of "theatricality" (cf. *Courbet's Realism*, 79). If that was Rops's intention, then with me he roundly succeeded—precisely by portraying a woman of the theater who is caught up in her own theatrical self-absorption!

8. Derrida makes much of Baudelaire's *Le peintre de la vie moderne* in *Memoirs of the Blind*, but focuses principally on Baudelaire's argument concerning the *mnemonic* character of drawing. My own reading of Baudelaire's essay is torn between section 5, "L'art mnémonique," and sections 9–12, on the dandy, on woman, "in praise of make-up," and on "women and daughters." See Baudelaire, *Œuvres complètes*, 559–64. Dandyism is a "cult of the self," particularly of the *homme blasé*, full of rebellion and yet a setting sun full of melancholy, while woman is "a being that is as terrible and as incommunicative as God." Further, Baudelaire is as interested in the feminine costume and ornament, the parergonal jewelry and the "paruregonal" makeup, as he is in the being who wears it. The folds of fashion on her are livelier than the skin of Saint Bartholomew, the flayed skin painted by Michelangelo into *The Last Judgment* as a self-portrait of his devastation. Eye shadow and rouge combine to make of the womanly eye "a window opening upon infinity," an infinity of which she alone is the priestess. Nevertheless, her temple is a secular "gallery" full of light and motion: "Elle a sa beauté, qui lui vient du Mal, toujours dénuée de spiritualité, mais quelquefois teintée d'une fatigue qui joue la mélancolie. Elle porte le regard à la horizon, comme la bête de proie; même égarement, même distraction indolente, et aussi, parfois, même fixité d'attention."

And, finally, I am caught by his portrait, after Constantin Guys, of *la comédienne:* "de la femme errante, de la femme révoltée à tous les étages. . . . Parmi celles-là, les unes . . . portent dans leurs têtes et dans leurs regards, audacieusement levés, le bonheur évident d'exister (en vérité pourquoi?). . . . Tantôt nous voyons . . . la maigreur enflammée de la phthisie . . . des nymphes macabres et des poupées vivantes dont l'œil enfantin laisse échapper une clarté sinistre . . . l'ombre de ses pointes sataniques . . . le regard du démon embusqué dans les ténèbres . . . rien que l'art pur, c'est-à-dire la beauté particulière du mal, le beau dans l'horrible . . . [la] fécondité morale" (564).

9. See Jacques Derrida, *Psyché: Inventions de l'autre* (Paris: Galilée, 1987), 275; this chapter is translated by Pascale-Anne Brault and Michael Naas, in *Continental Philosophy*, no. 1 (London: Routledge, 1987), 261–62. The following quotation appears on p. 281 of the French, p. 269 of the English. See Michael Fried's discussion of Roland Barthes's *Camera Lucida*, trans. Richard Howard (New York: Hill & Wang, 1981), a discussion that relates Barthes's *punctum* to Fried's thesis concerning resistance to theatricality, in *Courbet's Realism*, 282–83n.

10. On April 18, 1996, as I was preparing to read a paper on Derrida's "Circumfession" at another conference at DePaul, organized by Katherine Rudolph and Jason Drucker and devoted to contemporary readings of Augustine, I was called away by my own mother's death. Michael Naas read my paper for me. End of story. *Punctum. Punctum caecum.* What would it mean to be ready to write (about) this first and last story?

11. From the outset of *Courbet's Realism*, Michael Fried resists the notion "that Courbet's project, even in the self-portraits, was essentially narcissistic" (5). In his sixth chapter, "Courbet's 'Femininity,'" Fried suggests that "the painter-beholder—or his desire—is frequently thematized in Courbet's art as metaphorically feminine (or at least as bigendered), which suggests that the lesbianism of *Sleep* [Plate 12] may perhaps be seen as a transposition into an entirely feminine and manifestly erotic register of the aspiration toward merger that . . . was basic to Courbet's enterprise throughout his career" (206). Yet the *aspiration* of merger is not its fulfillment. Fried writes of Courbet's "quasi-corporeal movement into the painting" (212), *quasi* because, as Fried himself stresses, "*it was precisely the impossibility of literal or corporeal merger that made [Courbet's] project conceivable, or rather pursuable in the first place*" (269). Thus what one might take to be the painter's (masculist) possession of his (female) objects in a painting is made to tremble: Fried observes that "possession turns out to have unexpected consequences as the painter-beholder all but becomes his female surrogates" (222). Fried concedes that the assessment of the phrase *all but* remains difficult—and that such assessment is "inescapably political." Nevertheless, if the sexual embrace is "blind" (220, quoting Leo Steinberg), sexual identity is lost in the dark. It is not essential, it seems to me, to argue for the supremacy of the hand over the eye, for activity over passivity, as Fried does in "The Question of Narcissism" (274–78), in order to refute Narcissus. For both the desirous eye and the busy hand undo the very identity of Narcissus and leave us with Echo, or Echoes, of narcissism.

12. What I am here calling Freud's dream is, to be sure, what Lacan calls "fraud." *Fraud,* not *Freud.* In "The Signification of the Phallus" Lacan writes: "[T]o disguise this gap [i.e., the gap between subjects of need, objects of love, and causes of desire] by relying on the virtue of the 'genital' to resolve it through the maturation of tenderness (that is, by a recourse to the Other solely as reality), however piously intended, is none the less a fraud [*une escroquerie*]. Admittedly, it was French psychoanalysts with their hypocritical notion of genital oblativity who started up the moralizing trend, which, to the tune of Salvationist choirs [*au son d'orphéons salutistes*], is now followed everywhere." See Jacques Lacan, *Écrits* (Paris: Seuil,

1966), 692; English translation in *Feminine Sexuality*, ed. Juliet Mitchell and Jacqueline Rose (London: Macmillan, 1982), 81.

13. However much *Memoirs of the Blind* has to do with the father/son filiation, especially with regard to the great old (blind) men of the Bible, the drafts*woman* at the origin of all drawing *should*, as Derrida writes, "shed light on rather than threaten our point of view" (15/6 n. 1).

14. Euripides, *The Bacchae*, trans. William Arrowsmith, in *Euripides V* (Chicago: University of Chicago Press, 1959), 190, line 811.

15. Maurice Merleau-Ponty, *Le visible et l'invisible*, ed. Claude Lefort (Paris: Gallimard, 1964), 301–3; trans. Alphonso Lingis as *The Visible and the Invisible* (Evanston: Northwestern University Press, 1968), 248–49. This work will be cited as VI, with French and English pagination. The quote in the text may be found also in *Memoirs of the Blind*, 57/53.

16. Michael Fried notes that, however paradoxical it may seem, *sleep* is one of the most significant "absorptive states" for eighteenth-century French painting (*Absorption*, 31). For Courbet too, in the nineteenth century, images of sleep and "effects of virtual blindness" are vital to his project (*Courbet's Realism*, 13). Fried describes *The Wounded Man* as follows: "the upper half of the body of a wounded man, Courbet himself, reclining on his back in a wooded setting, his head propped against the base of a tree and his left hand grasping a fold of the dark brown cloak that covers much of his torso and presumably his lower body as well." Fried notes that the execution of this large painting "is broad and confident." He comments on the positioning of the body as follows: "[I]t almost seems we are obliged to look up at the sitter's head and face from below," as in the case of Rops's charcoal. "The wounded man's eyes are closed (though it is just possible that he is looking out from beneath his lids), and he appears on the verge of losing consciousness if he hasn't already done so. . . . At the same time we feel that the whole crepuscular scene expresses his condition, or to put this another way, that his consciousness although on the verge of extinction nevertheless flows out toward his surroundings. . . . [W]e seem to be dealing with a state of mind which, like intense reverie, involves both an extinguishing and a dilation of ordinary waking awareness" (*Courbet's Realism*, 57–58).

17. Note that I cite the *Confessions* by book (in Roman numeral) and chapter (in Arabic numeral) in my text, e.g., I, 7.

18. It was this highly mobile earring that absorbed Michael Fried in the discussion of Rops's charcoal that followed upon my initial presentation of this chapter. I thank him for his warm and insightful engagement, and above all for his published work, which I have been citing—though never enough—in these notes.

## Chapter 3: Mourning the Voice

1. See David Farrell Krell, "Engorged Philosophy: A Note on Freud, Derrida, and Differance," and idem, "Engorged Philosophy II," both cited in the Preface.

2. Jean-Paul Sartre, *La nausée* (Paris: Gallimard, 1938), 141.

3. Jacques Derrida, *Écriture et la différence* (Paris: Seuil, 1967), 335–37; trans. Alan Bass as *Writing and Difference* (Chicago: University of Chicago Press, 1978), 227–28.

4. Samuel Taylor Coleridge, "Dejection: An Ode," in *Selected Poetry and Prose of Samuel Taylor Coleridge*, ed. Donald A. Stauffer (New York: Modern Library, 1951), 79, lines 53–58.

5. I am indebted to David Wood for directing me to James's remarkable pages. See William James, *The Principles of Psychology*, 2 vols. (New York: Henry Holt, 1890), 1:299–302, henceforth cited in my text as PP, with page numbers.

6. See David Wood, "Time and the Sign," *Journal of the British Society of Phenomenology* 13, no. 2 (1982): 149; see also his book *The Deconstruction of Time* (Atlantic Highlands, N.J.: Humanities International, 1989).

7. Derrida cites Merleau-Ponty in *L'origine de la géométrie* (Paris: Presses Universitaires de France, 1962), 71, 116–18, 122, and in *De la grammatologie*, 155 n. 4 and 219 n. 6. In both places the bone of contention is Husserl's relation to ethnological science and the problem of historical-cultural relativism. Derrida rejects Merleau-Ponty's reading of the later Husserl, which would see a "striking difference" between the early and the late writings. Derrida is tempted to uphold a view that is "diametrically opposed" to Merleau-Ponty's: he argues that Husserl increasingly *excludes* the historical realm as his work proceeds—whatever the usual understanding of Husserl's *Krisis* may lead us to believe. Perhaps the most intriguing of these references is Derrida's rejection of an "existential" psychoanalysis of the style promoted by Merleau-Ponty. See G, 219 n. 6. Finally, see Derrida's forceful rejection of Sartre and Merleau-Ponty in *Philosophy in France Today*, ed. Alan Montefiore (Cambridge: Cambridge University Press, 1983), 38. (My thanks to Robert Bernasconi for these references.) For the more fruitful references to Merleau-Ponty in *Memoirs of the Blind*, see the preceding chapter.

8. However, it may be more true to say that for Husserl *memory* is closer to such evidence than *perception* is: see the discussion of Husserl in Chapter 6, which emphasizes the limits of both perception and memory with regard to evidence and which takes Husserl too to be a figure of *mourning*.

9. Of course, this only exacerbates the problem of accounting for boustrophedonic and other forms of writing—when the bodies that engage in them seem so similar to ours. It would be worthwhile to describe in great detail the Derridian and Leroi-Gourhanian "transaction" in terms of the spatiality of the lived body. The project would involve both of Husserl's assistants, Oscar Becker and Martin Heidegger, and would require an expansion of Derrida's remarks on indication (*Zeigen, Anzeichen*) and an introduction of *Greifen*, our grasp of the writing stylus, as a form of what Merleau-Ponty, after Gelb and Goldstein, calls "abstract movement."

10. See Maurice Merleau-Ponty, *Signes* (Paris: Gallimard, 1960), 110–11, for this and the following (henceforth cited as S, with page number).

11. See Maurice Merleau-Ponty, *Phénoménologie de la perception* (Paris: Gallimard, 1945), 461–62, on the word *sleet*. Note that henceforth Merleau-Ponty's *Phénoménologie* will be cited as P, with page number.

12. There is some value in thinking of Derrida's *Of Grammatology* as being situated at the point of convergence of these two fragments of Merleau-Ponty's project, even though *Of Grammatology* is doubtless more a reading of prose than a singing of the visible world.

13. See sections 299–302 of G. W. F. Hegel, *Enzyklopädie der philosophischen Wissenschaften im Grundrisse (1830)*, ed. Friedrich Nicolin and Otto Pöggeler (Hamburg: F. Meiner, 1969), 247–50. See also Jacques Derrida, "Le puits et la pyramide," in *Marges de la philosophie* (Paris: Minuit, 1972), 79–127, esp. 101–11; trans. Alan Bass as *Margins of Philosophy* (Chicago: University of Chicago Press, 1982), 69–108.

14. See David Farrell Krell, *Intimations of Mortality: Time, Truth, and Finitude in Heidegger's Thinking of Being*, 2d ed. (University Park: Pennsylvania State University Press, 1991), 44–46. Nowadays, I am more convinced by *frontality* than *ontology*.

# Chapter 4: Mourning Ultratranscendence

1. See JD, 267–84, discussed in this chapter; Rodolphe Gasché, *The Tain of the Mirror* (Cambridge, Mass.: Harvard University Press, 1986), 194–238 (henceforth referred to in the text as TM), discussed in this chapter; Irene Harvey, *Derrida and the Economy of Différance* (Bloomington: Indiana University Press, 1986); and John Llewelyn, *Derrida on the Threshold of Sense* (cited in the Introduction).

2. See David Farrell Krell, *Of Memory, Reminiscence, and Writing: On the Verge* (Bloomington: Indiana University Press, 1990), where "queasy-transcendentality" appears in chaps. 4 and 7.

3. Schelling, *Werke* (cited in the Introduction), 7:355.

4. See, for example, G, 69/47; 78/54; and 88/60.

5. Jacques Derrida, *De l'esprit: Heidegger et la question* (Paris: Galilée, 1987); trans. Geoff Bennington and Rachel Bowlby as *Of Spirit: Heidegger and the Question* (Chicago: University of Chicago Press, 1989); idem, "Interpreting Signatures (Nietzsche/Heidegger): Two Questions," in *Dialogue and Deconstruction: The Gadamer-Derrida Encounter,* ed. Diane P. Michelfelder and Richard E. Palmer (Albany: State University of New York Press, 1989), 58–71. Derrida discusses the issue of *lifedeath* in detail in "Spéculer—sur 'Freud,'" in *La Carte postale de Socrate à Freud et au-delà* (Paris: Aubier-Flammarion, 1980), 275–437; translated by Alan Bass as *The Post Card from Socrates to Freud and Beyond* (Chicago: University of Chicago Press, 1987), 257–386.

6. Hegel, *Enzyklopädie der philosophischen Wissenschaften,* 4.

7. Martin Heidegger, *Sein und Zeit,* 12th ed. (Tübingen: M. Niemeyer, 1972), 38, henceforth cited in the text as SZ; trans. in *Basic Writings,* 2d ed., rev. and exp. (San Francisco: HarperCollins, 1993), 85.

8. Immanuel Kant, *Kritik der reinen Vernunft,* ed. Raymund Schmidt (Hamburg: F. Meiner, 1971), A xii–xix; trans. Norman Kemp Smith as *Critique of Pure Reason* (New York: St. Martin's Press, 1965), 9–14.

9. See Krell, *Of Memory, Reminiscence, and Writing,* 179–87.

10. F. W. J. Schelling, *Die Weltalter, Erstes Buch,* ed. Karl Schelling for the *Sämmtliche Werke* (as cited in the Introduction) in 1861. See *Schriften von 1813–1830* (Darmstadt: Wissenschaftliche Buchgesellschaft, 1976), 1–150. This text, along with the supplement attached to it, *Über die Gottheiten von Samothrake (1815),* takes Schelling to the farthest reaches of his speculation. But see above all *Die Weltalter Fragmente,* ed. Manfred Schröter, which is a *Nachlaßband* to the Münchner Jubiläumsdruck of Schelling's works (Munich: Biederstein Verlag and Leibniz Verlag, 1946). This volume presents the original versions of *Die Weltalter,* set in print (but not released for publication) in 1811 and 1813; the first half of the 1811 version is, I believe, of special interest. Jason Wirth, of Ogelthorpe University, has recently published (with SUNY Press) an English translation of *Die Weltalter.*

11. Martin Heidegger, *Die Grundprobleme der Phänomenologie,* Gesamtausgabe vol. 24 (Frankfurt am Main: V. Klostermann, 1975), 463; see the discussion in Krell, *Intimations of Mortality,* 35.

12. Martin Heidegger, *Vorträge und Aufsätze* (Pfullingen: G. Neske, 1954), 116; see also idem, *Beiträge zur Philosophie (Vom Ereignis),* Gesamtausgabe vol. 65 (Frankfurt am Main: V. Klostermann, 1989), 406. For further discussion, see the following chapter.

## Chapter 5: Mourning the Perfect Future

1. In chaps. 2 and 3 of *Intimations of Mortality* and in chap. 6 of *Of Memory, Reminiscence, and Writing*, both cited above.
2. Martin Heidegger, *Metaphysische Anfangsgründe der Logik im Ausgang von Leibniz*, Gesamtausgabe vol. 26 (Frankfurt am Main: V. Klostermann, 1978), 268.
3. Martin Heidegger, *Zur Sache des Denkens* (Tübingen: V. Klostermann, 1969), 55.
4. Martin Heidegger, *Unterwegs zur Sprache* (Pfullingen: G. Neske, 1959), 57, for this and the following quotation. On Heidegger's reading of Trakl and the question of *Geschlecht*, see also chap. 8 of my *Daimon Life* and chap. 4 of my *Lunar Voices: Of Tragedy, Poetry, Fiction, and Thought* (Chicago: University of Chicago Press, 1995).
5. The occasion on which this chapter was first presented as a paper concluded with Derrida's presentation of "Geschlecht ii: Heidegger's Hand," now printed in *Philosophy and Deconstruction: The Texts of Jacques Derrida*, ed. John Sallis (Chicago: University of Chicago Press, 1987).
6. Georg Trakl, *Dichtungen und Briefe*, ed. Walther Killy and Hans Szklenar (Salzburg: Otto Müller, 1969), 26; cited henceforth by page number in the body of my text.
7. Martin Heidegger, *Vorträge und Aufsätze*, 116, for this and the following quotation. For the English translation, see idem, *Nietzsche*, vol. 2, *The Eternal Recurrence of the Same*, trans. David Farrell Krell (New York: Harper & Row, 1984), 224. See also Heidegger's *Was heißt Denken?* (Tübingen: M. Niemeyer, 1954), pt. 1.

## Chapter 6: Eight Labors of Mourning

1. Jacques Derrida, *Feu la cendre* (Paris: Des femmes, 1987); trans. Ned Lukacher as *Cinders* (Lincoln: University of Nebraska Press, 1991). The present chapter was first presented several years ago as a paper to the Society for Phenomenology and Existential Philosophy; this perhaps accounts for its desire to speak—however briefly—to as many varieties of contemporary European thought, from Husserl to Cixous, as possible, granted the limitations of my own narrow experience.
2. Edmund Husserl, *Analysen zur passiven Synthesis*, Husserliana, vol. 11, ed. Margot Fleischer from lecture and research manuscripts dating from 1918 to 1926 (The Hague: M. Nijhoff, 1966), esp. 172–222 and 364–85.
3. *Cinders*, 57. In the context of these labors of mourning, one ought to reread those pages of *La voix et le phénomène* (cited in Chapter 3) on the testamentary ego (104–9); and one ought to review once again the moments of Derrida's 1953–54 master's thesis, *Le problème de la genèse dans la philosophie de Husserl* (Paris: Presses Universitaires de France, 1990), where the genesis of temporality is at issue—and at crisis. See esp. 117–24, on "the point of introducing passivity into primordial constitution" and "the absolute beginning of time's arrival on the scene," as well as 163, on passive genesis. I have commented on some of these texts in an appendix to *Archeticture: Ecstasies of Space, Time, and the Human Body* (Albany: State University of New York Press, 1997), 175–88.
4. Jean-Paul Sartre, *Situations IV* (Paris: Gallimard, 1964); trans. Benita Eisler as *Situations* (Greenwich, Conn.: Fawcett, 1965), 169.

5. Walter Benjamin, *Illuminationen: Ausgewählte Schriften* (Frankfurt am Main: Suhrkamp, 1977), 258; cited henceforth by page number in my text.

6. Jacques Derrida, *Spectres de Marx* (Paris: Galilée, 1994), 47. Note that the invocation of a future that is "more ancient" than an imperfect past appears to bring Derrida's thought much closer to Heidegger's in this regard (see Chapter 5) than one might have anticipated. For "Force of Law," see now Jacques Derrida, *Force de loi* (Paris: Galilée, 1994).

7. See David Farrell Krell, "Everything Great Stands in the Storm That Blows from Paradise," *Cardozo Law Review* 13, no. 4 (1991): 301–7.

8. Martin Heidegger, *Phänomenologische Interpretationen zu Aristoteles: Einführung in die phänomenologische Forschung*, Gesamtausgabe vol. 61 (Frankfurt am Main: V. Klostermann, 1985), 131–55.

9. Martin Heidegger, *Die Grundbegriffe der Metaphysik: Welt—Endlichkeit—Einsamkeit*, Gesamtausgabe vol. 29/30 (Frankfurt am Main: V. Klostermann, 1983), 89 and 271; trans. William McNeill and Nicholas Walker as *The Fundamental Concepts of Metaphysics: World—Finitude—Solitude* (Bloomington: Indiana University Press, 1995); see also chap. 3 of Krell, *Daimon Life*.

10. Heidegger, *Unterwegs zur Sprache*, 235; cited hereinafter as US.

11. Derrida, *De l'esprit*, 173–76/105–8.

12. Personal communication. Irigaray's *L'oubli de l'air* was published in Paris by Minuit in 1983; an English translation by Mary Beth Mader for the University of Texas Press is now in progress. On the theme of mourning, *le deuil*, see esp. 14, 30–31, 43, 67–68, 98–99, 101–10, 113, 115, 125, 127, 140, and 153.

13. See David Farrell Krell, *Infectious Nietzsche* (Bloomington: Indiana University Press, 1995), chap. 8.

14. On "return without return," that is, without appeal to the "same," see Jacques Derrida, *Schibboleth: Pour Paul Celan* (Paris: Galilée, 1986).

15. Hélène Cixous, *Neutre* (Paris: B. Grasset, 1972), cited by page number in my text.

16. See Krell, *Lunar Voices*, chap. 2, "Hölderlin's Dissolution."

17. Friedrich Hölderlin, *Sämtliche Werke und Briefe*, ed. Michael Knaupp (Munich: Carl Hanser Verlag, 1992), 2:596.

18. See Zarathustra's "Prologue," 4:15, and Hölderlin's *Der Tod des Empedokles*, first version, lines 372–76, in Friedrich Hölderlin, *Sämtliche Werke*, ed. D. E. Sattler (Darmstadt: Luchterhand, 1986), 12:55 and 190.

## Chapter 7: Knell

1. Joyce, *Ulysses*, 433.

2. See, in the meantime, David Farrell Krell, *Contagion: Sexuality, Disease, and Death in German Idealism and Romanticism* (Bloomington: Indiana University Press, 1998), pt. 3.

3. Georges Bataille, *Visions of Excess: Selected Writings, 1927–1939*, ed. and trans. Allan Stoekl (Manchester: Manchester University Press, 1985), 20; cited hereinafter merely by page in the body of my text. Bataille is no doubt anticipating those two famous footnotes (foot notes?) that open and close chapter 4 of *Civilization and Its Discontents*. (Or it may also be that Freud is anticipating Bataille's lucubrations—for these texts both stem from the year

1929.) There Freud speculates on the erection of the human being, its partial removal from the surface of the earth, as the essential cause of what he calls "organic repression." See Freud, 9:229–30 and 235–36.

4. Both in vol. 1 of the Theorie-Werkausgabe (Frankfurt am Main: Suhrkamp, 1970), henceforth cited in the text by volume and page number from this edition.

5. Barbara G. Walker, *The Woman's Encyclopedia of Myths and Secrets* (San Francisco: Harper & Row, 1983), s.v. "Mary Magdalene." My thanks to Joseph Sullivan for the reference. Mari-Anna-Ishtar is precisely the figure presented to us in Georg Trakl's early dialogue *Maria Magdalena*. Although Trakl ignores the actual scene of christening, the anointing of Christ's feet (he writes merely that she "sank down at his feet"), he gives the goddess herself feet—along with a sense of the divine and a certain devotion to death. The Roman soldier Marcellus notes that when Mary Magdalene dances she touches all the ancient divinities:

> It happened on one of those glowing summer nights when fever haunts the winds and the moon confounds the senses. That is when I saw her. It was in a small taverna. She danced there, danced with naked feet on a precious carpet. I have never seen a woman dance more beautifully, with greater intoxication. The rhythm of her body caused me to see strange and obscure dream images; shivers of hot fever shook my own body. It seemed to me as though this woman in her dance was playing with invisible, precious, secret things, as though she were embracing creatures like unto gods that no one could see, as though she were kissing red lips that longed for her own. Her movements were those of supreme pleasure; it seemed as though she were showered with caresses. She seemed to see things we could not see, to play with them in her dance, to enjoy them in the unheard-of raptures of her own body. Perhaps when she tossed back her head and gazed longingly upward she was raising her mouth to precious, sweet fruits, and sipping fiery wine. No, I never comprehended it, and yet it was all so remarkably alive—it was *there*. And then she sank naked at our feet, inundated only by her hair.

When in Trakl's dialogue Christ is led off to be crucified, the Magdalene is right there at the front of the crowd; on Golgotha, she hovers close beneath the cross, "hearkening to the fleeing of his life—entranced" (117). Marcellus refuses to follow her there. "And in me it has remained dark," he says. See Georg Trakl, "Aus goldenem Kelch: Maria Magdalena, Ein Dialog," in *Das dichterische Werk*, ed. Walther Killy and Hans Szklenar (Munich: Deutscher Taschenbuch Verlag, 1972), 116.

6. Flannery O'Connor, "A Good Man Is Hard to Find," in *Major American Short Stories*, ed. A. Walton Litz (New York: Oxford University Press, 1975), 665.

7. G. W. F. Hegel, *Phänomenologie des Geistes* (cited in Chapter 1), 318–23; cited hereinafter as PG, with page.

## Chapter 8: Mourning Monica, Our (M)Other

1. I cite by volume and page number from the Heidegger Gesamtausgabe.

2. See now Martin Heidegger, *Phänomenologie des religiösen Lebens,* Gesamtausgabe vol. 60 (Frankfurt am Main: V. Klostermann, 1995), which contains (1) notes from an undelivered course of lectures from the years 1918–19 on the philosophical foundations of medieval mysticism, (2) an introduction to the phenomenology of religion from the winter semester of 1920–21, and (3) a course on Augustine and Neoplatonism taught during the summer semester of 1921. I do not find in any of these courses and sets of notes any explicit reference to *rapio, rapere,* or *raptim,* viewed in relation to ἐξαίφνης, "the sudden." Yet throughout these courses Heidegger emphasizes what he calls "history" in the factical experience of life as taking-trouble concerning the self. Taking-trouble, *Bekümmerung,* not yet *Sorge,* suggests our concern with our troubled existence. Such a "history" of troubled life is clearly bound up with time. Heidegger's question is, "What is temporality originally in factical experience?" (55). His interpretation of Pauline παρουσία is likewise guided by the question "When?" and the theme of "time and the moment," *Zeit und Augenblick* (99–100). The moment of the Second Coming is to be understood, not chronologically, but *kairotically,* as the "when" of the coming event, or *Ereignis* (119, 149). Even though Heidegger makes no explicit reference to ἐξαίφνης in these texts, there are several intriguing references to "suddenness" here, as though suddenness were the secret of the ecstatic temporal analysis to come in Heidegger's *Being and Time.* What is astonishing about such references is that they have to do with the suddenness of a fall—of temptation, corruption, and demise: "sudden corruption" (*plötzliches Verderben* in 2 Thessalonians) and the sudden and unexpected nature of "temptation," *tentatio, Versuchung,* in Augustine's *Confessions* (103, 151, 217) are the anticipatory moments of the kairotic Second Coming. What is familiar about the Augustine course of 1921, which is a reading of book X of the *Confessions,* is the interpretation of *Bekümmertsein* as Augustinian *curare,* such taking-trouble being the fundamental character of factical life (§ 12). What is striking is the phenomenological access to "dailiness" (*Täglichkeit*) and "dispersion" (*Zerstreuung*) in sexual temptation, which plagues both day and night. It is such temptation that brings together genealogy and ontology, but also genealogy and deconstruction, inasmuch as temptation alone compels us to see the irruption of temporality in our lives: "The very next moment [*Augenblick*] may cause me to fall" (217). If *continentia* reverses the tendency of falling, *molestia* is nonetheless the facticity of this troubled life. Only in temptation does history penetrate factical existence. Monica, as the (m)other, as the relic of Eve, has something to do with the self's becoming a problem for itself in the unfolding of time. To be sure, this is not yet an elaborated temporal interpretation, much less a fully developed ecstatic understanding of time. Yet because temptation is a *transitus,* a process (*Vollzug*), and a possibility (*Möglichkeit*) of factical life as such (248–49, 263, 280), the ecstatic temporal interpretation of Dasein is an accident that is waiting to happen. That accident will grant Heidegger the insights that inform *Being and Time,* and its shock waves will be felt throughout Derrida's *Circumfession.*

3. For Augustine I have used the translation by John K. Ryan, *The Confessions of Saint Augustine* (Garden City, N.Y.: Doubleday-Image, 1960), 50, and the Latin text of the Loeb Classical Library edition, with the 1631 translation by William Watts (Cambridge, Mass.: Harvard University Press, 1977). Note that I cite Derrida's *Circumfession,* contained in JD, by section, not page number.

4. Again I refer the reader to my *Of Memory, Reminiscence, and Writing* (cited in Chapter 4), esp. 52–55, which treats (very briefly) of Augustine in the context of typography, iconography, and engrammatology.

5. Friedrich Nietzsche, *Sämtliche Briefe: Kritische Studienausgabe,* ed. Giorgio Colli and Mazzino Montinari, 8 vols. (Berlin and Munich: Walter de Gruyter and Deutscher Taschenbuch Verlag, 1986), 7:34.

6. See *Kritische Studienausgabe,* 11:467 (cited in note 10 to Chapter 1); cf. 12:28. Nietzsche also refers to Augustine's "hysterical honesty" (11:69) and to his "comical" hysteria concerning his own sexuality (11:242). On Augustine as "revenge on the spirit, and other backgrounds to morality," see *The Gay Science,* no. 359 (3:605–7). On Augustine's slavishness, see *Beyond Good and Evil,* no. 50 (5:70–71), and *The Antichrist,* no. 59 (6:248–49). Finally, the earliest reference to Saint Augustine that I know of in Nietzsche's works is this one: "*The Darwinist.*—St. Augustine said, 'The Lord says, "I am the truth and the life"'; He did not say, "I am your habit!"'"—What a shame! The Lord is thus not the truth, and does not know what life is" (8:572).

7. See now Jacques Derrida, *Politiques de l'amitié* (Paris: Galilée, 1994).

8. The references to B. (Barthes) and M. P. (Merleau-Ponty?—Derrida cites the year of the latter's death as 1962, not 1961, so that M. P. may in fact refer to another mother's son) appear in section 40 of *Circumfession.*

9. Derrida is quick to observe that he does not write with the fetishistic pen, "the good old Sergeant-Major" (26, 42), and he sings the praises of the computer; yet the gray sky of the Macintosh screen ("Who was Macintosh?"—L. Boom) is both "marine and *high tech,*" both naked and precise, and it spreads open like the eye of a blind man (53) or a sky of skin stretched to the point of orgasm (46). The Macintosh should therefore be as ripe for inhibition as the Bic.

10. *Confessions* II, 2; cf. VIII, 1. A thinker prior to Nietzsche who has insight into the intimate connection between Christianity and *voluptas* is Novalis. A note from January–April 1800 reads as follows: "The Xian religion is the genuine religion of voluptuosity. Sin is the great stimulus to love of the Godhead. The more sinful one feels, the more Christian one is. Unconditioned unity with the Godhead is the goal of *sin* and *love.* Dythirambs [*sic*] are a genuinely Christian product." See Novalis, *Das philosophisch-theoretische Werk,* ed. Hans-Joachim Mähl, vol. 2 of *Werke, Tagebücher und Briefe Friedrich von Hardenbergs,* ed. Hans-Joachim Mähl and Richard Samuel (Munich: Carl Hanser, 1978), 814; cf. 788–89, on "Christian Dithyrams [*sic*] and Songs."

11. Cf. *Confessions* VII, 5: "It was as if there were a sea, one single sea, that was everywhere and on all sides infinite over boundless reaches. It held within itself a sort of sponge, huge indeed, but yet finite, and this sponge was filled in every part by that boundless sea. Thus did I conjecture that your finite creation was filled by you, the infinite, and I said: 'Behold God, and behold what God has created! God is good. . . . But being good, he has created good things. . . . Where then is evil, and whence and by what means has it crept in here? What is its root, and what is its seed?" Derrida notes the temptation that plagues him—to "expound this sublime chapter on the origin of evil." The thought of the seascape would dominate his exposition, and it would invoke Freud's notions of introjection and incorporation, in order to make the situation of mourning, like that of evil, incorrigible, "on this shore of introjection and incorporation from which even God, on the day of his death, will not be able to deliver us" (21).

12. The story of Zipporah is confusing, to say the least, and Luther at least reads it quite otherwise than Derrida does. In the Second Book of Moses (C.IIII.IV), when Zipporah rescues her son Elieser from the Lord's wrath by circumcising him, Luther interprets her words "You

are a blood-husband" in the following way: "That is to say, she was angry, and she meant to say, 'It costs me blood that you are my husband, so that I have to circumcise my son,' which is something she was loathe to do [*welches sie ungerne thet*], because it was a mark of shame among the pagans [Zipporah was a Mede]. Yet that was the sense of the law that God wanted for his people. Yet they did not want to bear the cross [*Aber es will das Creutze nicht leiden*], nor did they want old Adam to be circumcised [*noch den alten Adam beschneiten lassen*] until it had to be." D. Martin Luther, *Die gantze Heilige Schrift*, 3 vols., ed. Hans Volz et al. (Munich: Deutscher Taschenbuch Verlag, 1974), 1:129. As far as I can see, there is nothing about Zipporah's eating the foreskin. However, it remains strange that a Medean woman should enforce the law of Abraham on a husband who obviously feels himself to be as much an Egyptian as a Jew; strange also that the Lord should be motivated to strangle Moses' firstborn son, as though he (the Lord) could not mark the difference between a Jew, a Mede, or a son of Pharaoh until blood were spilled at that particular place; strange, finally, that a mother should do the bloody work of the Lord.

13. Derrida continues: "like so many *mohels* [who] for centuries had practiced suction, or *mezizah*, right on the glans, mixing wine and blood with it, until the thing was abolished in Paris in 1843 for reasons of hygiene" (13). Such erotic cannibalism became one of the themes of Derrida's 1990 lectures in Paris, "Eating the Other" (*Manger l'autre*) (32).

14. In his response to my Chapter 6, Derrida himself remarked that the cryptic phrase *il y a là cendre* may represent a proper name. If it does, the proper name is properly his own, but it is a secret name the bearer can never assume as his own—a mere trace, and the barest trace, of ashes.

15. On *obsequence* and the *logic of the living woman*, see Derrida, *Otobiographies: L'enseignement de Nietzsche et la politique du nom propre* (Paris: Galilée, 1984), "La logique de la vivante."

16. The picture, El Greco's *Burial of Count Orgaz*, with Derrida seeing himself as the painter's son (painted into the foreground of the painting, on the left), represents of course the burial of the *father*, not of the mother.

17. "Marrano," literally "pig," is the pejorative name the Spaniards bestowed on a large group of Sephardic Jews between 1391 and 1497. These Jews of the Iberian Peninsula, forced to convert to Christianity, feigned the requisite practice of Catholicism but retained their Jewish identity and practiced Jewish rites in secret. After the formal expulsion of the Jews in 1492, Sephardim dispersed to western Europe, the southern Mediterranean, the Near East, and northern Africa—where Derrida was born. See his *Aporias*, trans. Thomas Dutoit (Berkeley and Los Angeles: University of California Press, 1994), 74–81. On that final page Derrida writes:

> Let us figuratively call Marrano anyone who remains faithful to a secret that he has not chosen, in the very place where he lives . . . in the very place where he stays without saying no but without identifying himself as belonging to. In the unchallenged night where the radical absence of any historical witness keeps him or her, in the dominant culture that by definition has calendars, this secret keeps the Marrano even before the Marrano keeps it. Is it not possible to think that such a secret eludes history, age, and aging?
>
> Thanks to this anachronism, Marranos that we are, Marranos in any case, whether we want to be or not, whether we know it or not, Marranos having an

incalculable number of ages, hours, and years, of untimely histories, each both larger and smaller than the other, each still waiting for the other, we may incessantly be younger and older, in a last word, infinitely finished.

## Conclusion: Affirmation Without Issue

1. These words appear repeatedly as the concluding words to several of Hölderlin's sketches at the conclusion of the Homburger Folioheft, those devoted to "The Nymph," and "Mnemosyne"; see Hölderlin's *Sämtliche Werke*, edited by Michael Knaupp (cited in Chapter 6), 1:435–38, along with the commentary at 3:262. Knaupp understands the phrase to mean "the same mistake is made by those who mourn"; Derrida and Heidegger are more likely to be thinking of the *fehlet* as indicating the default or absence of mourning as such.

2. Pierre Klossowski, *Nietzsche et le cercle vicieux*, rev. ed. (Paris: Mercure de France, 1969), esp. 93–103; see chaps. 6–7 of my *Of Memory, Reminiscence, and Writing* (cited in Chapter 4), and chap. 11 of my *Infectious Nietzsche* (cited in Chapter 6).

3. Jacques Derrida, *Ulysse gramophone: Deux mots pour Joyce* (Paris: Galilée, 1987); see Krell, *Of Memory, Reminiscence, and Writing*, chap. 7, esp. 300–309.

4. Jacques Derrida, *La dissémination* (Paris: Seuil, 1972), 165; trans. Barbara Johnson as *Dissemination* (Chicago: University of Chicago Press, 1981), 143.

5. Did he ever see his father again? Derrida seems to think so: see *Glas*, 13/7: "At the end of his life, Hegel responds to a natural son come to be acknowledged: I know I had had something to do with your birth, but previously I was the accidental thing, now I am the essential one." I take the liberty of referring my readers to my novel, *Son of Spirit* (Albany: State University of New York Press, 1997), which tells the story of Louis Hegel-Fischer, who never did see his father again after he left for the Dutch East Indies.

6. In the following paragraphs, italicized passages are quotations from *The Post Card* (cited in Chapter 4). I cite them without page references because the point of the citations is not to demonstrate something about the particular contents of this text but to show what a bastard its author really and truly is.

7. I am referring to their papers presented at the conference "Mourning (and) the Political," held at DePaul University on October 7, 1996. My thanks to them and to Peg Birmingham, Bill Martin, and Will McNeill, as well as to the purest of bastards himself, for their contributions. I take it for granted that Brault and Naas will include versions of their papers in the edited volume, to be published by the University of Chicago Press.

# Index

Echo, echoes, 35, 49–52, 54, 56, 58,
    59–60, 62–63, 66, 67–68, 69, 72–77,
    80–81, 97–99, 113, 122, 134, 182,
    191, 196, 197, 204, 211, 218–20
*ecstasis*, ecstasy, 65, 67, 77, 92, 116,
    118–26, 129, 135, 175–79, 189,
    198–99, 224, 227. *See also*
    temporality
ego, 10, 11, 15, 16, 50, 61, 63, 68, 72, 99,
    131–32, 181–82, 224. *See also* self,
    the
El Greco, 229
Emerson, Ralph Waldo, 4
Empedocles of Acragas, 143–44, 210, 225
Enkidu, 3–4, 18
Ephraim (biblical), 74
Euripides, 72, 221
examples, exemplarity, 8, 25, 26, 28, 29,
    30–33, 34, 37, 41–47, 56, 60, 65, 86,
    96, 117, 124, 153, 162–64, 181, 182,
    192
eye(s), the, 2–3, 6, 8, 11, 37, 52, 56, 59,
    60, 65–68, 69–81, 92, 93, 95–97,
    104, 122, 144, 150, 154, 175, 179,
    182, 184–85, 191, 219–221, 228.
    *See also* blindness; visibility

familiarity, 8, 97, 99, 108, 110, 131, 146,
    211, 227
family, 4, 15, 150–56, 163, 166, 168–73,
    191–94, 196, 203, 206–8, 211
Fantin-Latour, Henri, 52–53, 56, 73, 77
father, the, 2, 4, 10, 14–16, 26, 74–75, 80,
    150, 157–61, 166–69, 178, 183–84,
    189, 191–94, 198, 206–8, 210, 213,
    221, 229, 230
Faulkner, William, 151
feminism, 143, 145, 151, 218. *See also*
    Cixous, Hèléne; Irigaray, Luce
Fichte, Wilhelm Gottlieb, 35, 49
Ficino, Marsilio, 209
Flaubert, Gustave, 136
Foucault, Michel, 95, 100
frames, 25–47, 50, 67, 75, 122, 216–17
Freud, Sigmund, 1, 14–17, 60–64, 73–74,
    85, 87, 101, 103, 117, 122, 145, 150,

163, 166, 168, 170, 175, 180–82,
    189, 190, 194, 195, 198, 201, 203–4,
    216, 220, 221, 223, 225–26, 228. *See
    also* psychoanalysis
Fried, Michael, 219–21
Frommann, Friedrich, 207
Fustel de Coulanges, 135
future, the, 8, 11, 18, 41, 50, 63, 116,
    117–27, 130, 131, 132, 135–37,
    176–78, 185, 198, 224, 225. See also
    *ecstasis*; temporality

Gasché, Rodolphe, 103, 114–15, 223
gaze, the, 2, 8, 37, 50–52, 65–67, 69,
    73–74, 77, 81, 102, 125, 144, 149,
    160, 191, 197, 208, 226. *See also*
    eye(s); visibility
genealogy, 6, 27, 37, 46, 134, 155, 165,
    175, 180–81, 183–87, 188, 195, 206,
    227
Genet, Jean, 99, 117, 145, 149–51,
    154–56, 172–73, 180
genitality, 80, 155, 157, 220–21. *See also*
    difference, sexual; sexuality
Gide, André, 195
Gilgamesh, 3–4, 166, 215
Goethe, Johann Wolfgang von, 35, 177,
    208
gorge, the, 56, 59, 66, 80–81, 86–87,
    91–94, 97, 98–101, 112, 115, 156,
    211, 221

Hades, 133, 189
Hamlet, 137, 181, 211
Harvey, Irene, 103, 223
heart, the, 1–3, 7, 13, 40, 42, 44, 47,
    50–51, 59, 77, 97, 99, 101, 121, 123,
    127, 132, 134–36, 144, 145, 156,
    162–65, 170, 184, 189, 192, 194–95,
    202, 204, 207–8. *See also* love
Hegel, Georg Wilhelm Friedrich, 4, 10, 13,
    27–28, 35, 39, 46, 52, 92, 97, 99–101,
    108–9, 145, 149–73, 176, 202, 206–9,
    217, 218, 222, 223, 226, 230
    *Phenomenology of Spirit*, 10, 150,
    155–56, 170–71, 207

1405159R0

Printed in Great Britain by
Amazon.co.uk, Ltd.,
Marston Gate.